Disability Rights and the American Social Safety Net

Disability Rights and the American Social Safety Net

Jennifer L. Erkulwater

CORNELL UNIVERSITY PRESS   Ithaca and London

Cornell University Press gratefully acknowledges a grant from the University of Richmond, which aided in the publication of this book.

First published 2006 by Cornell University Press

Printed in the United States of America

Library of Congress Cataloging-in-Publication Data
Erkulwater, Jennifer L.
    Disability rights and the American social safety net / Jennifer L. Erkulwater.
        p. cm.
    Includes bibliographical references and index.
    ISBN-13: 978-0-8014-4417-3 (cloth : alk. paper)
    ISBN-10: 0-8014-4417-9 (cloth : alk. paper)
    1. Insurance, Disability—United States.   2. Disability retirement —United States.   3. People with disabilities—Legal status, laws, etc. —United States.   4. Supplemental security income program—United States.   5. Social security—United States.   I. Title.
    HD7105.25.U6E75 2006
    368.38'2—dc22
2006001752

Cornell University Press strives to use environmentally responsible suppliers and materials to the fullest extent possible in the publishing of its books. Such materials include vegetable-based, low-VOC inks and acid-free papers that are recycled, totally chlorine-free, or partly composed of nonwood fibers. For further information, visit our website at www.cornellpress.cornell.edu.

Cloth printing   10 9 8 7 6 5 4 3 2 1

For Trent

you are my sun, my moon, and all my stars
—e. e. cummings

CONTENTS

PREFACE

The great pleasure of finishing this book is the opportunity to express my gratitude to the many individuals who helped make it possible. I owe a great debt to Dan Cullen, who taught me much about the relationship between justice and public policy, and to Catherine Guthrie Walker, my mentor at Memphis Area Legal Services and a trusted friend, who cultivated my early interest in poverty and social justice. As I finished the last chapters of this book, I thought of Catherine often and wished that she could have seen the final project come to fruition.

As I struggled to convert my early vague thoughts on antipoverty and disability politics into concrete words, I was fortunate to work with an outstanding group of scholars. First and foremost is Shep Melnick, who read and rigorously critiqued every word of this book, always balancing his pointed criticism with much-appreciated encouragement. He epitomizes all that an adviser should be. In addition, Kay Schlozman did me a great favor in showing me early in my career "how research is really done," and in my professional and personal life, I have benefited greatly from her guidance. Marc Landy patiently served as a sounding board for many of my initial hunches about the connections between individual rights and governmental policies. Deborah Stone honed my thinking and writing about disability policy, and her imprint is everywhere throughout these pages. My thanks extend as well to Martha Derthick and Kent Weaver, who kindly shared their research files on SSI, Disability Insurance, and welfare reform. Martha Derthick, Edward Berkowitz, and Mark Nadel read parts or all of the manuscript and provided their sage advice.

I would never have been able to reconstruct the events described in this book without the help of many government officials, doctors, advocates, and lawyers who agreed to be interviewed. Such busy people, such generous giving of time and experience. I am especially thankful to Leonard Rubenstein, Patricia Owens, Howard Goldman, and Barry Eigen. They answered with great candor and corrected many mistaken assumptions I had. They also saw the political story that lurked behind my questions and enthusiastically embraced the project when it was still in its infancy. Their support carried me through the long days I spent slogging through the mountains of mundane legal rules and medical facts pertaining to disability.

I extend my appreciation as well to the National Academy of Social Insurance for the recognition it gave to the dissertation on which this book is based and to Robert Hudson, who chaired the committee that reviewed the dissertation, for his thoughtful words of encouragement. I also thank the *Connecticut Insurance Law Journal* for allowing me to reprint my article, "The Judicial Transformation of Social Security Disability: The Case of Mental Disorders and Childhood Disability," *Connecticut Insurance Law Journal* 8, 2 (2001–2002): 401–34, on which Chapter 5 is based.

In the course of my research, I received invaluable assistance from the staff at the Thomas P. O'Neill, Jr., Library at Boston College, the Library of Congress, the Brookings Institution, and the University of Richmond's Boatwright Library. In addition, Larry DeWitt and Bob Krebs at the Social Security Administration's Office of the Historian warmly opened their archives to me and helped me comb through countless files brimming with memos, letters, and studies. Meanwhile, Keith Weimer and Daryl Weade at the University of Richmond pulled double duty as both friends and on-demand research and technical support. I would be deeply remiss, too, if I did not thank Valerie Richmond, who in the days and weeks following my son's birth made numerous trips to the library to retrieve journal articles for me and even hand-delivered them to my home. She was an invaluable and superb research assistant at an incredibly hectic time, and I am truly grateful for all she did for me.

Financial support from several institutions sped the progress of this book. A research fellowship from the Brookings Institution allowed me to take time off from teaching so that I could live in Washington, DC, near my archival sources and interviewees. Research grants from the University of Richmond helped me devote my summers to writing. And as the book neared completion, a grant from the Office of the Dean of Arts and Sciences at the University of Richmond aided with the costs of publication. I am grateful to Andy Newcomb, Dan Palazzolo, Terri Weaver, and Jessica Albertson for their help in securing the grant.

Someone once told me that your editor is your best friend during the long and sometimes agonizing process of publishing your first book. How right he was. I am eternally grateful to my editor at Cornell University Press, Roger Haydon, for shepherding me through the ordeal with humor and good cheer. I also wish to extend my heartfelt appreciation to the staff at Cornell University Press, in particular Priscilla Hurdle, Teresa Jesionowski, and Susan Barnett, and to my copyeditor, Jack Rummel, for the many hours of work they put into this book.

Finally, I owe a huge debt of gratitude to the circle of family and friends who have sustained me. First, special thanks go to my parents, Samard and Flor Erkulwater, and my brothers, Sam Erkulwater and Edson Erkulwater, and to my in-laws, David and JoAnne Taylor—I am certain they never could grasp why it took so long to write this book, but they were always kind enough to feign interest, ask how things were going, and bolster me with promises of displaying the book prominently on their coffee tables. Many thanks also to Sandy Carpenter, Jamie Edrington, Lyn Kyle, Angela Saba, Judd and Julie Peak, Buck Knott, Allison Beltz Butcher, Michael Auerbach, Hans Schattle, Grace Cho, Jessica Gerrity, Ruth Melkonian-Hoover, Dan Robison and Hadley Truettner, Daryl and Ana Weade, Keith Weimer, and Tracy Roof. They are constant reminders of how blessed and rich I truly am. I am especially grateful to Dan and Hadley for opening their home to me whenever I was in Washington, DC, for research trips or conferences.

Last but not least are my two favorite men: Trent Taylor and Will Taylor. Will came in the final stages of this project. Though his birth has made for many sleepless nights and chaotic days, he more than makes up for them with the joy that he brings me each and every day. Trent has always been by my side. He is a ruthless editor but an astute and gentle critic, and always my best friend and true love. He makes anything possible.

JENNIFER L. ERKULWATER

Richmond, Virginia

Disability Rights
and the
American Social
Safety Net

Introduction:
The Puzzle of Reform

A truism of American politics is that liberal policy reform can be accomplished rarely, only when the stars align and favorable political winds sweep aside previously immovable political obstacles. For this to happen, though, the prerequisites are many. There must be a crisis of such magnitude that the American people abandon their deep-seated mistrust of the federal government and turn for help to a charismatic presidential candidate who promises change. Elected by a landslide, the new president must then storm into office, quickly drawing up his reform agenda and forwarding it to Congress. Lawmakers then enact it in short order, in part because many rode into office on the president's coattails and now feel they owe their seats to him and in part because the opposition has been scattered and demoralized by its crushing electoral defeat. Hence, the programs of the American welfare state were established and expanded in two "big bangs." The first of these was Franklin Roosevelt's New Deal in 1933–36, in response to the economic dislocation caused by the Great Depression; the second, Lyndon Johnson's Great Society and War on Poverty in 1964–66, in response to widespread social and racial unrest. But momentum is soon lost, and the gridlock and inaction that typifies American politics return.[1] As a result, outside these two extraordinary periods of liberal activism, there is little policy innovation. Viewed from a historical perspective, this pattern of policymaking explains why, compared to its Western European counterparts, the American welfare state has remained exceptional—exception-

---

1. Christopher Leman, *The Collapse of Welfare Reform: Political Institutions, Policy, and the Poor in Canada and the United States* (Cambridge: MIT Press, 1980), 23, 26–33.

ally spartan, exceptionally stingy, exceptionally punitive toward the poor.

Yet this truism of American politics is not necessarily true. In fact, this book recounts the expansion of disability benefit programs since 1970, just one occasion in which conventional wisdom is misleading. But how can we account for these successful episodes of liberal reform? How do we explain instances when liberal advocates were able to navigate around political impediments and reach their goals despite the odds? How do we account for the growth of some social welfare programs in a political environment hostile to such innovations? The answers to these questions provide important lessons about how policy innovation occurs in American politics notwithstanding daunting political hurdles.

In some ways, of course, the history of disability benefits in the United States confirms the nation's reputation as a welfare laggard. With the exception of small programs for railroad workers, veterans, and civil servants, until the mid twentieth century, help for sick or injured people was not a national concern. States and local governments retained primary responsibility for running workers' compensation funds, institutions for people with mental illness or developmental disabilities, and the various aid programs for the blind and crippled. It was not until 1956 that Congress extended social insurance coverage to disability, marking the first time that most (but not all) workers were protected against the vagaries of injury and illness. Even then, the new Social Security Disability Insurance program was a strict one, limited to workers over age fifty who had been rendered completely and permanently unable to work with no provision made for temporary sickness or partial disablement.

Disability benefits have come a long way from these modest beginnings. Throughout the 1960s, Congress raised the value of disability payments, dropped the age restriction, covered impairments that were not permanent but lasted longer than one year, reduced the length of time a worker had to be employed before he qualified, and extended public health insurance to some people with disabilities. In 1972, lawmakers expanded cash assistance to disabled adults and children living in poverty. Not surprisingly, in the decades since, spending for entitlements for the disabled has soared, and the programs have grown to encompass larger numbers of younger workers, children, and people with mental disorders—groups that were only a marginal part of early programs. Today benefits for the disabled represent one of the fastest growing segments of the social safety net. As a result, the pendulum has swung from largesse to circumspection. Politicians who once worried about deserving individuals being turned away now fret that too many people who enter the rolls are not really disabled at all.

What is so remarkable about this transformation in social welfare policy is that the years since 1970 hardly seem a time to expect liberal policy change. The era saw the resurgence of a staunchly conservative Republican Party and increasing public doubts about governmental activism. During this time, maturing entitlement programs and slower economic growth enhanced fiscal pressures for spending cuts, and the optimism that launched the War on Poverty in 1964 gave way to dramatic efforts in the late 1970s to scale back the reach of most social welfare programs.[2] When Democrats in the 1990s adopted a pragmatic approach to antipoverty policy, characterized as a "third way" between the ideological excesses of the Left and the Right, their emphasis on promoting employment and ending long-term dependency on the state seemed to make the expansion of social welfare commitments a dubious enterprise.

In this book, I examine how the expansion in disability benefits occurred in this rather inauspicious political climate. I focus attention on the mobilization of people with disabilities under the banner of a new civil rights movement and on the influence this movement had on social welfare policy. More specifically, I explore three related developments. First, I recount how initially disability benefits policy was closely tied to a medical understanding of disability, a policymaking framework that kept benefit programs limited to a relatively small number of recipients and, in the eyes of disability rights activists, maintained the isolation and inferior social status of people with disabilities. Second, I show how advocates for the disabled challenged the prevailing medical view of disability, advancing in its place a rights-based understanding of disability that eventually encouraged the expansion of benefit programs. Advocates argued that disability—that is, the inability to work and provide for one's needs because of a medical impairment—was not an inherent feature of a person, but a socially constructed phenomenon that excused discriminatory treatment against anyone who was physically or mentally different from the able-bodied majority. Insisting that the disabled had a right to take part in mainstream society, advocates pressed for the recognition of employment rights, the creation of accessible transportation systems and buildings, and the deinstitutionalization of mental patients. Seizing on the idea of social inclusion, some antipoverty and disability advocates sought to end the "warehousing" of the disabled poor in state residential

2. Thomas Bryne Edsall and Mary D. Edsall, *Chain Reaction: The Impact of Race, Rights, and Taxes on American Politics* (New York: Norton, 1992), and Michael B. Katz, *The Undeserving Poor: From the War on Poverty to the War on Welfare* (New York: Knopf, 1989).

hospitals and group homes and to erect in their place a "new asylum" of income support, health care, and social services. For these advocates, embracing this new rights-based understanding of disability meant that government should not provide income support programs for the disabled because people with disabilities were automatically and utterly incapable of caring for themselves, but because such programs would allow the disabled to live a life of dignity and autonomy within their home communities alongside the able-bodied. Finally, I explain how advocates incorporated their new views into policy, leading to an expansion of disability benefit programs, and why conservatives could not halt program growth but were able to block the establishment of the broad social safety net that advocates for the disabled hoped would make full community integration possible.

This perspective on policy change is fundamentally political. It emphasizes the central importance of conflicting ideas about disability, the strategies and tactics of advocates, and the political hurdles that the advocates had to overcome. This political interpretation is a different approach than that taken by much of the literature on disability benefits policy. There, scholars assume that there is no political conflict because everyone agrees that the disabled deserve social assistance, or they give politics only a brief mention, focusing instead on the economic or demographic reasons for program change. While these approaches have merit, they cannot account fully for the scale of innovation that has taken place in income support programs for the disabled. It is not simply the case that the program expansion was "natural," the expected outcome of increases in the size of a program's target population or inflation. Instead, the expansion was "real" in the sense that it resulted from purposeful policy actions designed to "enlarge the scope or function of a program in relation to its social or economic base."[3] Program expansion of this sort is not merely a change in degree. Instead, it represents an effort "to redefine the relationship" between government and the private sector and "an aspiration for change in the institutions and processes as well as the substance and direction" of policy.[4] Because I seek to explain program change that cannot be accounted for by quantifiable trends, understanding this sort of real growth requires an approach that is, at bottom, historical and qualitative. I focus on the mobilization of social movements, watershed political events, and departures from the policy norm rather

3. Martha Derthick, *Policymaking for Social Security* (Washington, DC: Brookings Institution Press, 1979), 295.

4. Richard A. Harris and Sidney M. Milkis, *The Politics of Regulatory Change: A Tale of Two Agencies*, 2d ed. (Oxford: Oxford University Press, 1996), 23.

than shifts in the population or labor market. I attend not only to variations in the size of benefit programs but also to transformations in their character and meaning over time.

The Quiet Revolution in Disability Benefits

In this book, I concentrate on developments in America's largest disability benefit program, Social Security. Social Security actually includes two programs for the disabled: Disability Insurance (DI) and Supplemental Security Income (SSI). The two programs share the same definition of disability and rules for certification. The difference is that DI is a social insurance program that provides benefits only to workers who have paid into the program's trust fund and to the dependents of those workers. SSI, on the other hand, is a source of cash support for individuals who live in poverty. In addition, how much a worker and his family receive from DI depends on the amount the worker contributed in payroll taxes, while SSI benefits, meager by comparison, are designed only to bring the recipient's income close to the poverty line. By any measure used, DI has expanded significantly since 1956 when Congress agreed to insure workers against the economic risks of disablement. SSI, added in 1972, has also grown by leaps and bounds. As illustrated by figure I.1, the number of persons awarded DI and SSI was especially pronounced in the years 1972–75 and 1984–95. A commensurate increase in program costs matched this expansion in program participation. Total federal and state spending for SSI increased from $3.8 billion in 1974 to $35 billion in 2003, with particularly rapid growth taking place during the 1990s. Meanwhile, total spending for DI benefits tripled from $3.2 billion in 1970 to $10.4 billion in 1976. By 1986, costs had nearly doubled to $20.5 billion; they then more than doubled again to $42.0 billion in 1996. In 2003, spending on benefits for disabled workers and their families reached $66 billion.[5]

More important than sheer enrollment numbers and expenditure levels, however, were three trends that accompanied growth. First was the fact that this expansion in spending and enrollment did not occur evenly

5. U.S. Social Security Administration, *Annual Statistical Supplement*, 2001, table 4.A2, 152 (hereafter SSA, 2001 Supplement); Program Highlights from U.S. Social Security Administration, *SSI Annual Statistical Report*, 2003, http://www.ssa.gov/policy/docs/statcomps/ssi_asr/2003/index.html#highlights; and Program Highlights from U.S. Social Security Administration, *Annual Statistical Report on the Social Security Disability Insurance Program*, 2003, http://www.ssa.gov/policy/docs/statcomps/di_asr/2003/index.html#highlights.

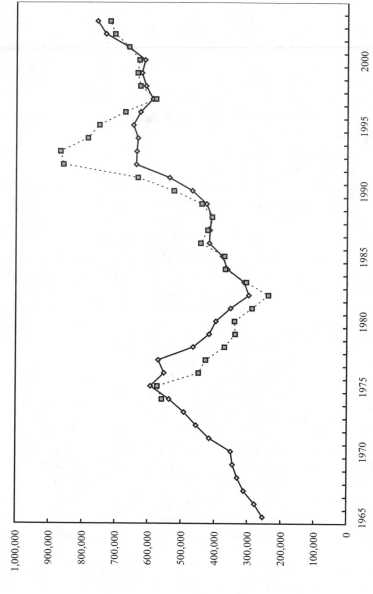

Figure 1.1 Number of Disabled Workers Awarded DI Benefits and Number of Disabled Persons Awarded SSI Benefits by Year, 1965–2003. (*Sources:* For DI, see U.S. Social Security Administration, *Annual Statistical Report on the Social Security Disability Insurance Program,* 2003, table 31, 89; for SSI, U.S. Social Security Administration, *SSI Annual Statistical Report,* 2003, table 47, 105, taking the total awards for all ages and removing those for persons age 65 and older.)

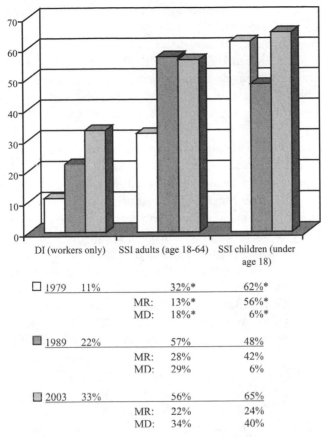

	DI (workers only)		SSI adults (age 18-64)	SSI children (under age 18)
☐ 1979	11%		32%*	62%*
		MR:	13%*	56%*
		MD:	18%*	6%*
■ 1989	22%		57%	48%
		MR:	28%	42%
		MD:	29%	6%
▨ 2003	33%		56%	65%
		MR:	22%	24%
		MD:	34%	40%

Figure I.2 Proportion of Persons with Mental Retardation (MR) and Other Mental Disorders (MD) on the Social Security Disability Rolls, Selected Years. (*Source*: For DI, see U.S. House of Representatives, Committee on Ways and Means, *Background Material and Data on Programs within the Jurisdiction of the Committee on Ways and Means (2001 Green Book)*, table I-43, 81, and U.S. Social Security Administration, *Annual Statistical Report on the Social Security Disability Insurance Program* 2003, table 6, 37. For SSI, see U.S. Social Security Administration, *Annual Statistical Supplement*, 1980, table 131, 229; *Annual Statistical Supplement*, 1989, table 9.F1, 336; and *SSI Annual Statistical Report*, 2003, table 25, 57. Figures on the percentage of SSI recipients currently receiving payments by diagnostic category are not available for 1979. Instead, figures presented are for the percentage of awards made that year by diagnostic category.)

among groups of the disabled. Instead, it was concentrated among impairments that are difficult to measure and verify—impairments such as chronic pain, backaches, fatigue, muscle weakness, and anxiety. Mental disorders are the most common of these "soft" impairments. Figure I.2 shows the growth in the proportion of the mentally disabled in the DI and SSI programs over time. Presently, one in three disabled workers and nearly two out of three SSI recipients suffer from a mental disorder; respectively, these are double and triple the proportions since the 1970s. The prevalence of mental disabilities is even more striking among children enrolled in SSI. Between 1989 and 2001, the proportion of children with a mental impairment grew more than fivefold, increasing from only 6 percent of all children receiving SSI to 32 percent. Today, children and adults with mental disorders outnumber beneficiaries in all other diagnostic categories.[6]

The rising numbers of beneficiaries with mental disorders contributed to a second trend that accompanied the expansion of DI and SSI—that is, the growing presence of younger people on the disability rolls. Because some of the most severe mental illnesses occur in young adulthood and can disrupt education plans and budding careers in a way that will have a lasting impact on future employment prospects, beneficiaries with mental impairments are, on the whole, younger than beneficiaries with other conditions.[7] Thus, as mental disorders became more prominent on the disability rolls, the age of the typical person receiving disability payments dropped precipitously. Between 1960 and 1993, the average age of workers enrolled in DI fell from 54.5 years to an all-time low of 47.7 years. (It has since rebounded to 51.3 years).[8] Because SSI pays benefits to children, its recipients, on average, tend to be even younger than DI beneficiaries. Currently, one-third of SSI recipients are under the age of 40 compared to only 14 percent of disabled workers. But even when children are excluded from the calculations, almost twice as many adult SSI recipients as disabled workers are under the age of 40, largely because

6. U.S. Social Security Administration, *SSI Annual Statistical Report*, 2001, tables 45 and 46, 98, 99.

7. Ronald C. Kessler, C. L. Foster, W. B. Saunders, and P. E. Stang, "Social Consequences of Psychiatric Disorders I: Educational Attainment," *American Journal of Psychiatry* 152, 7 (1995): 1026–32; JoAnne E. Turnbull, Linda K. George, Richard Landerman, Marvin S. Swartz, and Dan G. Blazer, "Social Outcomes Related to Age of Onset among Psychiatric Disorders," *Journal of Consulting and Clinical Psychology* 58, 6 (1990): 832–39; Ann Vander Stoep, Shirley A. Beresford, Noel S. Weiss, Barbara McKnight, Ana Mari Cance, and Patricia Cohen, "Community-Based Study of the Transition to Adulthood for Adolescents with Psychiatric Disorder," *American Journal of Epidemiology* 152, 4 (2000): 352–62; and Sue E. Estroff, Catherine Zimmer, William S. Lachicotte, Julie Benoit, and Donald L. Patrick, " 'No Other Way to Go': Pathways to Disability Income Application among Persons with Severe Persistent Mental Illness," in *Mental Disorder, Work Disability, and the Law,* ed. Richard J. Bonnie and John Monahan (Chicago: University of Chicago Press, 1997), 61.

8. U.S. Social Security Administration, *Annual Statistical Report on the Social Security Disability Insurance Program*, 2000, table 15, 52 (hereafter SSA, 2000 DI Report), and U.S. Social Security Administration, *Annual Statistical Report on the Social Security Disability Insurance Program*, 2003, table 19, 66.

SSI enrolls a larger proportion of people with mental impairments than DI does and because DI claimants must show a history of employment before they qualify while SSI applicants do not.[9]

The larger proportion of mental disorders and the relative youth of current DI and SSI beneficiaries contributed to a third trend associated with program expansion. Given that persons with mental disorders tend to stay on the disability rolls longer than anyone else, as the average age of beneficiaries dropped, the length of time that the typical beneficiary received disability payments increased.[10] According to Kalman Rupp and Charles Scott, a disabled worker entering Disability Insurance today is expected to collect benefits for an average of 10.9 years, up from an expected duration of 9.5 years in 1975.[11] SSI recipients are expected to stay on the rolls even longer. Rupp and Scott estimate that the adults and children presently enrolled in SSI will, on average, spend the next 17.8 years receiving payments.[12]

Taken together, these three trends—the growing prevalence of mental disorders and other soft impairments, the increasing youth of beneficiaries, and longer spells on the disability rolls—add up to administrative and political trouble. In recent decades, the Social Security Administration (SSA) has struggled to find a reliable way of evaluating mental disorders, one that will adequately separate true medical conditions from mere personality flaws. Critics, meanwhile, remain dissatisfied, arguing that people who are found disabled today simply do not meet the strict standard of disability that Congress intended when it created DI in the 1950s. At the same time, given the relative youth of DI and SSI beneficiaries,

9. Author's calculations based on SSA, 2001 Supplement, table 7.E3, 290 (includes aged recipients), and author's calculations based on SSA, 2000 DI Report, table 8, 39.

10. Scott Kochlar and Charles G. Scott, "Disability Patterns among SSI Recipients," *Social Security Bulletin* 58, 1 (1995): 3–14, and Kalman Rupp and Charles G. Scott, "Trends in the Characteristics of DI and SSI Disability Awards and Duration of Program Participation," *Social Security Bulletin* 59, 1 (1996): 3–21.

11. Kalman Rupp and Charles G. Scott, "Determinants of Duration on the Disability Rolls and Program Trends," in *Growth in Disability Benefits: Explanations and Policy Implications*, ed. Kalman Rupp and David C. Stapleton (Kalamazoo, MI: W. E. Upjohn, 1998), table 4.2, 150.

12. Because SSI is a means-tested program, the figures for SSI are arrived at after correcting for exits resulting from income changes rather than recovery, death, or retirement. When exits due to income changes are not taken into account, the average length of stay on SSI is substantially lower, reflecting the volatility in family income of SSI recipients. When the analysis is limited to adult SSI recipients, the average length of stay drops to 11.3 years, still higher than the average duration on the DI rolls but now more closely in line with it. Rupp and Scott, "Determinants of Duration," table 4.5, 159.

some lawmakers have urged the SSA to intensify its rehabilitation and employment support efforts rather than simply send out disability checks. Indeed, some elected officials now worry that the long stretches that DI beneficiaries and especially SSI recipients spend collecting payments will not only encourage long-term "welfare" dependency among the disabled, a term once reserved for single mothers, but also push program costs higher far into the future.

Trying to Explain the Growth of Disability Programs

How did this extraordinary change in Social Security disability benefits take place? Typically, sociologists and economists attribute the growth in benefit programs to increased public demand. This demand, in turn, is the result of either demographic changes or the state of the economy. The two most consequential demographic shifts are the growth of the U.S. population and the "graying" of the Baby Boom generation, both of which are expected to lead naturally to higher incidences of chronic illnesses, limited mobility, and senility. Yet, while population shifts are certainly a factor, the enrollment increases in DI and SSI that occurred during the 1980s and 1990s were far out of proportion with demographic changes. Although the U.S. population increased by 11 percent between 1984 and 1993, the number of DI and SSI recipients grew by 60 percent over the same time period.[13] In addition, since the 1970s, the most dramatic growth in the Social Security disability programs has taken place, not among beneficiaries nearing retirement, as anticipated, but among younger workers.[14]

Economic explanations are, likewise, incomplete. All studies clearly show that when the economy slides into recession, applications for disability payments increase. Though the impact of unemployment varies widely from study to study, none have found the opposite effect.[15] Much

13. U.S. Congressional Research Service (CRS), prepared by David Koitz, Geoffrey Kollman, and Jennifer Neisner, *Status of the Disability Programs of the Social Security Administration*, 1992, 51.

14. Between 1980 and 1990, the median age of the population rose from 30.0 to 32.9 years old, an increase attributable in large part to longevity among the oldest cohort. These individuals, however, tend to receive Social Security retirement pensions rather than disability payments. In the age brackets where dependence on disability pensions is expected to be the most pronounced, age 50–64 years, the population actually fell, reflecting the low birth rates of the 1930s. Ibid., 3 n. 5.

15. A review of studies that have investigated the effect of the unemployment rate on the Social Security disability programs can be found in Kalman Rupp and David C. Stapleton, Introduction to *Growth in Disability Benefits*, ed. Rupp and Stapleton, 15–16.

more muddled, however, is the relationship between unemployment and the number of applications actually approved for benefits. Historically, economic changes track imperfectly the trends in awards. For example, enrollment in the Social Security disability programs was far below what economists would have predicted during the recessions of 1980 and 1981–82. On the other hand, increases in DI and SSI enrollment continued well after the 1990–91 recession ended.[16] Noting that unemployment had receded by 1993 while enrollment in SSI and DI still stood at an "all-time high," congressional researchers argued that "it would be misleading to conclude that the dominant factor behind recent growth . . . was a poor economic picture."[17] Moreover, studies found that during the economic boom of the mid to late 1990s, the employment rate for persons with disabilities declined significantly even though employment increased for the general population. This decline occurred despite the fact that the enactment of the Americans with Disabilities Act (ADA) in 1990 was supposed to have opened the workplace to the disabled and ended their need to depend on welfare.[18] In short, employment of the disabled, enrollment in disability benefit programs, and the state of the economy remain rather loosely related.

Concentrating primarily on explaining the growth that took place between 1980 and 1994, a study conducted by David C. Stapleton and his colleagues placed these social and economic conditions in context. Accounting for the effect of population growth, the aging of the population, unemployment, economic restructuring, cuts in state general assistance programs, the HIV/AIDS epidemic, and rates of immigration and poverty, the researchers concluded that the three major reasons for the growth of the programs after 1989 were the 1990–91 recession, efforts by state and local governments to shift the costs of welfare spending onto federal programs, and changes in the "supply" of benefits. With their model, Stapleton and his colleagues could explain almost half the annual increases in applications filed for DI and SSI, but they found it much more difficult to account for the increasing share of applications approved for payment. Altogether their variables accounted for one-

16. David Stapleton, Kevin Coleman, Kimberly Dietrich, and Gina Livermore, "Empirical Analysis of DI and SSI Application and Award Growth," in *Growth in Disability Benefits*, ed. Rupp and Stapleton, 56–58.

17. CRS, *Status of the Disability Programs*, 51.

18. Richard V. Burkhauser, Andrew J. Houtenville, and David C. Wittenburg, "A User's Guide to Current Statistics on the Employment of People with Disabilities," in *The Decline in Employment of People with Disabilities: A Policy Puzzle*, ed. David C. Stapleton and Richard V. Burkhauser (Kalamazoo, MI: W. E. Upjohn Institute, 2003), 72–73.

quarter of the annual growth in awards for DI but just 7 percent of the annual growth in SSI awards. The model also was unable to explain a large proportion of the growth in applications from workers under the age of fifty, persons with mental disorders or musculoskeletal impairments, and individuals claiming SSI. Yet these were the very groups of the disabled that most interested policymakers, because they represented the most rapidly increasing parts of the Social Security disability programs.[19] Stapleton and his colleagues attributed the growth that they could not explain to changes in policy, changes that encouraged individuals to apply for benefits and administrators to grant awards. Though these factors were exceedingly difficult to measure with the same precision as economic factors were, the researchers concluded that they undoubtedly mattered.[20]

While theories that focus on population shifts and labor market transformations explain an important piece of the puzzle, these approaches are incomplete. Because politics is outside the purview of these researchers and because policy changes are difficult to measure in a quantitative manner, one is left with the impression that the programs serve only as conduits through which larger changes in the population or business cycle are translated into policy outcomes. How these social conditions are mediated by governing institutions, political actors, and even the programs themselves remains obscured. Disability programs, however, are far from static, black boxes, automatically converting external inputs into policy outputs. On the contrary, they are politically dynamic and highly responsive to legislative, judicial, and administrative actions. As congressional researchers have noted, "the programs' volatility probably results from . . . what many view as subtle rule and process changes."[21] Though seemingly small and inconsequential, these "subtle rule and process changes" have had a profound and far-reaching impact on disability programs.

In this book I emphasize the central importance of political contests regarding the meaning and scope of disability. Of course, given the com-

---

19. Stapleton et al., "Empirical Analysis," 71–74, and Exhibit 2A.4, 92.

20. Ibid., 72, 74–75. Similarly, two researchers trace rising levels of unemployment among people with disabilities to the policy liberalizations made to DI in the 1980s and 1990s. See Nanette Goodman and Timothy Waidmann, "Social Security Disability Insurance and the Recent Decline in the Employment Rate of People with Disabilities," in *Decline in Employment of People with Disabilities*, ed. Stapleton and Burkhauser, 339–68. See also Richard V. Burkhauser and David C. Stapleton, "A Review of the Evidence and Its Implications for Policy Change," in *Decline in Employment of People with Disabilities*, ed. Stapleton and Burkhauser, 389–93.

21. CRS, *Status of the Disability Programs*, 53–54.

plexity of a phenomenon like disability, complete explanations are likely to be multifaceted.[22] Political interpretations, therefore, are best seen as a complement to, rather than a competitor with, social and economic analyses. My intention is not to displace these theories but to enhance them with an approach that is decidedly political and that accounts for program expansion that cannot be accounted for by the conventional explanations. Only by turning our attention to how program rules and processes are shaped by political conflict can we make sense of the vast changes that have occurred and continue to occur in disability and social welfare policy.

Why Study the Politics of Disability

Ideally, political scientists would balance the attention that economists and demographers place on quantifiable economic and social factors with comparable attention to the political origins of the growth in disability benefits programs. This has not been the case, however. Political scientists rarely examine disability as an important chapter in the development of American social welfare policy. There are two reasons for this neglect. First, disability is an exceedingly complex policy area, which until recently discouraged interest in its politics. Spread over law, economics, sociology, rehabilitation studies, and medicine, issues of disability have spawned a thicket of policy complexities that few have dared to tread. As historian Edward Berkowitz points out, disability policy is a jumble of disconnected programs "born in many different eras," frequently working at odds with one another and "reflect[ing] many styles of policymaking." Workers' compensation, veterans' pensions, special education, health care, civil rights, income-support, and legal torts all address disability issues. Yet they are seen as separate and discrete policy areas and rarely viewed as a whole.[23] One observer declared in frustration, "From

22. Other reasons suggested for the growth in DI and SSI in the early 1990s are structural changes in the economy that had a particularly adverse impact on the employment opportunities of the disabled, the lack of any other income support available for people with disabilities, and the incentives to enroll provided by the linking of disability benefits to public health care coverage. Edward Yelin, *Disability and the Displaced Worker* (New Brunswick, NJ: Rutgers University Press, 1992); Richard V. Burkhauser, Robert Haveman, and Barbara Wolfe, "How People with Disabilities Fare When Public Policies Change," *Journal of Policy Analysis and Management* 12, 2 (1993): 251–69; and Aaron Yelowitz, *Why Did the SSI-Disabled Program Grow So Much? Disentangling the Effect of Medicaid* (Cambridge: National Bureau of Economic Research, 1997).

23. Edward D. Berkowitz, *Disabled Policy: America's Programs for the Handicapped* (Cambridge: Cambridge University Press, 1987), 1.

this welter of programs, no policy emerges, only inconsistency and conflict."[24] Trying to make sense of this morass is exceedingly difficult, and the need to master countless medical and legal concepts and the details of the many disparate programs that comprise our nation's disability policy poses a formidable challenge. Scholars are deterred from tackling the subject, which, more often than not, has been left to specialists whose technical language has obscured broader political trends. As a result, "disability has not received the attention it deserves as a policy problem."[25]

The second reason that the politics of disability have not received the scholarly consideration it warrants is because political scientists are generally interested in explaining controversy, and they see very little of it in disability programs. The literature on American social welfare policy draws a sharp distinction between programs for the deserving poor and those for the undeserving poor. The latter receives a great deal of attention, and indeed, much of what we know is based largely on studies of Aid to Families with Dependent Children (AFDC, now called Temporary Assistance for Needy Families or TANF), the cash assistance program that most Americans had in mind when they used the word "welfare" in its most pejorative sense. But as Steven Teles points out, the politics of family assistance is not indicative of the broader patterns of welfare state politics in the United States. "AFDC is different," he explains. "No other program of the American welfare state is so unpopular." No other program raises, to the same degree, the acrimonious issues of race, gender roles, and sexual and personal responsibility. Turning his attention to the other programs that comprise America's social safety net, Teles notes, "Although there are occasional political debates about these parts of the original American welfare state, they are for the most part uncontroversial and politically stable."[26] Yet scholars tend to dismiss these programs, including programs for the disabled, as requiring little critical scrutiny

24. Editorial introduction to "The Right to an Adequate Income and Employment," in *The Mentally Retarded Citizen and the Law*, ed. Michael Kindred, Julius Cohen, David Penrod, Thomas L. Shaffer, report sponsored by the President's Committee on Mental Retardation (New York: Free Press, 1976), 271.

25. Berkowitz, *Disabled Policy*, 225–26.

26. Steven Teles, *Whose Welfare? AFDC and Elite Politics* (Lawrence: University Press of Kansas, 1994), 1, 2. Robert Greenstein, in fact, points out that contrary to what many scholars write about means-tested programs, many including the Earning Income Tax Credit, SSI, Food Stamps, and Medicaid have been quite resilient in the face of retrenchment. See Robert Greenstein, "Universal and Targeted Approaches to Relieving Poverty: An Alternative View," in *The Urban Underclass*, ed. Christopher Jencks and Paul E. Peterson (Washington, DC: Brookings Institution Press, 1991), 437–59.

because they are targeted at a group that everyone agrees merits social assistance. Supposedly, there is no political conflict to explain.[27]

Scholars connect the privileged moral status of the disabled to American cultural values prizing hard work and self-sufficiency. Government programs use administrative categories like disability or age as mechanisms to enforce social judgments about who should work and who is allowed to receive social aid. Only those individuals who are considered infirm are entitled to assistance; all others must find employment. According to this line of reasoning, because their medical condition renders them functionally incapacitated, the disabled are not expected to work, and since their infirmity is not their fault, providing social assistance to them does not violate social norms.[28]

Applying this simplistic distinction, scholars find it all too easy to account for policy outcomes. For instance, Daniel Patrick Moynihan noted that in 1972, federal aid to the elderly and disabled poor easily passed Congress while reforms designed to enhance assistance to poor families collapsed. The reason, he wrote, "was not only a matter of equity but of politics": The elderly and disabled "were the 'deserving poor,' and they were voters"; poor mothers and their children were neither.[29] Striking a similar refrain, historian Walter Trattner dismissed the enactment of SSI as nothing more than an effort targeted at individuals "who are clearly unemployable," thus demonstrating "the lasting strength of America's work ethic."[30] Likewise, Paul Pierson notes that in the United States and Great Britain conservative attempts in the 1980s to cut disability programs faltered because "few groups are more deserving of public support than the sick and disabled."[31] But he goes no further in explaining how the deservingness of the disabled is translated into the political clout necessary to withstand retrenchment pressures.

No doubt, to the extent that the American people and politicians make judgments about the moral worth of supplicants for social assistance, no-

27. Arthur W. Blaser, "Taking Disability Rights Seriously," *New Political Science* 25, 4 (2003): 594.

28. Lance Liebman, "The Definition of Disability in Social Security and Supplemental Security Income: Drawing the Bounds of Social Welfare Estates," *Harvard Law Review* 89, 5 (1976): 853. See also Deborah A. Stone, *The Disabled State* (Philadelphia: Temple University Press, 1984), 15–28.

29. Daniel Patrick Moynihan, *The Politics of a Guaranteed Income: The Nixon Administration and the Family Assistance Plan* (New York: Vintage, 1973), 198.

30. Walter I. Trattner, *From Poor Law to Welfare State: A History of Social Welfare in America* (New York: Free Press, 1974), 271.

31. Paul Pierson, *Dismantling the Welfare State? Reagan, Thatcher, and the Politics of Retrenchment* (Cambridge: Cambridge University Press, 1994), 139.

tions of deservingness are worth taking into consideration. But a stark dichotomy is too simplistic. To begin with, the emphasis placed on deservingness treats disability as a monolithic category when, in fact, impairments are diverse in nature and their relative deservingness is equally as varied. People in wheelchairs are regarded as the deserving disabled by most Americans, but mental disabilities, childhood behavioral and learning disorders, and chronic pain are poorly understood impairments that elicit as much skepticism as they do empathy. Indeed, the disabled often encompasses individuals whom most of us might judge as decidedly undeserving—drug addicts, alcoholics, troubled children, and persons with personality disorders, for instance. Moreover, far from being fixed, the distinction between the deserving and undeserving varies over time. Old age, disability, and childhood are valid reasons to stay out of the labor market, and the old, disabled, and children are supported by public assistance or private charity. Motherhood once was seen this way, too, but this exception is hotly contested today, particularly in the case of single mothers living in poverty. The boundaries of deserving categories are often uncertain as well. Age is easy to determine, but there is no widely accepted definition of "disability." The condition can easily be feigned, and because different people have different ideas about what constitutes a disability, even well-intentioned individuals using the same standards find it difficult to reach the same conclusion in specific cases.[32] Disability, in short, is inescapably subjective, and attention to these issues soon reveals that who is "clearly employable" and who is deserving of social assistance is not necessarily so clear a demarcation after all.[33]

Although boundary questions are resolved for the time being when programs are enacted and legal definitions crafted, the subjective nature of disability opens the door to recurring political contests during the administration and amendment of programs. So while judgments of moral worth no doubt matter, policy outcomes are not simply the straightforward consequence of those judgments. Focusing exclusively on a specific group's moral worth fails to examine how government policies and political debate shape our understanding of deservingness. The delineation of this crucial distinction—who is deserving and who is not—is a decidedly

32. Stone, *Disabled State*, 23.
33. See, among others, Liebman, "Definition of Disability," 833–68; Stone, *Disabled State*; Claire H. Liachowitz, *Disability as a Social Construct: Legislative Roots* (Philadelphia: University of Pennsylvania Press, 1988); Matthew Diller, "Entitlement and Exclusion: The Role of Disability in the Social Welfare System," *UCLA Law Review* 44 (1996): 361–465; and Lars Noah, "Pigeonholing Illness: Medical Diagnosis as a Legal Construct," *Hastings Law Journal* 50 (1999): 241–307.

political enterprise, one that reveals a great deal about the ideas that animate American antipoverty efforts.

Readers familiar with the literature on disability will immediately recognize my argument as reminiscent of Deborah Stone's seminal work on disability policy, *The Disabled State*.[34] Seeking to explain the puzzle of program expansion, Stone argues that the pressure for liberalization is, to a great degree, inherent in the nature of disability benefit programs. While government programs attempt to ground disability on something objective, such as the presence of a medical illness or injury, the condition is intrinsically subjective. Consequently, no matter how tightly policymakers try to define disability, as an administrative category, disability is elastic; it can be stretched or contracted over time. Yet restrictive disability programs require constant vigilance against lax interpretations of disability as well as against those applicants who would feign the condition for pecuniary gain while expansive pressures continually emanate from the political, legal, and social contexts. Thus, in all nations, the trend has been inexorably in the direction of programmatic growth regardless of time or place.

This book serves as a complement to *The Disabled State*. Taking Stone's analysis of the subjectivity of disability as a starting point, this study investigates the specific actions political actors and interest groups undertook in their efforts to mold the interpretation of disability to serve their policy ends. Stone argues that disability as an administrative concept is inherently expansive; this study analyzes how advocates took advantage of this conceptual opening.

Incorporating a deeper understanding of disability into our picture of the American social welfare policy serves a much-needed corrective purpose. Scholars have long compared programs in the United States to the extensive welfare states of Western Europe and found America wanting. The possible reasons for this disparity are many, ranging from theories that point to the weakness of the labor movement in the United States, the lack of a political voice among the poor, the disruptive effects of race on efforts to build coalitions between poor and working class citizens, and institutional obstacles—such as the Senate filibuster, the presidential veto, and the tradition of judicial review—which allow small but well-organized conservative groups to block popular legislative initiatives.[35]

---

34. Stone, *Disabled State*.

35. For a review of the various explanations of American welfare state development, see Edwin Amenta and Theda Skocpol, "States and Social Policies," *Annual Review of Sociology* 12 (1986): 131–57; Jill Quadagno, "Theories of the Welfare State," *Annual Review of Sociology* 13 (1987): 109–28; Hugh Heclo, "The Political Foundations of An-

The common thread behind these scholarly works is the premise that the American welfare state is a failure or, at best, an unrealized project. Rather than a universal welfare state that aids all (or most) citizens as a matter of right, the United States is stuck with a residual welfare state, one that does little to redistribute resources equitably among rich and poor and that provides only the bare minimum (if that) to citizens who fall through the cracks of the market-driven economy.

This book is different. I contend that what is exceptional about the United States is not its failure to conform to a specified trajectory of welfare state advancement but instead the peculiar way in which policy is made. Explanations that focus primarily on political constraints do little to account for those instances when progressive reformers triumphed despite the odds, other than to view them as unusual and infrequent events. I argue, however, that in many ways the United States is particularly open to the demands of organized interests, including liberal public interest groups representing weak and marginalized people, like the disabled. Throughout the book, I examine the struggle of advocates to circumvent institutional barriers and ideological opposition in order to end discrimination against the disabled and further their integration into mainstream society. But I also consider how the American attachment to work and self-sufficiency, the shift of American politics to the right in the late 1970s, and the fragmentation of its governing institutions shaped and ultimately constrained the effectiveness of these advocacy efforts. What emerges from this analysis of disability policy is a richer picture of social welfare politics than admitted by simplistic characterizations of the United States as a welfare laggard.

The Plan of the Book

In order to illustrate the ebbs and flows of social welfare and disability politics, I examine Social Security and disability rights policy from the 1960s to the present. This period begins with the federal government assuming greater responsibility for poverty and economic inequality in the 1960s and early 1970s and ends with policymakers placing increased emphasis on ending dependency and scaling back social welfare spending in

---

tipoverty Policy," in *Fighting Poverty: What Works and What Doesn't*, ed. Sheldon H. Danzinger and Daniel H. Weinberg (Cambridge: Harvard University Press, 1986), 312–40; and Francis Fox Piven and Richard Cloward, *Regulating the Poor: The Functions of Public Welfare*, 2d ed. (New York: Vintage, 1993).

the late 1990s. I argue that policy decisions made in the 1950s as disability was added to the array of risks covered by social insurance set the limits within which future welfare and disability reform would take place. By defining disability as a medical condition that precluded work, policymakers erected a set of institutions that was not easily adapted to the "human rights" or "social" model of disability championed in the 1970s by advocates seeking to overcome the exclusion and secondary social status of the disabled. Still, even within these constraints, advocates were able to open Social Security to previously excluded groups of the disabled by taking advantage of judicial activism and congressional deadlock. But the reform interpretation of disability, which I call the "functional approach," made peace with rather than challenged Social Security's medicalized notion of disability. The key difference between the medical model and functional approach was that the functional approach allowed maladaptive and inappropriate behaviors to qualify as disabilities while the medical model often demanded more rigorous evidence in the form of clinical observations or laboratory tests. Because the functional approach took an expansive view of disability, advocates then sought to apply it to DI and SSI in order to bring more people under the protective umbrella of the welfare state. Their goal was to transform Social Security from a strictly compensatory program for middle-class workers into a safety net for disadvantaged persons with disabilities, many of whom were plagued by mental impairments that were not easily measured according to clinical criteria. Nevertheless, advocates did not entirely displace the medical paradigm. Rather than argue that disability was a social construct—a key underpinning of the rights model—the functional approach accepted that medical impairments were inherently debilitating and limiting, a compromise that, as I explain in later chapters, left policy reform incomplete.

In chapter 1, I begin with a discussion of the political and policy environment that served as the backdrop to efforts to restructure disability and social welfare policy. I highlight the shifts in the ideas that framed how society approached the problem of disability, transformations in American politics that made government accessible to newly mobilized disability groups, and the conditions that set limits on the ability of the advocates to realize their larger policy goals. I focus on the factors that leave American government open to initiatives of reform-minded actors as well as those that continue to frustrate their ambitions.

In chapter 2, I describe the advocates who are the protagonists of this political history. I trace their origins to the disability rights movement of the late 1960s and early 1970s. Or perhaps, I should say "movements," for as I make clear, the disability rights movement was actually a banner encompassing smaller movements of people with disabilities, including the patients' rights movement and the independent living movement. Not all activists were of the same mind regarding what policy reforms would best bring an end to the many disadvantages that the disabled confronted. Nevertheless, what activists shared in common was a strong belief that people with disabilities had a right to social inclusion—that is, the right to be full participants in the social life of their communities as equals with able-bodied people. Social inclusion, however, meant the ability to live free of the confines of residential hospitals and other medical institutions, and this required the establishment of a broad social safety net of income support, assistive services, and health care. I illustrate how advocates for mental patients drew from these new ideas about disability to argue for a shift from asylums toward community mental health care. I trace how the interest that patients' rights reformers had in community mental health care inspired their antipoverty activism and ultimately led them to organize around Social Security issues.

In chapter 3, I turn the focus from social movements outside of government to policy entrepreneurs within government. While advocates were formulating their plans for an expanded system of social supports for disabled people, a small circle of executive officials and lawmakers made it happen by pushing the Supplemental Security Income program through Congress in 1972. The irony, however, is that though SSI eventually became a vital part of the social safety net that advocates envisioned, neither they nor their rhetoric of disability rights had anything to do with the program's passage. SSI became law precisely because it was not framed as a rights or a disability issue, thus underscoring the difficulties disability advocates would face in creating a broad safety net based on the principle of inclusion. I explore why elected officials created SSI despite the fact that the disabled did not demand it as well as how the program opened Social Security policymaking to previously excluded groups of the disadvantaged disabled. As I explain, SSI inadvertently pushed Social Security policy toward the expansive understanding of disability that the advocates favored and became a cornerstone of the social safety net they hoped to erect.

In chapter 4, my narrative moves from the liberal confidence that characterized the years of the Great Society and the early years of the disability rights movement to the fiscal austerity and cost consciousness of the Carter and Reagan years, and shows how advocates traversed this adverse setting. I explain why advocates turned their attention from disability rights and patients' rights to Social Security and how they sought to reorient the program to serve the needs of the deinstitutionalized and disabled poor. I recount the frustrations advocates faced as President Reagan attempted to retrench social welfare programs across the board and the strategies they used to resist these moves.

In chapters 5, 6, and 7, I examine the strategy of the advocates and their opponents across three political forums: litigation, legislation, and administration. In chapter 5, I look at the role that federal judges played in shielding DI and SSI from budget cuts and pushing the boundaries of the programs beyond the strict medical interpretation of disability that Congress had sanctioned when it first created DI in the 1950s. Covering the years between 1982 and 1991, I explain how the federal courts were politicized by the Reagan administration's retrenchment efforts and why judges were receptive to the advocates' arguments for program expansion.

In chapter 6, I focus on how Congress dealt with social welfare and disability policies in light of the demands made by advocates. I explain why, throughout the mid and late 1980s, conservatives could not halt the judicially driven program expansion nor could liberals muster enough political support to build legislatively on the court decisions. With Congress deadlocked and divided until the mid 1990s, advocates were nonetheless adept at locking in the gains they had made in the courts and sneaking additional expansive measures past skeptical lawmakers. Judicial activism, cost-shifting by state governments, and administrative reforms pursued by sympathetic bureaucrats at the Social Security Administration facilitated program expansion even in the absence of congressional agreement. In addition, I examine why, despite their success with Social Security, advocates failed to build congressional support for a comprehensive system of income support and social services for disabled people living in the community. I trace this failure, in part, to the fight to win the enactment of another prize sought by the disabled community, the Americans with Disabilities Act, a broad bill designed to guarantee equal access rights for people with disabilities.

In chapter 7, I consider developments within the Social Security Administration that helped the advocates further open DI and SSI to deinstitutionalized adults and children. I chronicle how between 1985 and 1991 the SSA translated judicial and congressional decrees into administrative rules and practices that ultimately pushed program expansion even further than the courts or Congress anticipated. I also examine why these reforms to DI and SSI led to administrative breakdown and controversy by the early 1990s.

By 1993, with the Social Security disability programs growing rapidly and clearly in disarray, lawmakers tried to assert order and arrest the rising tide of disability claims. In chapter 8, I examine conservative efforts to roll back the liberalizations of the 1980s and early 1990s. Although retrenchment proponents were able to make significant headway, they were unable to realize their more far-reaching ambitions. In fact, many of the liberalizations that advocates had achieved remained embedded in administrative rules and practices, sheltered from the reach of opponents. The chapter explains why retrenchment proponents were able to scale back some aspects of DI and SSI while leaving others untouched.

Finally, in the conclusion, I balance the ledger by turning attention from the advocates' triumphs to their disappointments. While advocates were able to expand the DI and SSI programs, their larger hopes of an extensive array of community clinics, health care benefits, income support, sheltered work programs, and social services was not to be. This chapter explains why advocates were unable to bring about more expansive reforms to American social welfare policy. I argue that the most significant limitation advocates confronted emerged out the interaction between their strategic choices and the political climate in which they operated. Because no institution wholeheartedly supported their quest for social inclusion, advocates framed the establishment of employment and equal access rights as an alternative to spending for entitlements. Thus, policymakers, even some activists themselves, came to see disability rights and social welfare assistance as mutually exclusive policy approaches, a development that undercut the logic for a comprehensive social safety net. As a result, many individuals with disabilities still remain vulnerable to joblessness, poverty, and social isolation. This chapter shows what advocates lost in their drive for disability rights, as institutional constraints compromised their efforts, and by turning attention to the more comprehensive policies of Western Europe, it attempts to shed light on the possibilities for American disability policy.

A Word on Studying Social Security and Disability

Although there are more than seventy federal programs targeted at people with disabilities, I focus on Social Security's Disability Insurance and SSI programs. I chose these two programs because their size and scope make them important in their own right. Unlike the many smaller income support programs targeted at specific occupational groups, DI and SSI are open to the public, thus making them the largest of the disability benefit programs. Excluding outlays for health care, DI and SSI together account for almost three-quarters of the federal government's annual spending for disability programs. No other program comes close to rivaling their size regardless of whether the measure is total persons enrolled or annual expenditures.[36] Also, because eligibility for disability benefits is tied to eligibility for public health care programs, growth in these two programs drives up spending for Medicare and Medicaid as well. What happens in Social Security disability policy, therefore, has considerable fiscal consequences for the other parts of our nation's welfare state.

In addition, the fact that DI and SSI are individual entitlements brings to the fore the importance of categorical boundary drawing. Unlike discretionary programs, entitlements are "legal obligations that require the payment of benefits to any person . . . that meets the eligibility requirements established by law."[37] Thus, each person who satisfies Social Security's eligibility requirements is entitled to benefits regardless of cost. How much the federal government spends in a given year is determined by how many persons qualify and how the benefit payments are calculated rather than by annual congressional appropriations. Consequently, lawmakers cannot hold the line on program growth by simply capping spending, as they might for community mental health programs and other social services block grants. If Congress wants to limit the number of persons on the Social Security disability rolls, it must tighten the standards used or change the formula for computing benefit levels. As a result, the categorical boundary of disability—that is, how disability is defined statutorily and administratively—emerges as vitally important in regulating the scope of the DI and SSI programs. This book explores how this boundary is drawn and redrawn over time.

Furthermore, although the range and types of impairments is vast, this study concentrates on programmatic growth in the following three areas: (1) adults with mental disorders, (2) children with disabilities, and (3) adults disabled by alcoholism or drug addiction. There are two reasons for this approach. First, by looking specifically at these groups, I can evaluate how notions of moral worth are disputed and refined through politics. Although the disabled are widely regarded as deserving of social assistance, the mentally disabled, substance abusers, and disabled children—at least those children with emotional, learning, and behavioral problems—put this assertion to the test. Moreover, these groups are

36. U.S. General Accounting Office, *Adults with Severe Disabilities: Federal and State Approaches for Personal Care and Other Services*, HEHS-99–101, 1999, 2.

37. Aaron Wildavsky, "The Politics of the Entitlement Process," in *The New Politics of Public Policy*, ed. Marc K. Landy and Martin A. Levin (Baltimore: Johns Hopkins University Press, 1995), 143.

what make disability benefits controversial. Of all the diagnostic groups eligible for Disability Insurance and SSI, mental disorders, childhood disabilities, and substance addiction grew the fastest during the 1980s and 1990s. This development defies conventional wisdom since program expansion has taken place precisely among those groups of the disabled whose status as "deserving" is most vigorously contested. Singling out these three groups, therefore, takes us into those aspects of policy that have been at the forefront of political conflict.

Of course, there are other areas of disability that are not explored in this book. For example, the number of claims filed for musculoskeletal impairments, like chronic back pain, and infectious diseases, in particular HIV/AIDS, has grown rapidly in recent years. But I do not examine advocacy on behalf of individuals with these impairments. Thus, it is possible that by focusing on mental disability, addiction, and childhood disability, I present a picture of policy reform that is exaggerated in its coherence. Indeed, deinstitutionalization and the patients' rights movement may have given advocates for children and the mentally disabled an integrity and consistent rationale that representatives for other impairments lacked. Other areas of disability may not be as well organized as they were, and groups in those areas perhaps did not draw on the same ideas or use the same tactics as the advocates in this study do.

With these caveats in mind, I still believe that the advantages of focusing on these three groups outweigh the shortcomings. I am explaining the increase in disability awards and expenditures that cannot be accounted for by the standard statistical studies. Thus, rather than examine a large sample of individual cases covering all impairment groups, I have chosen to concentrate on those that will allow me to explore more fully and intensely the connections between advocacy movements, political institutions, and ideas. In addition, I do not necessarily try to present a picture representative of all disability groups so much as I strive to cover the central issues at the crossroads of disability and social welfare politics. To the extent that mental disorders, addictions, and childhood disabilities represent the largest, the fastest growing, and the most controversial aspects of the Social Security disability programs, these areas are most indicative of the political debate surrounding disability and welfare issues. Where appropriate, however, I draw connections between Social Security and additional disability and social welfare programs. The purpose of this two-track approach is to give the reader the rich detail necessary to comprehend how policy reforms occurred while at the same time arrive at an appreciation of the larger political forces driving social policy making.

1

The Politics of
Disability and Welfare

During a 1995 hearing, Alan Simpson, Republican senator from Wyoming, questioned Dr. Shirley Chater, the commissioner of the Social Security Administration, about the reasons for the rapid growth in spending for the two Social Security disability benefit programs, Disability Insurance and SSI, that had occurred over the previous decade.

Complaining that the agency's disability standards were too vague, Simpson read down a list of qualifying conditions. "Loss of interest in activities, trouble sleeping, agitation, decreased energy, feelings of guilt or low self-esteem, difficulty concentrating. . . . Some of these," Simpson pointed out, "afflict all of us in some way every day of our lives."

In a jovial mood, his Democratic colleague, Senator Kent Conrad of North Dakota, asked, "Could you read the ones that apply to you every day?"

Simpson happily obliged. "Yes, I could. Agitation. . . . Then decreased energy from the schedule they give us. Feelings of guilt. A little bit of that flips back and forth in this place. Difficulty concentrating." Chuckling, he added, "Trouble sleeping. I do not have that, at least according to my wife."

Turning to the commissioner, Conrad asked, "Dr. Chater, do you have an application with you?" The hearing room erupted into laughter.[1]

Though lighthearted, senators Simpson and Conrad had broached a weighty subject. Their comments reflected a concern that the DI and SSI

1. U.S. Senate, Committee on Finance, Subcommittee on Social Security and Family Policy, *Rising Costs of Social Security's Disability Programs*, 104th Congress, 1st Session, 1995, 37.

programs, intended to remain limited to the most severely impaired workers, were growing out of control, their standards for evaluating disability so loose that they were compensating people for personality faults, bad behavior, or common everyday problems rather than for true medical illnesses or injuries. How did this policy transformation occur?

To answer this question, I offer an account of the nation's social support for the disabled in the wake of the disability rights movement: what this policy looks like overall, how it has changed, and above all, how the politics of these programs are different from the conventional picture we have of antipoverty politics. My approach is both institutional and historical, emphasizing the role of ideas and political institutions in structuring opportunities for policy innovation over time. Works that share this perspective assume that the behavior of political actors and interest groups is not open-ended but is instead mediated by institutional arrangements. To borrow Harold Lasswell's famous adage, institutions profoundly influence how government decides "who gets what, when, and how."[2] Institutions might be understood as the formal organizations and rules of government—constitutions and constitutional structures, for instance—or, according to a much looser definition, as simply "stable, recurring and valued patterns of behavior," such as administrative practices or party rules for choosing candidates for office.[3] By examining the efforts of antipoverty advocates, disability rights activists, and champions of patients' rights, I show how institutions shape the ability of social groups to realize consciousness and mobilize and, once mobilized, to access power. I also explore how institutions affect the strategies that reformers adopt, the points of leverage they enjoy, and the hurdles they confront.

In addition, my analysis is historical insofar as the timing and sequencing of events matter. I assume that contemporary decisions are shaped by the context in which they are made, and that this context is determined by its construction over time. Decisions made early in a temporal sequence are consequential, Margaret Weir argues, because they "can restrict future possibilities by sending policy off particular tracks." As historical patterns reproduce themselves, "some avenues become increasingly blocked if not entirely cut off."[4] It matters, therefore, that advocates

2. Harold D. Lasswell, *Politics: Who Gets What, When, and How* (New York: McGraw-Hill, 1936).

3. Paul Pierson, *Dismantling the Welfare State?: Reagan, Thatcher, and the Politics of Retrenchment* (Cambridge: Cambridge University Press, 1994), 46.

4. Margaret Weir, *Politics and Jobs: The Boundaries of Employment Policy in the United States* (Princeton: Princeton University Press, 1992), 18, 19. See also Paul Pierson, "Not Just What, but When: Timing and Sequence in Political Processes," *Studies in American Political Development* 14, 1 (2000): 72–92.

did not mobilize until after a dense web of income support and rehabilitation programs had already been firmly established. Coming later in time, the advocates articulated a compelling critique of the medical model on which these program were based. But their ability to remake existing programs was hampered by the institutions and interests that had crystallized around current practices and by policymakers' attachment to the prevailing medicalized way of thinking about disability as a policy problem. It also matters that the move to reform DI and SSI coincided with the rise of retrenchment politics. The increasingly harsh political and fiscal climate in which advocates operated influenced their political strategies and tactical choices and greatly constrained their efforts to build a comprehensive safety net. By taking a historical view of policy, we can see how social ideas, policy structures, and political institutions interact with one another over time to direct the course of policy reform.

A New Way of Thinking about Disability

No study of disability policy would be complete without attention to the upheaval that occurred in the 1960s and 1970s in the way that society viewed disability. Indeed, it is not surprising that ideas about disability as a social and political problem would play such a central role in policy change. Ideas are integral to politics, serving as the motive and instrument of reform. In the words of Deborah Stone, "People fight about ideas, fight for them, and fight against them. . . . Moreover, people fight *with* ideas as well as about them."[5] They are the glue that holds coalitions together, a tool deployed to win votes, and a device to embarrass and pressure opponents. But ideas serve normative purposes as well as instrumental ones. Ideas influence how groups define their interests and how decision makers interpret events in the world around them. They also provide moral guidance on what "good" public policy should look like. They can either "reaffirm and thus support elements of the status quo" or "give eloquent voice to a previously inarticulate sense among members of the public that social values and ways of thinking are changing and that policies therefore need to be brought into harmony with these new practices."[6]

5. Deborah A. Stone, *Policy Paradox: The Art of Political Decision Making* (New York: W. W. Norton, 1997), 32, 34.
6. Peter H. Schuck, "The Politics of Rapid Legal Change: Immigration Policy in the 1980s," in *The New Politics of Public Policy*, ed. Marc K. Landy and Martin A. Levin (Baltimore: Johns Hopkins University Press, 1995), 50–51, 77–80.

This book focuses on two rival ideas that framed how policymakers understood the problem of disability. The first of these two rival ideas, known as the medical model of disability, was the prevailing approach to disability prior to the 1960s. According to the model, disability is an unfortunate biological defect in the body that leaves an individual functionally incapacitated.[7] As such, society expects a disabled person to follow a variant of what sociologist Talcott Parsons called the "sick role." The role is a form of social deviance in which individuals do not fulfill the major social responsibilities expected of everyone else, responsibilities such as maintaining employment and economic self-sufficiency or caring for one's family. This form of deviance is socially acceptable because it is both temporary and medically sanctioned. The patient is not blamed for his condition or his neglect of social duties, but in exchange, he is expected to regard his condition as undesirable and to strive to recover, which means following the advice of the physicians charged with "curing" him, even if medical treatment is unpleasant and uncomfortable.[8] The sick role, however, is problematic when applied to the disabled. Their impairment is a permanent condition, not a temporary illness. Insofar as disability does not hold out the possibility of recovery, the sick role dictates that an individual with a disability remain a "permanent patient," forever under the tutelage of medical professionals and excluded from both the duties and the privileges that define citizenship and social belonging: education, marriage, career, and family.

Programs enacted prior to the late 1960s adopted one of two approaches. The first was rehabilitation, a process by which specialists taught the individual how to adapt to and ultimately overcome the limitations of his medical condition. Workers who were successfully rehabilitated reentered the workforce and were no longer considered disabled. But those who could not adapt themselves to the demands of the able-bodied world were relegated to the welfare state, the second of the two approaches to disability. Workers' compensation programs, income support and pension programs, and institutionalization were all premised on the medical model's core assumption that a disability rendered a person completely unfit for productive labor. Since people with disabilities could not care for themselves, they became wards of the state, as either lifelong recipients of public assistance or residents of public hospitals and asylums. In each case, people with disabilities were separated from main-

    7. Paul K. Longmore, "Medical Decision Making and People with Disabilities: A Clash of Cultures," *Journal of Law, Medicine, and Ethics* 23 (1995): 82.
    8. Talcott Parsons, *The Social System* (Glencoe, IL: Free Press, 1951).

stream society and their able-bodied peers. Because the "problems" posed by disability were inherent in the individual, there was no attempt at social reform; the individual had to adapt to meet the needs of society, not the other way around. "This public policy," historian Paul K. Longmore observed, "created a large stigmatized and segregated category of persons and held it in a permanent state of clientage."[9]

The second view of disability, known as the social model, emerged in the late 1960s and early 1970s to challenge the medical model. Also sometimes called the human rights or minority model of disability, the social model asserted that disability was not an objective characteristic or defect of a person but rather a socially constructed category used to justify discrimination against individuals whose bodies made them different from the social norm. According to this perspective, there was nothing inherently deviant about disability, nor did the condition necessarily translate into incapacity and helplessness. Instead, the functional limitations of disability arose from the interplay between a person's mental or physical attributes and an environment that was structurally or socially arranged to be unreceptive and inaccessible to individuals with disabilities. In other words, an individual's medical condition might be given but the hardships resulting from it were not an inevitable consequence of that condition. Indeed, disability rights activists liked to argue that the disabled were impeded "more by the prejudicial attitudes of others than by their own functional limitations." In a society that was "compatible with a broad range of human capabilities" or "designed to meet the needs of each of its members," disability would cease to be a disadvantage.[10] Thus, according to the social model, the problem that government should be addressing lay not with the disabled but with society. Programs that compelled the disabled to adapt to a society structured by the able-bodied for the benefit of the able-bodied were misguided. Instead, disability activists argued, morally just public policy should seek to change society so that it would accept and accommodate the physical and mental capabilities of all of its individual members.

The political ramifications of this change in perspective were enormous. First, the social model and the movement for disability rights that it gave rise to allowed individuals with disabilities to gain self-awareness and mobilize in pursuit of their shared interests. In the past, the disabled divided along impairment lines with groups lobbying separately for pro-

9. Longmore, "Medical Decision Making and People with Disabilities," 83.
10. Harlan Hahn, "Disability Policy and the Problem of Discrimination," *American Behavioral Scientist* 28, 3 (1985): 297, 304.

grams that served their specific needs. There were distinct organizations representing the deaf, the blind, paralyzed veterans, crippled children, and parents of children with mental retardation, and each viewed the others as competitors for attention and funding. At the same time, stigmatized groups like alcoholics or mentally ill adults had few organizations to speak on their on behalf. With the rise of the disability rights movement in the early 1970s, however, people with disabilities regarded their impairments not as tragic defects that one should be ashamed of, but as a part of their identity that, like race or gender, should be proudly claimed. Moreover, rather than competing with one another, disability organizations saw themselves as all having a common stake in ending the discriminatory treatment that all people with disabilities confronted, whatever their impairment. Thus, the rhetoric of rights helped to smooth the differences between groups and build a cross-disability movement. As Robert Katzmann explained, when demands were reframed in terms of rights, "questions of costs became irrelevant: each group could champion the demands of others without financial sacrifice."[11] The impairments might be different, but the exclusion was the same.

The second political consequence of the shift from the medical to the social model of disability is policy-related. The social model and the idea of disability rights reoriented the focus of disability advocacy. Prior to the late 1960s, disability organizations were primarily concerned with securing better funding of rehabilitation, social services, and income support programs. Many activists who came of age during the disability rights movement, however, rejected this approach. Some argued that existing social welfare programs were oppressive because they placed people with disabilities under the all-encompassing control of patronizing bureaucrats, doctors, and vocational counselors, who knew nothing about what it was like to be disabled. While some tried to restructure existing programs so that they were attentive to the demands of disabled clients, other activists denounced the very concept of social welfare programs. Evan Kemp, for instance, contended that any form of charity, whether public programs or private donations, was inherently flawed because it mistakenly equated disability with incapacity and helplessness. The sense of pity that motivated giving, Kemp argued in an editorial to the *New York Times* in 1981, reinforced the notion that disability was a tragedy. Pity, however well-intentioned, "raise[d] walls of fear between the public and us" and fostered negative stereotypes of people with disabilities as ut-

11. Robert A. Katzmann, *Institutional Disability: The Saga of Transportation Policy for the Disabled* (Washington, DC: Brookings Institution Press, 1986), 111.

terly incapable of providing for themselves.[12] In place of more services, these new disability activists called for the enactment of civil rights protections that would end discrimination against the disabled and guarantee equal access. During debate over the Americans with Disabilities Act in 1990, wheelchair activist Bob Kafka gave voice to this new attitude when he proudly proclaimed, "We're not going to be passive recipients of charity anymore. We're changing our image. We're demanding our rights."[13]

Legislation passed after the late 1960s—the Architectural Barriers Act of 1968, Section 504 of the 1973 Rehabilitation Act, the Education for All Handicapped Children Act (EAHCA, now called the Individuals with Disabilities Education Act or IDEA), and the Americans with Disabilities Act of 1990—reflected this demand for rights. These laws created legal protections that not only prevented public and private parties from barring or excluding an individual "solely by reason of his handicap," but later laws, such as Section 504 and the ADA, also went much further by requiring state and local governments, building contractors, and employers to accommodate the functional capacities of the disabled. As this book demonstrates, however, the idea of disability rights did not stop with civil rights laws. It also influenced the older, first-generation income support programs, like Social Security, that had been founded on the medical model. The idea that disabled people could and should become productive members of society called into question the very purpose of income support. Moreover, even when advocates did not attack the premises of first-generation programs, hoping instead to use existing programs to support disabled people living outside institutions, they found it difficult to reconcile the specter of "welfare dependency" with the disability rights movement's rhetoric of independence. Thus, policymaking since the 1970s has been a struggle to find ways to transform old programs, designed for a society in which the disabled were segregated and cared for, into new programs that will serve the ends of inclusion and independence.

A New Politics of Public Policymaking

The activists of the late 1960s and early 1970s were not the first to challenge the medical model's assumption that disabilities were inher-

12. Evan J. Kemp, "Aiding the Disabled: No Pity, Please," *New York Times*, September 3, 1981, A19.
13. Joseph P. Shapiro, *No Pity: People with Disabilities Forging a New Civil Rights Movement* (New York: Times Books, 1993), 135.

ently incapacitating. More than thirty years earlier, the League of the Physically Handicapped had complained that New Deal work programs lacked enough slots for people with disabilities who wanted to participate.[14] But it was not until the late 1960s that the disabled mobilized into a cross-cutting movement on behalf of their rights to employment, equal access, and deinstitutionalization and, more importantly, that the American political system had altered in ways that made government leaders much more accessible to advocates and more amenable to their demands. The difference between the New Deal and the post-1960 period can be seen in the contrast between, on the one hand, the politics surrounding the enactment and subsequent expansion of Disability Insurance in the early 1950s and, on the other, the contemporary institutional environment.

Scholars have long argued that, because of its institutional decentralization, the American political system is far from receptive to the demands of progressive reformers. Federalism, separation of powers, checks and balances, and bicameralism—all these features of American democracy combine to create a government replete with "veto points"— "points in the policy process where the mobilization of opposition can thwart policy innovation."[15] According to conventional wisdom, if reformers secured liberal policy advances, it was because they managed through extraordinary measures to counteract those veto points. The "big bangs" of the 1930s and 1960s are two occasions in which the political momentum generated by a Democratic president's decisive electoral victory allowed a brief window of opportunity for reform. Of course, attention to the politics of Social Security soon reveals that even outside these periods, the decentralization of the American political system did not necessarily inhibit the expansion of social welfare programs. Instead, as Martha Derthick argues in her seminal political history of Social Security, the program grew precisely because its proponents operated in an institutional space that overcame institutional decentralization.

According to Derthick, between 1940 and 1970, an insular "subgovernment" controlled program politics and nurtured the steady expansion of social insurance. This subgovernment was comprised of a small band

14. Paul K. Longmore and David Goldberger, "The League of the Physically Handicapped and the Great Depression: A Case Study in the New Disability History," *Journal of American History* 87 (2000): 888–992.

15. Kathleen Thelen and Sven Steinmo, "Historical Institutionalism in Comparative Politics," in *Structuring Politics: Historical Institutionalism in Comparative Analysis*, ed. Sven Steinmo, Kathleen Thelen, and Frank Longstreth (Cambridge: Cambridge University Press, 1992), 7, stressing the need for a more dynamic view of politics.

of SSA officials and the lawmakers who sat on the House Ways and Means Committee and the Senate Finance Committee, the two congressional tax committees overseeing Social Security issues. By centralizing decision making in the hands of a few, this institutional arrangement neutralized the political system's many veto points. It essentially insulated Social Security from partisan divisions, public opinion, or presidential politics—all of which might have prevented the program from becoming the sacred entitlement it is today. The SSA officials and members of Congress who shared responsibility for Social Security were all experts in the technical nuances of social insurance policy, but they were nevertheless guided by a common vision of what Social Security should be, a vision that was largely shaped by the bureaucrats. SSA officials and lawmakers alike engaged in careful examination of expansion options, and when the committees' recommendations were sent to the floor, they were voted on up or down without amendments. This meant that measures that expanded Social Security—the enlargement of the wage base, extended coverage to dependents and new occupations, increases in benefit levels, and the addition of Disability Insurance and Medicare—all took place within the trajectory that the SSA and tax committees had in mind. On the other hand, proposals that ran contrary to this shared vision, such as occasional suggestions that general revenues be used to pay for retirement benefits or that all elderly Americans be folded into the program at once rather than gradually, made little headway. While the SSA and the tax committees were certainly aware of political currents, rarely did the president, interest group adversaries, or public opinion intrude on the give-and-take that took place within the confines of this tight-knit circle of officials. In evocative imagery, Derthick describes policymaking as "a prolonged symphony in which the movements were conceived by the executive 'composers.'" The tax committees played their parts, "rejecting now, accepting later, and selecting to suit their collective preferences and the preferences of the whole legislature, pertinent interest groups, and the public as the committees perceived them." The growth of Social Security, therefore, was a carefully planned and deliberately paced endeavor in which "there was an exceptional degree of symbiosis" between members of Congress and the officials at the SSA.[16]

The inception and expansion of Disability Insurance between 1954 and 1972 illustrates how this dynamic worked.[17] Following World War

---

16. Martha Derthick, *Policymaking for Social Security* (Washington, DC: Brookings Institution Press, 1979), 46–47, 58, 60.

17. This section draws from ibid., 295–315.

II, after having firmly established Old Age and Survivors Insurance (OASI), SSA officials decided to press for extending social insurance coverage to disability. The problem was that while everyone agreed that disability was a major threat to the economic security of American workers, not everyone agreed that disability compensation was feasible. The government's War Risk Insurance program for veterans of World War I and commercial insurance plans during the 1930s had both begun with narrow definitions of disability. But these tight boundaries were promptly swept aside as adverse labor market conditions and courts sympathetic to the plight of down-and-out workers conspired to stretch even the strictest disability plans into general compensation programs for the unemployed.[18]

Sensing strong resistance in Congress, SSA officials decided to start small. They pared back their initial plans for a broad pension plan, agreeing instead to drop coverage of temporary and partial impairments and limit eligibility to only the most severe medical conditions. Proponents of Disability Insurance suggested two additional restrictive devices to further assuage the skeptics. First, SSA officials proposed a strict definition of disability, one grounded on the medical model's assumptions that the disabled could be objectively distinguished from the nondisabled and that people found disabled were necessarily functionally incapable of work. As the report of the 1948 Social Security Advisory Council explained, if "compensable disabilities" were "restricted to those which can be objectively determined by medical examination or tests," then "the adjudication of claims based on purely subjective symptoms can be avoided." Said the council, "Unless demonstrable though objective tests, such ailments as lumbago, rheumatism, and various nervous disorders would not be compensable."[19] The definition of disability that Congress finally approved reflected the faith that lawmakers had in the power of medicine to root out questionable claims and restrict program growth. According to the statutory language, claimants would be awarded disability benefits only if they could show an "inability to engage in any substantial gainful activity by reason of any medically determinable physical or mental impairment" that was expected to last indefinitely. In addition, the disability certification process would rely heavily on the observations and tools of physicians. Medical impairments qualified only if they were "anatomical, physiological, or psychological abnormalities which are demonstrable by medically acceptable clinical and laboratory diagnostic techniques."[20] Not

18. Deborah A. Stone, *The Disabled State* (Philadelphia: Temple University Press, 1984), 72–76.
19. Ibid., 79.
20. Social Security Act, Title II, section 223(d)(1). See 42 U.S.C. 423.

only would this statutory definition supposedly keep the number of disability awards small and manageable, but it would also ensure that benefits remained limited to people who, through no fault of their own, could not provide for themselves and their families.

The striking irony of this episode, however, was that even though Congress expected medicine to ferret out fraudulent cases of disability, lawmakers dismissed objections from physicians that what government was asking of them was impossible. Physicians opposed to the new program pointed out the flaws with this approach. They testified that they could do a reasonable job of determining whether a person suffered from a medical impairment. But they were adamant that extrapolating from the impairment to a person's work capacity was an entirely different matter and one beyond their field of expertise.[21] It was to no avail. "I don't know of anybody as well qualified as the medical profession to pass on a man's disability," said Senator Alben Barkley during debate over Disability Insurance in 1956. "Is it not a medical question after all?" The senator later added, "I am not willing to concede that after all the years of experience and growth and investigation and practice in the medical profession that they cannot with some reasonable degree of certainty arrive at a medically determinable point where a man is totally and permanently disabled."[22] Nothing could shake Congress's belief that medical science had the power to render the political struggle over program boundaries into an apolitical application of specialized expertise.

Perhaps it was easy for lawmakers to ignore the cautionary tale of physicians. The American Medical Association had made it clear that it opposed Disability Insurance, fearing that the new program was the first step toward government control of the medical profession, and the doctors' newfound modesty, thus, appeared self-interested. Moreover, clinical evidence was not the only restrictive device the new disability program would employ. Besides a statutory definition premised on the medical model, lawmakers relied on an age limit that would bar benefits to younger workers. This age limit had the added advantage of allowing proponents to draw parallels between disability pensions and their well-established and popular retirement counterpart. Using Old Age Insurance (OAI) as a political base from which to launch the campaign for Disability Insurance, SSA executives repeatedly compared disability to premature aging. After a lifetime of grueling labor, they argued, workers in physically demanding occupations faced infirmities similar to the frailties of advancing age, and like aged retirees, many older, impaired work-

21. Stone, *Disabled State*, 81–83.
22. Quoted in ibid., 82.

ers simply could not continue, forced by their bodies to curtail the number of hours they worked or drop out of the labor force entirely. It made sense, therefore, to establish a disability pension at least for workers over age fifty, since they would have a difficult time switching occupations and were unlikely to benefit from rehabilitation.[23]

This reasoning allowed SSA officials to establish Disability Insurance piecemeal, using OAI as the entering wedge. In 1954, SSA officials and their allies in Congress secured a "freeze" on wage calculations so that workers over age fifty who became disabled before they became eligible for retirement at age sixty-five would not have their benefits reduced because of an extended period of lost work. This, of course, required the SSA to draw up a definition of disability and contract with the state agencies that would make the disability determinations, nullifying complaints from opponents that a disability benefit program was inherently unworkable. The age limit also hid the fact that Disability Insurance was a significant step forward. In 1956, Congress took up the issue of disability benefits and a related measure to lower the retirement age for women from sixty-five to sixty-two. Taking advantage of the conceptual link between disability and age, supporters of disability benefits "presented the measure as a reduction in the age of eligibility for women and the disabled rather than as a major new program of aid to the disabled."[24]

The compromises related to the age limit and clinical methods of certification were designed to soften the opposition, but because Disability Insurance was something new, it was intensely controversial. President Dwight Eisenhower spoke out against it, and though he did not veto the program, he remained skeptical of it. The insurance industry and the American Medical Association lobbied against it, and labor lobbied for it. Congress remained divided, and the measure barely passed, clearing the Senate by only one vote. Once Congress enacted DI, though, conflict subsided, and a period of incremental growth, similar to the pattern of subgovernment politics that had characterized the expansion of retirement benefits, prevailed. Congress liberalized eligibility for Disability Insurance in 1958, 1960, 1965, 1967, and 1972, removing the age restriction, shortening the period of required work, and allowing payments for temporary impairments that lasted a year or more. None of these expansions generated the same discord as the inception of the program. Of this period, Martha Derthick writes, "Congressional committees that had la-

---

23. Edward D. Berkowitz, *Disabled Policy: America's Programs for the Handicapped* (Cambridge: Cambridge University Press, 1987), 46–47.
24. Derthick, *Policymaking for Social Security*, 305.

bored to write suitably restrictive language could not recall that they had written it, or why, and instead began asking administrators why it took so long to adjudicate disability claims and why seemingly disabled claimants sometimes had their claims denied."[25] Once deeply contested, DI came to exemplify constituent politics, another program with benefits that members of Congress liked to distribute to voters back home.

This form of subgovernment policymaking soon came to an end, however. In the early 1970s, institutional power in Congress fragmented, and the bipartisan support that fueled the postwar expansion of Social Security disintegrated. Yet avenues for liberal policy reform were not necessarily closed. On the contrary, the increased fragmentation of power that followed party and congressional reforms in the late 1960s and early 1970s opened new possibilities for policy innovation. House reforms stripped the prerogatives of the conservative southern Democrats who had long dominated powerful congressional committees and devolved them to a proliferating number of subcommittees chaired by junior (and more liberal) rank-and-file legislators, who served as policy entrepreneurs promoting their favored programs. Meanwhile, electoral reforms weakened the influence of party bosses and empowered grassroots New Left activists. As a result, opportunities for participatory access were opened for the proliferating number of organizations that arose in the 1970s to represent the poor, the elderly, the disabled, children, and a range of other public interest causes. Whereas once only a few officials set the pace of Social Security policymaking, by the 1980s, hundreds of interest groups were involved.[26]

The democratization of the policy process coincided with the end of the political harmony that had characterized Social Security's formative years. The maturity of Old Age and Survivors Insurance meant that the program, once small and inconsequential, now had a major redistributive effect and a sizable impact on the federal budget. What is worse, it also experienced occasional predicted shortfalls in the trust funds that demanded immediate attention and pushed Social Security policymaking into presidential politics. Moreover, deteriorating administrative capacities, frequent changes in the leadership of the Social Security Administration, and mixed signals from Congress exacerbated the difficulties as-

25. Ibid., 311.
26. See, for instance, the changes described in David W. Rodhe, *Parties and Leaders in the Post-Reform House* (Chicago: University of Chicago Press, 1991); James Q. Wilson, "American Politics, Then and Now," *Commentary* 67 (February 1979): 18–21; and Marc K. Landy and Martin A. Levin, "The New Politics of Public Policy," in *New Politics of Public Policy*, ed. Landy and Levin, 280.

sociated with properly managing and carefully administering Disability Insurance and Supplemental Security Income.[27] By the mid 1970s, the growth of the disability and retirement pension programs was neither planned nor paced. Politicians who had once talked about expanding DI now scrambled for ways to rein it in, much to the chagrin of constituent groups.

Thus, the old, insular patterns of political interaction dissolved and were replaced by a more fluid and contentious policy environment. Just as the American political system is replete with veto points so too is it peppered with "strategic openings," opportunities for organized groups to take part in decision making.[28] By the 1980s, the growing fragmentation of government multiplied the number of strategic openings available to the newly mobilized disability advocates, allowing them to press their case in many venues and before many political decision makers. As I will illustrate in my analysis of the debate about the 1984 Social Security disability amendments in chapter 6, opposition from political actors who had once formed the inner circle of Social Security policymaking no longer doomed proposals. Advocacy groups found that if the legislators on the overseeing tax committees were unsympathetic to their concerns, they could find support among other powerbrokers in Congress. And if Congress itself were indifferent or locked in a stalemate, advocates could turn to other institutions, such as the courts, to accomplish their goals. Indeed, institutional fragmentation allowed advocates to leapfrog from one institution to the next to build on their victories. Famed liberal political strategist Wilbur Cohen had once remarked that incremental legislating was akin to "salami slicing" so that by the end, one arrived at "a very good sandwich." In a variant on this salami-slicing technique, disability advocates used victories in one forum to leverage an advantage in the next. This allowed them to ratchet up the reforms. Eventually, they

27. Martha Derthick, "The Plight of the Social Security Administration," in *Social Security after Fifty: Success and Failures*, ed. Edward D. Berkowitz (Westport, CT: Greenwood Press, 1987), 101–117, and Martha Derthick, *Agency under Stress: The Social Security Administration in American Government* (Washington, DC: Brookings Institution Press, 1990).

28. Thelen and Steinmo, "Historical Institutionalism in Comparative Perspective," 6–7. Among the works that make this point are Ellen M. Immergut, *The Political Construction of Interests: National Health Insurance Politics in Switzerland, France, and Sweden* (Cambridge: Cambridge University Press, 1992); Edwin Amenta, *Bold Relief: Institutional Politics and the Origins of Modern American Social Policy* (Princeton: Princeton University Press, 1998); and Sven Steinmo, *Taxation and Democracy: Swedish, British, and American Approaches to Financing the Modern State* (New Haven, CT: Yale University Press, 1993).

accomplished a significant liberalization of policy outcomes despite the fact that there was neither elite consensus nor widespread public support behind the expansion of disability entitlements.[29]

The Limits of Innovation

The possibilities for reform, however, are not without limit. Indeed, policy reform is best seen as a glass both half-full and half-empty. This book concentrates of the efforts of disability advocates to pry open Disability Insurance and SSI to controversial and previously excluded groups. But their aspirations reached beyond these two programs. Ultimately, advocates wanted to remake all of disability and social welfare policy so that people with disabilities were no longer segregated into dehumanizing asylums or inadequate welfare programs. These advocates hoped to supplant the medical model of disability, which they believed contributed to prejudice against the disabled, with the social model's emphasis on social inclusion and individual rights. They wanted programs that would end exclusion and discrimination and allow the disabled to live autonomously in their home communities and take part in important social activities like education and employment. The effort to bring DI and SSI in line with disability rights was only one piece of this much more ambitious plan. But these grand hopes for a disability policy premised on the right to social inclusion were met with disappointment. Even as advocates succeeded in making DI and SSI more accommodating of people with mental disorders and children, they could not fully ingrain disability rights into existing social welfare policy. Thus, one purpose of this book is to highlight the successes as well as failures of the advocates and explain why some opportunities for reform were available while others were not.

The reform efforts discussed in this book, therefore, are a case of what Margaret Weir called "bounded innovation," a term that captures both the possibilities for remaking policy as well as the limits on change.[30] Even though advocates wanted to do away with the medical model, because ideas become formalized in policy, they have a way of persisting even as new ideas arise to challenge old ways of viewing the social world. In the case of DI and SSI, the influence of the medical model is clearly

29. For a description of this strategy with respect to children's issues, see Sheryl Dicker, *Stepping Stones: Successful Advocacy for Children* (New York: Foundation for Child Development, 1990), 2, 7–8.

30. Weir, *Politics and Jobs*, 18–19, 164–68.

seen in the fact that Social Security treats disability as an all-or-nothing concept. Someone is either disabled and therefore unable to support herself, or she is able-bodied and is fully capable of employment. Within the two programs, there is little recognition of the social model's contention that disability emerges from the interaction between a person's functional capacities and the structural environment. Thus, neither DI nor SSI takes into consideration whether an employer has made job accommodations for the claimant, and neither recognizes degrees of disability. Instead, the two programs equate disability with productive incapacity, expect claimants to show medical evidence of their impairments, and do little to promote work and rehabilitation. This interlocking constellation of ideas and institutions built around the assumptions of the medical model can be thought of as forming a policy paradigm, "a framework of ideas and standards that specifies not only the goals of policy and kind of instruments that can be used to attain them, but also the very nature of the problems they are meant to be addressing."[31]

Because advocates wanted to make benefits widely available so that people with disabilities could have a source of income outside of public asylums, they had to challenge the prevailing paradigm that guided disability policy. Yet even though politics is "routinely refreshed with ideas outside government," policy paradigms are difficult to displace because of the inertial forces present in American government. Weir explains, "As resources, expertise, and institutions become invested in particular courses of action, ideas that envision substantial reorganizations of these elements may be blocked by institutional obstacles."[32] Advocates faced two formidable constraints.

The first was the rise of retrenchment politics. By the late 1970s, elected officials had turned from expanding government's social welfare commitments to curtailing rapidly increasing entitlement spending. Adapting to an adverse ideological and budgetary environment, disability advocates struck a compromise. Rather than attempting to displace the medical model from Social Security policy—a tall order, indeed—they tried instead to harness its rhetoric in support of their cause by advancing a functional approach to disability determination, which was an easier sell during a time of fiscal unease. Thus, when in 1980, President Reagan attempted a sweeping purge of the Social Security disability rolls, advocates claimed that the administration was using the wrong method for

31. Peter A. Hall, "Policy Paradigms, Social Learning, and the State: The Case of Economic Policymaking in Britain," *Comparative Politics* 25, 3 (1993): 279.

32. Weir, *Politics and Jobs*, 19–20. On the difficulty of replacing policy paradigms, see Hall, "Policy Paradigms, Social Learning, and the State," 279–81.

determining who was disabled. The SSA, advocates asserted, was relying too heavily on clinical evidence and thus adopting an overly restrictive view of disability, one that left many legitimately disabled people off the DI and SSI rules. In place of the SSA's clinical approach, the advocates proposed a functional interpretation of disability, one that took an expansive view of mental and childhood disorders by placing emphasis on an individual's behavior and functioning in a particular setting, such as the workplace or school. Because it relaxed the categorical eligibility standards for SSI and DI, this method of determining disability could be used to liberalize social welfare programs and thus provide more social supports to disabled people living in the community. Nevertheless, it differed from the medicalized approach used by the SSA only insofar as it placed its emphasis on behavior rather than on laboratory tests or the objectively verifiable clinical signs of a medical disorder.

With the functional model, advocates gave up the opportunity to press for a disability determination process that recognized the socially constructed aspects of disability. They also gave up the stirring rhetoric of social justice. They dropped their calls for a broad social safety net to support the deinstitutionalized disabled and instead portrayed their desired policy changes as small adjustments to existing programs based on the latest scientific findings. The move is counterintuitive but understandable. As I will explore in chapter 4, the functional approach to measuring disability was grounded in the emerging norms of the psychiatric, pediatric, and rehabilitation professions, and the fact that medical experts endorsed this approach provided advocacy groups a crucial advantage. Indeed, in many policy areas, from tax to trade policy, professionals and experts outside of government exercise a great deal of authority in policymaking. Timothy Conlan notes that these experts "are the natural generators and propagators of ideas. Where experts and professionals are employed in and around government itself, they can influence policy quickly and directly."[33] Lawmakers are especially inclined to turn to experts for advice when policy is as technically daunting as disability or as ideologically divisive as welfare. To borrow the words of Alice O'Connor, the conviction that the "scientific knowledge" of experts can resolve vexing social problems "has long been an article of faith in American liberalism."[34] Yet though they were experts, the medical professionals who

33. Timothy J. Conlan, David R. Beam, and Margaret T. Wrightson, "Policy Models and Policy Change: Insights from the Passage of Tax Reform," in *New Politics of Public Policy*, ed. Landy and Levin, 130.

34. Alice O'Connor, *Poverty Knowledge: Social Science, Social Policy, and the Poor in Twentieth-Century U.S. History* (Princeton: Princeton University Press, 2002), 3.

joined with disability advocates to expand DI and SSI were by no means detached. They supported the advocates' goals for a broad social safety net and formed what Paul Sabatier calls an "advocacy coalition," an alliance comprised of political actors, researchers, and analysts who shared common perceptions regarding policy problems and appropriate remedies.[35] At the same time, however, their status as outside experts gave these reform-minded medical professionals a privileged voice in policy debates. Informed by the medical model, lawmakers viewed no one better qualified to speak on matters of disability than physicians and their professional organizations.

Recasting questions about the appropriate scope of income support programs into a narrow and technical debate about the proper methods for measuring disability served to dampen political resistance. But it also complicated efforts to align Social Security with disability rights. Functionalism did not stray far from the medical model's expectation that disability was akin to sickness, a condition that was tragic, debilitating, and relatively rare. Although functionalism permitted a more liberal approach to disability certification than the clinical approach did, it did not call into question the medical model's premise that disability was an all-or-nothing concept, that it was equivalent to incapacity, and that it was, at bottom, an individual shortcoming rather than a discriminatory social construct. The functional approach also retained the assumption that because disability was the exception rather than the norm, disability benefit programs should remain small. This way of framing the policy problem, in turn, constrained efforts to expand the social safety net.

In addition to the hold that the medical model exercised over policymaking, advocates faced a second constraint, one rooted in political institutions rather than ideas. Simply put, the very fragmentation that made policymaking accessible to advocacy groups also frustrated their ability to remake disability programs wholesale. Scholars often speak of public policies forming regimes of interlocking institutions, interests, and ideas that reinforce an established pattern of behavior and way of thinking about a policy problem.[36] Robert Lieberman, however, argues that public policy is seldom, if ever, this coherent. To the contrary, most policies encompass internal contradictions that create ongoing political friction. Entrenched institutions or programs outlive their missions as ideas or social circumstances shift beneath them, or new policies are layered on top

35. Paul A. Sabatier, "An Advocacy Coalition Framework of Policy Change and the Role of Policy-Oriented Learning Therein," *Policy Sciences* 21 (1988): 138, 139.

36. Richard A. Harris and Sidney M. Milkis, *The Politics of Regulatory Change: A Tale of Two Agencies*, 2d ed. (Oxford: Oxford University Press, 1996), 25–31.

of them. As a result, policy goals sometimes "collide and chafe, creating an ungainly configuration of political circumstances that has no clear resolution, presenting actors with contradictory and multidirectional imperatives and opportunities."[37] Sometimes these discontinuities lead to policy change; at other times, they leave policy a mess by spawning a confusing web of uncoordinated and cross-cutting programs.

This confusion is certainly characteristic of disability policy. If policy is conceived of as a set of programs serving a common purpose, then historian Edward Berkowitz concludes, "America has no disability policy." Instead, disability policy is an eclectic collection of programs created during different time periods, serving vastly different social groups that may have little in common other than their disability. Among income support programs, separate plans exist for railroad employees, veterans, federal employees, middle-class workers, and the poor. No common purpose vision of disability animates policy. Instead, "retirement policy intended primarily for the elderly, civil rights policy for blacks and women, welfare policy aimed at the poor, and the legal system of torts and damages all govern disability programs."[38]

The disparate nature of our nation's disability policy had far-reaching consequences for reformers. In their efforts to build a social safety net compatible with the inclusive ideals of disability rights, advocates were forced to navigate through many policy areas that, while they addressed the problem of disability, had not been formulated with the specific needs of the disabled in mind. Doing so, however, was complicated by the same institutional fragmentation that had aided advocates in remaking Social Security. In other words, while the decentralized and disjointed nature of the American political system opened new avenues of opportunity for reform-minded groups, it also impeded their ability to build supportive legislative coalitions in pursuit of comprehensive action. Advocates could pry open DI and SSI, but they were less successful in joining them to a larger, coherent safety net of disability rights laws and social support programs. In the end, there was no question that the advocates had brought about profound changes in how society thinks about and treats disability as a policy problem, yet their grand ambitions for a "new asylum" of community-based programs to advance the autonomy and integration of people with disabilities remained unfulfilled.

37. Robert C. Lieberman, "Ideas, Institutions, and Political Order: Explaining Political Change," *American Political Science Review* 96, 4 (2002): 702.
38. Berkowitz, *Disabled Policy*, 1.

2

The Advocates Mobilize
for Rights

Disability policy was not always concerned about empowering people with disabilities. In its earliest years, policy took the form of rehabilitation, welfare, or asylums. Though some programs provided services and others cash, though some were run by state and local governments and others by the federal government, what these early programs shared was a medical orientation toward disability that assumed that people with disabilities were incapable of earning a living or caring for themselves. In the late 1960s and early 1970s, however, the language of individual rights transformed the landscape of disability policy. Activists, many of whom were disabled themselves, found the medical model and the programs premised on its assumptions debilitating and patronizing, and they endorsed instead the social model of disability. What the medical model took for granted—that is, the limitations confronted by people with disabilities—the social model viewed as convention. It emphasized society's discriminatory treatment of people with disabilities, which consisted of locking them away in mental asylums, hospitals, or private homes, out of sight and out of mind, all in the name of "caring" for them. According to the social model, the disabled did not need charity or pity from others; what they needed was recognition of their rights to equality and social inclusion. After 1970, this new approach to disability became the guiding force behind many pieces of federal legislation that, rather than isolate people with disabilities on welfare programs or in hospitals, now sought to integrate the disabled into community life by making schools, workplaces, and local neighborhoods accessible. The idea of disability rights also infiltrated, to a lesser extent, older disability programs, like DI and SSI. Although they had been founded on the principles of the medical model, advocates sought to re-orient these programs to further the ends of the social model.

The advocacy community grew out of the enormous changes in mental health and disability policy that began in the Kennedy and Johnson administrations. Between 1963 and 1968, reformers affiliated with the patients' rights movement sought to establish an extensive array of rights that would not only protect individuals who had been institutionalized but also challenge the complete control that medical professionals exercised over their patients. Above all, they wanted to shift the provision of mental health care from the large, impersonal, and dehumanizing asylums that they believed isolated patients and contributed to their neglect to community-based programs that would allow patients to live and work alongside the able-bodied and able-minded. In the early 1970s, these patients' rights reformers joined the ranks of the budding disability rights movement, a social movement that brought people with disabilities under a common banner despite differences of age, class, race, gender, and impairment. Yet, whereas some disability rights activists, especially those associated with the independent living movement, attacked existing income support programs and the professionals that staffed them as vestiges of the patronizing and prejudicial social order they were trying to overthrow, the reformers who had fought for patients' rights and community mental health were not so quick to dismiss welfare. They came to realize that without generous social assistance, rights had little meaning for the destitute ex-mental patients they represented. In describing the advocates—who they were, where they came from, and why they cared about welfare policy, I explain how support for community mental health care took advocates from their initial interest in patients' rights to a wider concern for the adequacy of the nation's social safety net and, in particular, Social Security.

Before beginning, two important qualifications are in order. First, I speak of the social movements in this book as if they were coherent entities, especially when I discuss their principles and beliefs. I realize, however, that with any collection of individuals, particularly those that form a nascent movement, amid the recognizable set of ideas that motivates their activism there are also disagreements and differing schools of thought. I refer to these movements as singular and cohesive units largely as a matter of convenience, but I also try to capture the prevailing sentiment of the activists and point out where there are differences of thought. Second, several related movements form the backdrop of the advocacy efforts covered in this book: the independent living movement, the patients' rights movement, the larger disability rights movement, and to a lesser extent, the welfare rights movement. Doing justice to any of these movements—much less all four—is well beyond the manageable scope of this book.[1] Instead, I concentrate only on explaining how the Social Security advocates fit into this burgeoning activism on behalf of disabled and poor people.

Who Were the Advocates?

The advocacy groups that sought to expand DI and SSI in the 1980s and 1990s were as diverse as the clientele the two programs served, and they reflected a dual concern for the disadvantages of disability and poverty. The disability groups included organizations like the Arc (formerly, the Association of Retarded Citizens), Easter Seals, United Cerebral Palsy, and the National Mental Health Association, to name just a few. Considerably older than the disability rights groups like ADAPT (American Disabled for Attendant Programs Today) and the Disability Rights Education and Defense Fund, which arose in the 1970s, many of these traditional disability organizations were founded by parents of people with disabilities and professionals. Most got their start lobbying for increased spending for disability-related social services, yet by the early 1970s, they too had adopted the self-help and civil rights orientation of the disability rights movement. In 1972, for instance, local chapters of the Arc were the plaintiffs in *Mills v. Board of Education* and *Pennsylvania Association of Retarded Children (PARC) v. Pennsylvania*, the first

1. There are several books on each of these movements, but I found the following most useful. On deinstitutionalization and mental health policy in general, see Gerald N. Grob, *The Mad among Us: A History of the Care of America's Mentally Ill* (New York: Free Press, 1994), and David A. Rochefort, *From Poorhouses to Homelessness: Policy Analysis and Mental Health Care*, 2d ed. (Westport, CT: Auburn House, 1997). On the patients' rights movement, see Rael Jean Isaac and Virginia C. Armat, *Madness in the Streets: How Psychiatry and the Law Abandoned the Mentally Ill* (New York: Free Press, 1990). On the disability rights movement and independent living, see Stephen L. Percy, *Disability, Civil Rights, and Public Policy: The Politics of Implementation* (Tuscaloosa: University of Alabama Press, 1989); Richard K. Scotch, *From Goodwill to Civil Rights: Transforming Federal Disability Policy* (Philadelphia: Temple University Press, 1984); Joseph P. Shapiro, *No Pity: People with Disabilities Forging a New Civil Rights Movement* (New York: Times Books, 1993); and Doris Zames Fleischer and Frieda Zames, *The Disability Rights Movement: From Charity to Confrontation* (Philadelphia: Temple University Press, 2001). Finally, on the welfare rights movement, see Frances Fox Piven and Richard Cloward, *Poor People's Movements: Why They Succeed, How They Fail* (New York: Pantheon Books, 1977), and Martha F. Davis, *Brutal Need: Lawyers and the Welfare Rights Movement, 1960–1973* (New Haven, CT: Yale University Press, 1993).

cases recognizing that disabled children had a right to an education in the public schools.[2] The coalition also included various antipoverty organizations, especially Legal Services. In fact, attorneys for Community Legal Services of Philadelphia, a particularly vocal and committed Legal Services office, brought *Sullivan v. Zebley*, one of the most important Social Security cases, to the Supreme Court. Similarly, the SSI Coalition for a Responsible Safety Net (now called Health and Disability Advocates) was another advocacy group, formed by Legal Services attorneys and dedicated to enhancing health care and income support programs for the aged and disabled. Aiding Legal Services attorneys were the backup centers. The National Senior Citizens Law Center, the Children's Defense Fund, and the Mental Health Law Project (MHLP, today called the Bazelon Center for Mental Health Law) were all public interest law firms that at one point or another provided logistical coordination and litigation support to local Legal Services offices contesting restrictive Social Security and welfare rules. These antipoverty attorneys infused the debate over disability policy, long dominated by the middle-class parents of disabled children, with a concern for the poor.

At the center of this broad and varied coalition was the Mental Health Law Project, an organization that embodied the coalition's interest in disability rights and welfare as well as its tendency to use litigation as a catalyst for policy reform.[3] Three attorneys formed the MHLP 1972: Paul Friedman, Bruce Ennis, and Charles Halpern. Halpern developed an interest in mental health law when in 1966 in the case of *Rouse v. Cameron*, he convinced the Washington, DC, district court to recognize for the first time a patient's right to treatment.[4] Then in 1971, Halpern along with Ennis and Friedman took part in *Wyatt v. Stickney*, a class-action lawsuit aimed at forcing the state of Alabama to improve the quality of care in its mental health asylums. Working with a team of reform-

2. *Mills v. Board of Education*, 348 F. Supp. 866 (D.D.C. 1972), and *Pennsylvania Association of Retarded Children v. Pennsylvania*, 334 F. Supp. 1257 (E.D.P.A. 1972).

3. This history of the Mental Health Law Project draws heavily from the following documents: Walter Goodman, "The Constitution versus the Snake Pit," *New York Times Magazine*, March 17, 1974, 21–22, 34; Lee S. Carty, "The Mental Health Project's 20 Years," *Clearinghouse Review: 25th Anniversary Review of Legal Services* (1992): 57–65; the Mental Health Law Project, "Mental Health Law Project, 1972–1992: Twentieth Anniversary Report," (1993), 4–17; and the Bazelon Center for Mental Health Law, *Civil Rights and Human Dignity: Three Decades of Leadership in Advocacy for People with Mental Disabilities*, 2002. The MHLP was renamed the Bazelon Center for Mental Health Law in 1993 in honor of Judge David Bazelon's ground-breaking decision in *Rouse* and other patients' rights cases.

4. *Rouse v. Cameron*, 373 F.2d 451 (D.C. Cir. 1966).

minded psychiatrists, the three attorneys drafted an amicus curiae brief
that spelled out the guidelines that asylums should have to follow. District court judge Frank Johnson, Jr., borrowed heavily from their amicus
brief in his opinion imposing detailed and rigorous minimum standards
of care on Alabama's mental institutions.[5] Inspired by his success in *Rouse*
and *Wyatt*, Halpern was convinced of the power of the law to bring about
progressive political change. A few years earlier, he had set up the Center
for Law and Social Policy, a public interest law firm devoted to bringing
"systematic attention" to social problems that lawyers had been trying to
remedy on a "hit-or-miss" basis. Halpern decided to do the same for
mental health issues. He found an eager partner in Bruce Ennis, a lawyer
at the American Civil Liberties Union. A committed libertarian, Ennis
objected to the inordinate control the state and treating psychiatrists exercised over individuals deemed mentally ill. The year after *Wyatt*, the
two attorneys along with Friedman created the MHLP with the goal of
developing a corps of legal specialists in the field of mental health who
would bring test cases and educate the public, states, and Congress on
the injustices done to people with mental disorders.[6] Because the MHLP
was first founded with a commitment to patients' rights, it was a latecomer to antipoverty advocacy. But concern for patients' rights soon led
the MHLP and other disability advocates from a narrow interest in negative rights to support for broad entitlements to social aid.

Disability Advocates Mobilize around the Idea of Rights

Prior to the 1960s, policy responded to the concerns of professionals
who worked with the disabled—physicians, vocational rehabilitation specialists, physical therapists, and other service providers—rather than to
the wants of the disabled themselves. There were a handful of vocal
groups representing veterans, the blind, and the deaf, but rarely did
people with disabilities raise their voice on political matters. Most individuals with disabilities did not attend schools, work, or even vote. This
changed in the late 1960s when a diverse array of groups questioned
America's attitudes toward its "hidden minority."[7] Several social develop-

5. *Wyatt v. Stickney*, 325 F. Supp. 781 (M.D. Ala. 1971).
6. Goodman, "Constitution versus the Snake Pit," 22.
7. Frank Bowe, quoted in Thomas Burke, "On the Rights Track: The Americans
with Disabilities Act," in *Comparative Disadvantage: Social Regulations and the Global
Economy*, ed. Pietro Nivola (Washington, DC: Brookings Institution Press, 1997), 252–
53.

ments led to the rise of the disability rights movement in the late 1960s. Some activists had come of age during the civil rights movement and identified with the struggles of African-Americans. Other activists had served in the Vietnam War and brought their antiwar fervor to disability issues. Also playing a role were advances in medical technology that permitted disabled persons to live longer, survive traumatic injury, and participate more fully in everyday life despite their functional limitations. Having once been able-bodied, these individuals were acutely aware of how their social status had changed once they had become disabled, and they felt the loss acutely. This new generation of activists was more politicized, better educated, and less accepting of society's limits than older generations of disabled persons.[8]

The framework of disability rights altered how individuals with disabilities looked at themselves and their social situation. Drawing from the tenants of the social model, activists argued that the disadvantages of disability were not a given. Instead, disability was a social construct used to subordinate one group to the majority. According to this perspective, because all disabled individuals were subject to social prejudice, they formed a minority group in the same way that women or people of color did. Likening the situation of the disabled to that of African-Americans in the Jim Crow South, activists argued that the disabled were oppressed by social institutions that had been constructed to facilitate, even enforce, the exclusion of the disabled. People with physical disabilities were kept apart by buildings, transportation systems, and sidewalks that were inaccessible to wheelchairs. The mentally disabled were locked away in asylums. Disabled children were cut off from other students, relegated to special education classrooms in which little learning took place. Disability activist Frank Bowe explained that as American cities grew around them, "disabled people were hidden away in attics, 'special' programs, and institutions, unseen and their voices unheard."[9] Once social institutions and public spaces had been constructed to exclude people with disabilities, this structural situation was then treated as the inevitable consequence of disability rather than as a conscious societal choice. The segregation and silencing of the disabled, therefore, was not a historical accident but the direct result of society's prejudice toward individuals with functional differences. To be sure, prejudice against the disabled did not resemble the vehement animosity that blacks encountered. Instead it took the form of a debilitating pity, one that regarded the disabled as

8. Scotch, *From Goodwill to Civil Rights*, 5–7, 31–35.
9. Quoted in Burke, "On the Rights Track," 253.

childlike, helpless, and incapacitated.[10] But, to the activists, it was an injustice all the same.

Unlike older disability organizations, the newly mobilized disability rights groups did not seek better services delivered in a segregated setting. Instead, they demanded autonomy, equality, and inclusion as a matter of right. Thus, activists rejected the control that professionals, even well-meaning ones, exercised over their personal decisions and the course of their lives. In place of enhanced service programs, disability rights activists promoted the concept of equal access, which would pave the way for the social inclusion of the disabled. They argued for laws that would not only ban discrimination, but also take civil rights law one step further by requiring accommodations to ensure that people with disabilities would no longer be excluded from public places. In their eyes, providing architectural modifications, adaptive devices, and special services, such as sign-language interpreters or personal attendants, was not preferential treatment, but instead different treatment that served as a necessary step toward social equality. These services, in other words, were reasonable and just accommodations that allowed people with "different modes of functioning" equal access to public places that had in years past been designed to enforce their exclusion. Equal access, in turn, would bring disabled people out of the "attics, 'special' programs, and institutions" that had been their prisons for so long. Only by integrating the disabled in the fabric of everyday life could people with disabilities achieve equal regard and full citizenship in a world that had largely been structured according to the needs and capabilities of the able-bodied.[11]

Applying Disability Rights to the Plight of Mental Patients

Disability rights found early and eloquent expression in the cause of mental patients, as a coalition of civil libertarians and poverty lawyers in the late 1960s imbued mental health policy with the rhetoric of patients' rights. These patients' rights reformers were deeply influenced by the troubled state of psychiatric medicine at the time, which seemed to confirm the social model's central tenet that disability was not rooted in ob-

10. Evan J. Kemp, "Aiding the Disabled: No Pity, Please," *New York Times*, September 3, 1981, A19.
11. These goals are summarized in Paul K. Longmore, "The Second Phase: From Disability Rights to Disability Culture," an online document from 1995, the Independent Living Institute, http://www.independentliving.org/docs3/longm95.html.

jective reality. Several studies of psychiatric diagnosis published in the late 1960s and early 1970s were highly critical of the state of medical knowledge, arguing that psychiatrists could not adequately distinguish sanity from insanity, much less measure the degree of mental limitation. In an example that was particularly embarrassing to the medical establishment, a team of social science researchers feigned hallucinations, checked themselves into a mental hospital, and then proceeded to act "normal." Although the patients in the facility quickly recognized the ruse, neither the staff nor the doctors at the hospital noticed that the "pseudopatients" were not really ill (a finding that did not surprise critics who pointed to the large number of patients the hospital cared for).[12] Sociologists of the labeling school further undermined the medical credentials of psychiatry by arguing that mental illness was not a pathology at all but a label used for social deviants.[13] An example of how extreme this critique of psychiatry could become is R. D. Laing's *The Politics of Experience*. Laing argued that schizophrenia was an adaptive response to a disordered society. Thus, only the insane are truly sane because they at least recognize the turmoil of reality.[14]

Given these findings, patients' advocates were disturbed by the ease with which states could forcibly commit individuals diagnosed as mentally ill. While treatment might be acceptable if it could cure someone who was truly sick, it was inexcusable if, as the social science literature suggested, mental illness were nothing more than a label given to the disadvantaged and the different. To the MHLP's Bruce Ennis, therefore, it came as no surprise then that racial minorities and the poor were the most likely to be found mentally ill. In his famous 1972 book, *Prisoners of Psychiatry*, Ennis laid out the intellectual foundations of the patients' rights movement, denouncing psychiatry as a tool used by the majority to "tame our rebellious youth, rid ourselves of doddering parents, or clear the streets of the offensive poor." Mental patients, he argued, were simply individuals whom society deemed "useless, unproductive, 'odd,' or 'different.'" Because of this judgment, they were stripped of their rights

12. D. L. Rosenhan, "On Being Sane in Insane Places," *Science* 179 (1973): 250–58.

13. Thomas J. Scheff, *Being Mentally Ill* (Chicago: Aldine, 1966). See also Thomas J. Scheff, "The Societal Reaction to Deviance: Ascriptive Elements in the Psychiatric Screening of Mental Patients in a Midwestern State," in *The Mental Patient*, ed. Stephan P. Spitzer and Norman K. Denzin (New York: McGraw-Hill, 1968), 276–90; and Thomas J. Scheff, "The Role of the Mentally Ill and the Dynamics of Mental Disorder: A Research Framework," *Sociometry* 26 (1963): 436–53.

14. R. D. Laing, *The Politics of Experience* (Baltimore: Penguin Books, 1967).

and locked in asylums, despicable places where "sick people get sicker and sane people go mad," all under the guise of compassionate medicine.[15]

Like their fellow disability rights activists, the patients' rights reformers saw their movement as continuing the tradition of the civil rights movement. Drawing on the minority metaphor, Judi Chamberlain, a former mental patient and rights activist, argued that the mentally ill, like African-Americans, were "an oppressed group, oppressed by laws and public attitudes, relegated to legalized second class citizenship." To her, "involuntary commitment to institutions and forced psychiatric treatment" were the epitome of "legalized discrimination" and served as "the biggest barrier" to the "full equality" for people with mental illness.[16] Thomas Gilhool, a key architect of many welfare rights and right to treatment lawsuits, also compared the virulent injustice done to African-Americans to the treatment mental patients received in asylums. "Slavery, segregation, and what has come to be called 'institutionalization,'" he asserted, "are functional equivalents; they are the historic expression of the judgment of inferiority taken to its furthest conclusion."[17]

Of course, confidence in the therapeutic value of institutionalized mental health care had been waning for many years before patients' rights reformers come on the scene.[18] Following World War II, books such as Albert Deutsch's *The Shame of the States*, Mike Gorman's *Every Other Bed*, and Erving Goffman's *Asylums* exposed the filthy and dehumanizing conditions prevalent in many mental hospitals and residential homes. In 1966, the publication of Burton Blatt and Fred Kaplan's

15. Bruce Ennis, *Prisoners of Psychiatry: Mental Patients, Psychiatrists, and the Law* (New York: Harcourt Brace Jovanovich, 1972), vii–viii, 82, 230. Among the works that attack psychiatrists and mental hospitals as institutions of social control with little interest in the well-being of the patient, see David J. Rothman, *The Discovery of the Asylum: Social Order and Disorder in the New Republic* (Boston: Little, Brown, 1971); Andrew T. Scull, *Decarceration: Community Treatment and the Deviant—A Radical View* (New Brunswick, NJ: Rutgers University, 1977); Thomas S. Szasz, *The Myth of Mental Illness* (New York: Harper Collins, 1974); Thomas S. Szasz, *Law, Liberty, and Psychiatry* (New York: Macmillan, 1963); and Thomas S. Szasz, *The Manufacture of Madness* (New York: Harper and Row, 1970).

16. Judi Chamberlain, "Psychiatric Survivors: Are We Part of the Disability Rights Movement?" *Disability Rag* 16, 2 (1995): 4.

17. Thomas K. Gilhool, "The Right to Community Services," in *The Mentally Retarded Citizen and the Law*, ed. Michael Kindred, Julius Cohen, David Penrod, and Thomas L. Shaffer, report sponsored by the President's Committee on Mental Retardation (New York: Free Press, 1976), 176 n. 9.

18. Peter S. Appelbaum, *Almost a Revolution: Mental Health Law and the Limits of Change* (Oxford: Oxford University Press, 1994), 4–10.

Christmas in Purgatory shocked the nation with its visceral photographs of patients locked in crumbling and overcrowded institutions.[19] After touring the facilities of Partlow State School, the institution that became the test case in the landmark lawsuit, *Wyatt v. Stickney*, Judge Johnson confirmed what the critics had uncovered. He recounted the stories of a resident who "died when soapy water was forced into his mouth" and one "authorities restrained . . . in a strait jacket for nine years to prevent him from sucking his hands and fingers." Appalled, Johnson characterized Partlow as "barbaric and primitive," noting that "some residents had no place to sit to eat meals, and coffee cans served as toilets in some areas."[20] But Partlow was not unique. Critics of the mental health system argued that treatment in asylums amounted to little more than the "warehousing" of patients. Much worse, because of neglect and frequent abuse at the hands of custodians and other patients, conditions in these hospitals were actually detrimental to the health of people committed for long periods of time. The irony was that state asylums had been founded in the 1840s as a humanitarian alternative to the poorhouses and prisons that, until then, had served as the holding pens of people with mental illness and developmental disorders. These were places where, to the dismay of reformer Dorthea Dix, people were locked "in cages, closets, cellars, stalls, and pens" and lived each day "chained, naked, beaten with rods, and lashed into obedience."[21] By 1965, however, the asylum had degenerated into a shameful symbol of the nation's continued disregard for the mentally disabled, discredited as little better than the poorhouses and prisons it had replaced.

By the time the patients' rights reformers entered the picture, federal officials, encouraged by the development of effective antipsychotic drugs, had already began experimenting with deinstitutionalization. In 1962, the Department of Health, Education, and Welfare (HEW) allowed state governments to use federal funds to supplement state disability assistance payments to patients on "conditional release" from mental institutions. Entrepreneurial state officials quickly realized that if patients were let go, they could be supported with some federal money. On the other hand, if

19. Albert Deutsch, *The Shame of the States* (New York: Harcourt, Brace, 1948); Mike Gorman, *Every Other Bed* (Cleveland, OH: World Publishing, 1956); Erving Goffman, *Asylums: Essays on the Social Situation of Mental Patients and Other Inmates* (New York: Doubleday, 1961); and Burton Blatt and Fred Kaplan, *Christmas Purgatory: A Photographic Essay on Mental Retardation* (Boston: Allyn and Bacon, 1966).

20. Quoted in Mark C. Weber, "Home and Community-Based Services, *Olmstead*, and Positive Rights: A Preliminary Discussion," *Wake Forest Law Review* 39 (2004): 266.

21. Grob, *Mad among Us*, 23–54, and Dix quoted in Shapiro, *No Pity*, 59.

they remained institutionalized, the costs of their care fell solely on the state. States seized on the opportunity to transfer patients from public hospitals to "alternative living arrangements wherever facilities could be found."[22] The following year, President John F. Kennedy signed the Community Mental Health Centers Construction Act. Signaling a move away from mental asylums and a federal preference for community placement, the law authorized federal funds for the development of a national network of small, locally based community mental health centers that would take the place of the large state hospitals and provide preventive care to the general population in order to avert the emergence of more serious disorders.

Patients' rights reformers, therefore, did not instigate deinstitutionalization, nor were they the first to voice concern for the plight of people with mental disorders. Their emphasis on individual rights, however, did instill the issue with a strong sense of social justice. Their goal was threefold. Insofar as they viewed psychiatry as a flawed and sometimes discriminatory enterprise, the reformers wanted, first, to weaken the ability of states to commit individuals involuntarily, which many of them did with nothing more than the certification of a lone psychiatrist. Reformers also wanted to arm patients, once inside an asylum, with basic protections that would preclude abuse and neglect at the hands of their doctors and custodians. The right to treatment, the right to refuse treatment, and the right to treatment in the least restrictive setting were legal guarantees designed to ensure that states provided patients with meaningful care. Reformers sought to prevent states from warehousing patients or, worse yet, subjecting them to forced medication, insulin shock therapy, electroshock therapy, and surgical lobotomy, treatments that reformers considered inhumane and degrading. The ultimate goal of the reformers, however, reached beyond merely improving the quality of custodial care. If the mental asylum was society's means of separating out and segregating people with mental disorders, then justice demanded its eradication. Thus, reformers sought as a final goal to replace the asylum with a community-based system of mental health care, a policy that would allow people with mental disorders to live in their home neighborhoods and to enjoy all the rights and social privileges offered to the able-bodied.[23]

22. Paul Lerman, *Deinstitutionalization and the Welfare State* (New Brunswick, NJ: Rutgers University Press, 1982), 14.

23. Gilhool, "The Right to Community Services," 19; David Rothman, "The Right to Habilitation: Reaction Comment," in *Mentally Retarded Citizen and the Law*, ed. Kindred et al., 407; and Robert A. Burt, "Beyond the Right to Habilitation," in *Mentally Retarded Citizen and the Law*, ed. Kindred et al., 422–24.

How Disability and Patients' Rights Became Policy

In the late 1960s, patients' rights reformers initiated legal challenges to the open-ended authority states and doctors exercised over patients, and they found the federal courts ready and willing allies. In 1966, David Bazelon, a federal district court judge in Washington, DC, handed down *Rouse v. Cameron*, the first in a long series of patients' rights cases. Persuaded by attorney Charles Halpern's arguments on behalf of a right to treatment, Judge Bazelon ruled that if states were going to commit individuals like Charles Rouse against their will, then they had to provide therapeutic medical care as well. By increasing the financial costs of involuntary commitment, the right to treatment weakened states' enthusiasm for locking patients away. Seeking to build on the *Rouse* precedent, reformers quickly brought the courts into decisions that had once been the exclusive province of state governments and medical professionals. Throughout the 1970s, attorneys affiliated with the MHLP, Halpern's new center, had a hand in practically every major court decision in the field of mental health. In 1972, the MHLP's inaugural year, its lawyers assisted with the pivotal right to education case, *Mills v. Board of Education*. The following year, in *New York State Association for Retarded Children v. Rockefeller*, they filed suit against the state of New York for the deplorable conditions at Willowbrook State School for the Mentally Retarded. In the Willowbrook case, the district court extended the right to treatment by recognizing that mental patients had a constitutional right to protection from harm and were entitled to therapeutic care designed to prepare them for life outside the institution.[24] Over the next several years, federal judges elaborated a detailed list of procedures that states had to follow before involuntarily committing someone, curtailed the ability of doctors to forcibly medicate patients, crafted exacting standards that had to be met before medical treatment was considered adequate, and required doctors to provide treatment in the least restrictive setting possible.

Indeed, given the parallels reformers drew between the civil rights and patients' rights movement, the federal courts were a forum well-suited to the manner in which patients' rights reformers framed their cause. The symbolism of *Wyatt v. Stickney*, the seminal patients' rights case decided in 1972, was particularly striking. Not only was the *Wyatt* case brought in Alabama, home of ardent segregationist governor, George Wallace, but

---

24. *The New York State Association for Retarded Children v. Rockefeller*, 357 F. Supp. 752 (E.D.N.Y. 1973).

the presiding judge, Frank Johnson, had been a staunch proponent of racial integration and a perennial thorn in the side of the Wallace administration. One writer wryly remarked that "the case looked like a conflict between the forces of humanitarian liberalism and redneck conservatism."[25]

At the same time that reformers made headway in the courts, the broader disability rights movement took form. The battle over Section 504 of the 1973 Rehabilitation Act became the catalyzing event for this movement. In 1972, senators Hubert Humphrey and Charles Percy and Representative Charles Vanik tried but failed to add disability to the protected classes covered by the 1964 Civil Rights Act. The following year, however, liberal congressional staffers accomplished what the three lawmakers could not. They inserted Section 504 into amendments to rehabilitation legislation. Attracting little attention when it became law, the provision built on the Architectural Barriers Act of 1968, which required buildings financed with federal funds to be accessible to the disabled. Section 504 went further by barring discrimination in any federally financed program. The law stated simply that "no otherwise qualified individual . . . shall, solely by reason of his handicap, be excluded from participation in, be denied the benefits of, or be subjected to discrimination under any program or activity receiving Federal assistance."[26] As drafted by the Office of Civil Rights in the Department of Health, Education, and Welfare, the regulations enforcing Section 504 made inaccessible facilities and the failure to accommodate the disabled a civil rights violation. The Nixon and Ford administrations, however, kept the rules needed to implement Section 504 bottled up in HEW for four years. When President Jimmy Carter entered office, disability rights activists had high hopes that HEW would finally issue the rules. They were outraged when Carter's new HEW secretary Joseph Califano delayed after business complained about the costs of compliance. In the spring of 1977, activists representing a variety of impairments staged protests in several major cities, including one at Califano's home and another at the San Francisco HEW office that lasted for twenty-five days, the longest sit-in ever at a federal building. Under intense pressure, Califano backed down and issued the 504 rules, and activists who in the past had worked separately learned the power of their combined strength.[27] As Doris Zames Fleischer and Frieda Zames recount, "Until this point, the dis-

---

25. Isaac and Armat, *Madness in the Streets*, 129.

26. 29 U.S.C. 794.

27. Shapiro, *No Pity*, 66–69, and Fleischer and Zames, *Disability Rights Movement*, 49–56.

ability rights movement had been local and disparate." But after the battle for Section 504, "the movement became national and focused."[28]

Given the growing activism of patients' rights reformers and disability rights activists, the elected branches of government came to second what the federal courts did by enshrining protections for people with disabilities into federal law. Presidents John Kennedy, Lyndon Johnson, and Jimmy Carter especially were attuned to the ideas of the advocates. Two expert committees, President Kennedy's Committee on Mental Retardation and President Carter's Commission on Mental Health, served as forums for reformers and like-minded professionals to recommend many of their policy aspirations. At the same time, the federal government became increasingly involved in mental health policy, an area in which state and local governments had once held wide discretion. In 1970, Congress reauthorized the Developmental Disabilities Assistance and Bill of Rights Act, creating councils to coordinate social services for people with developmental disabilities and ensure that these services were provided in the least restrictive setting. Five years later, lawmakers established protection and advocacy systems designed to safeguard the rights to treatment, services, and habilitation. Similarly, the struggle for education rights for disabled children, which began with the two court cases brought by the Arc, *Mills v. Board of Education* and *PARC v. Pennsylvania*, culminated in passage of the Education for All Handicapped Children Act in 1975. In addition, throughout the 1960s and into the early 1970s, Congress repeatedly increased spending for community support services, such as halfway houses, day care centers, drug and alcohol treatment facilities, and community-based mental health clinics, even expanding expenditures in 1973 over the strong objections of the Nixon White House. By the end of the 1970s, the total amount that the federal government devoted to community mental health care programs reached a peak of $298 million, almost ten times the amount appropriated in 1965.[29] Finally, in 1980, Congress enacted the Civil Rights of Institutionalized Persons Act, authorizing the U.S. Justice Department to intervene against a state or local government to protect the rights of institutionalized patients or nursing home residents, a step that was reminiscent of the power granted the department in the late 1960s to enforce the provisions of the Civil Rights Act and the Voting Rights Act on behalf of African-Americans in the South.

28. Fleischer and Zames, *Disability Rights Movement*, 52.
29. Martha R. Burt and Karen J. Pittman, *Testing the Social Safety Net: The Impact of Changes in Support Programs during the Reagan Administration* (Washington, DC: Urban Institute Press, 1985), 77.

Why Advocates Cared about the Social Safety Net

Despite their success in convincing federal judges to recognize the rights of mental patients, the reformers were not content. Their ultimate goal was not the improvement of mental asylums but their abolition. Insofar as it represented society's desire to be rid of the mentally disabled, MHLP founder Charles Halpern argued, the very existence of the asylum, no matter how well-staffed or humanely run, was "antithetical" to the right of people with disabilities to inclusion in society.[30] Reformers wanted to replace institutional care with community mental health care, and they viewed the string of patients' rights lawsuits as an interim step toward that end. As Bruce Ennis of the MHLP noted in 1974, patients' rights litigation was the "best method for deinstitutionalizing thousands of persons" and hastening the shift toward community-based care.[31] He explained that if courts broadly applied the mandated reforms articulated in *Wyatt* and other patients' rights cases, then many state mental institutions would be unable to meet the increased costs, thus forcing them to close their doors forever.[32]

But, as advocate David Rothman pointed out, there was a risk entailed in this strategy. By fighting to "protect the rights of persons inside the institutions," he argued, reformers also risked "legitimating the institutions themselves." If states were willing to commit the resources necessary to meet judicial requirements, then the court mandates could end up creating "newer, bigger, ostensibly better institutions" and that would weaken the impetus for providing care in the community.[33] It was for these reasons that the MHLP decided against taking part in a lawsuit brought by Morton Birnbaum, a physician and lawyer who was the original architect of the right to treatment doctrine. Birnbaum's lawsuit challenged Medicaid's refusal to reimburse states for the medical care of persons under age sixty-five who lived in institutions and resident hospitals.[34] MHLP attorneys feared that if the lawsuit were successful, Medicaid funds would allow the states to enhance the quality of care in their asylums and thus

30. Charles Halpern, "The Right to Habilitation," in *Mentally Retarded Citizen and the Law*, ed. Kindred et al., 387, 405–6.

31. Quoted in Isaac and Armat, *Madness in the Streets*, 128.

32. Ibid., 128–29. This belief is also voiced in Gilhool, "Right to Community Services," 192.

33. Rothman, "Right to Habilitation," in *Mentally Retarded Citizen and the Law*, ed. Kindred et al., 407, and Robert A. Burt, "Beyond the Right to Habilitation," in *Mentally Retarded Citizen and the Law*, ed. Kindred et al., 422–24.

34. *Legion v. Richardson*, 354 F. Supp. 456 (S.D.N.Y. 1973).

make community care less attractive by comparison. Though a strong proponent of the right to treatment, the MHLP refused to help Birnbaum, and his lawsuit failed. Rather than aid existing asylums, the MHLP sought instead to persuade federal lawmakers to redirect spending for institutionalized care to community mental health care.

The commitment to community mental health care, therefore, became the bridge that took patients' rights reformers into social welfare advocacy. Illustrating the connections between patient autonomy and equality, on the one hand, and the social safety net, on the other, mental health lawyer Thomas Gilhool argued, "Behind every question of access to services in the community, and not distantly, is the question of . . . liberty."[35] Releasing former mental patients into the community required the creation of a social safety net to take the place of the care that state custodians had provided within the asylum. Only with an expanded federal commitment to providing social assistance outside the asylum could reformers succeed in integrating former patients to community life. Although acute care for psychiatric emergencies could still be offered at large hospitals on a short-term basis, people with mental disorders would no longer be committed to institutions far from their homes, friends, and families for indefinite periods of time. Instead, reformers envisioned a comprehensive and integrated system in which out-patient mental health care and case management would be provided through a network of small and personal clinics located throughout communities. These facilities would provide care that was both less restrictive and more rehabilitative than that provided in the asylums. Complementing community mental health centers would be an array of programs that would serve as a safety net for deinstitutionalized patients.[36] This alternative mode of mental health care would be, one advocate claimed, a "new asylum, the 'asylum of the community.'" This new asylum would be, not a building, but a dense web of public programs replete with income support, housing assistance, sheltered work initiatives, and social services.[37]

35. Gilhool, "Right to Community Services," 191.

36. These goals are aptly stated in John A. Talbot, ed., prepared by the American Psychiatric Association, Ad Hoc Committee on the Chronic Mental Patient, *The Chronic Mental Patient: Problems, Solutions, and Recommendations for a Public Policy* (Washington, DC: American Psychiatric Association, 1978), especially 142–46. See also Bruce J. Ennis and Richard D. Emery, *The Rights of Mental Patients* (New York: Avon, 1978), 18, and Leslie Scallet, "The Clash between Advocacy and Implementation," in *Disability: Challenges for Social Insurance, Health Care, Financing, and Labor Market Policy*, ed. Virginia Reno, Jerry Mashaw, and Bill Gradison (Washington, DC: National Academy of Social Insurance, 1997), 179–83.

37. Monroe E. Price, "The Right to Community Services: Reaction Comment," in *Mentally Retarded Citizen and the Law*, ed. Kindred et al., 210–13, 211.

In 1976, in a report sponsored by the President's Committee on Mental Retardation, Charles Halpern called for the "next generation of litigation" to "develop community services as an alternative to institutionalization." He urged reformers to build on the promise of the right to treatment articulated in *Wyatt* and the right to an education in *Mills*. These two cases were significant because they articulated affirmative state obligations to provide adequate services to the disabled.[38] Thus, *Mills* and the Education for All Handicapped Children Act, the law that enshrined the right to education into statutory law, were welfare as well as civil rights initiatives. They called for integration of disabled students into mainstream public schools, but to do so, required states to pay for the services that made this integration possible. Sign language interpreters, personal assistants, and specialized equipment were among the many services states had to provide. Equally important, *Mills* and the EAHCA entitled disabled children to assistance even though many of these children lived outside mental institutions and therefore were not wards of the state.

Extending the positive rights to social aid that disabled students had won to all people with disabilities, however, proved difficult. Two developments complicated these efforts. First, the litigation strategy that had been the backbone of the patients' rights movement floundered on the shoals of community mental health care. The federal courts recognized the rights of patients only so long as they were under the power of the state. But as two mental health attorneys admitted, "Once the institution is left behind and the individual is in the community, the issues are not as neatly framed." In the community, "disabled individuals are no longer deprived of liberty or subject to harm by custodians who control all aspects of their lives."[39] As a result, the courts narrowly interpreted the state's obligations to former patients released into the community. The courts, put simply, had not signed on to the idea of social inclusion; it was state power, not societal discrimination that they worried about. Thus, once the patient was released, he was on his own. In 1982, the Supreme Court followed the lead of the lower courts when, in *Youngberg v. Romeo*, the justices reiterated that "a duty to provide certain services does exist" when "a person is institutionalized," but "as a general matter, a state is

38. Halpern, "The Right to Habilitation," 387, 405–4, 406.
39. Leonard S. Rubenstein and Jane Yohalem Bloom, "The Courts and the Psychiatric Disability," in *Psychiatric Disability: Clinical, Legal, and Administrative Dimensions*, ed. Arthur T. Meyerson and Theodora Fine (Washington, DC: American Psychiatric Association, 1987), 438–39.

under no constitutional duty to provide substantive services."[40] Throughout the 1980s, the court continued to undermine the judicial logic for positive state obligations to people living outside mental institutions. In 1985, the justices refused to recognize disability as a suspect class, thus denying people with disabilities the same protections afforded women and racial minorities, and they allowed states to slash health care programs even though such cuts would have a disproportionately adverse impact on the disabled.[41] Finally, in the 1989 case of *DeShaney v. Winnebago County*, the Supreme Court put the final nail in the coffin of constitutional guarantees to state assistance. In a narrowly split opinion, the justices held that a state's failure to protect a person from harm caused by private actors was not a violation of rights if the state itself was not the cause of those harms. The Constitution, said the court, "is phrased as a limitation on the State's power to act, not as a guarantee of certain minimal levels of safety and security; while it forbids the State itself to deprive individuals of life, liberty, and property without due process of law," it does not "impose an affirmative obligation on the State to ensure that those interests do not come to harm through other means."[42] Because courts viewed the lack or inadequacy of community support services as "a deficiency of the welfare state" rather than "as a problem resulting from a denial of legal rights," they refused to compel states to set up community care programs or fund existing ones, preferring to leave these matters to legislators.[43]

Second, some disabled activists, particularly those affiliated with the independent living movement, were ambivalent about endorsing enhanced social welfare programs, a division within the disabled community that impeded advocacy efforts to present a united front on behalf of an expanded safety net.[44] There were several reasons for this ambivalence. As some disability rights activists pointed out, social welfare programs were premised on the assumption that a disabled person was helpless, and the state offered support out of a sense of charity or pity. This reinforced all the negative stereotypes that rights activists were trying to

40. *Youngberg v. Romeo*, 457 U.S. 307 (1982).

41. *Cleburne v. Cleburne Living Center*, 473 U.S. 432 (1985), and *Alexander v. Choate*, 469 U.S. 287 (1985).

42. *DeShaney v. Winnebago County*, 489 U.S. 189 (1989), at 189.

43. Rubenstein and Bloom, "Courts and the Psychiatric Disability," 439.

44. Samuel R. Bagenstos, "The Americans with Disabilities Act as Welfare Reform," *William and Mary Law Review* 44 (2003): 985, and William Johnson, "The Future of Disability Policy: Benefit Payments or Civil Rights?" *Annals of the American Academy of Political and Social Science* 549 (1997): 160–72.

overthrow. In their eyes, to argue for both equal rights for the disabled and welfare would be to present a mixed message.

Moreover, social welfare programs often placed disabled persons under the thumb of bureaucrats and medical professionals who had no direct experience with disability. For example, wheelchair-bound activist Ed Roberts resented the fact that the vocational rehabilitation counselors he had worked with were narrowly focused on ensuring that participants in their programs find employment. Thus, they did little to help people with severe handicaps like him, essentially writing them off as poor job prospects. When he founded the Center for Independent Living in Berkeley, California, in 1972, he insisted that disabled people, rather than able-bodied medical and rehabilitation professionals, manage the center's referral programs for jobs, personal attendants, housing, and income support to ensure that the perspective of people with disabilities was ever present.[45] Having been constructed by professionals, traditionally structured social welfare programs did not share this disability-centered perspective.

A final reason disability rights activists were divided over the question of welfare was that some of them, like the MHLP's Bruce Ennis and prominent leaders of the disability rights movement, distrusted state power whatever its form. Committed libertarians, they valued individual autonomy and self-sufficiency and were uncomfortable with long-term reliance on public assistance. For instance, Ed Roberts urged people with disabilities to reject the "welfare mentality." Others, like disability rights activist Justin Dart, condemned " 'the "give me" socialist view' that 'society should and can provide certain benefits to each human with no corresponding obligation on the part of the individuals.' "[46] Even less radical rights activists tended to accept this "small government" mentality. Appealing to lawmakers' desire to hold the line on social welfare expenditures, patients' rights reformers often claimed that "high quality integrated programs based on a . . . full service model" would not cost more than the current practice of "state hospital incarceration."[47] Not only was this disingenuous—after all, public asylums were deplorable precisely because states would not commit the resources necessary for proper care—but it was also self-defeating. Thus, unlike some older disability organizations that had lobbied for both assistance and civil rights, a significant contingent of the contemporary disability community came to view wel-

45. Shapiro, *No Pity*, 49–55.
46. Quoted in Samuel R. Bagenstos, "The Future of Disability Law," *Yale Law Journal* 114 (2004): 16.
47. Talbot, *Chronic Mental Patient*, 216.

fare expansion and disability rights as mutually exclusive rather than re-
ciprocally supportive policy approaches.[48]

Perhaps because of this ambivalence, reformers never devoted the same
attention to the development of the social safety net that they had to the
patients' rights litigation. What made deinstitutionalization and indeed
some semblance of community living possible, however, was not the
courts or community mental health programs but the expansion of federal
social welfare spending that took place during Johnson's War on Poverty
and the early years of the Nixon administration. Deinstitutionalization
simply would not have proceeded as fast as it did without growth in the
programs that comprised the core of the American welfare state, programs like Social Security Disability Insurance, SSI, Medicare, and Medicaid. For all the attention that patients' rights reformers paid to community mental health grants, spending for them paled in comparison to
federal outlays for these mainstream programs. But with expenditures for
community mental health grants and conventional social welfare programs on the rise, it was all too easy for reformers to neglect reorienting
existing social welfare programs and instead focus on enacting new programs targeted specifically at people with mental disorders. As a result,
patients' rights reformers and other disability advocates made little at
tempt to coordinate the existing programs with community mental health
initiatives. Reformers spoke about a "new asylum" of social welfare supports based in the community, but even up until the mid 1970s, few had
given much thought to how to make this social safety net a reality.

Patients' rights reformers began with a desire to protect the mentally ill
and mentally retarded from the neglect and harm they suffered at the
hands of state custodians. But beyond simply improving conditions
within mental institutions, reformers had much more ambitious goals.
They wanted to give individuals with mental disabilities the opportunity
to live outside the confines of the asylum alongside able-bodied and able-
minded people. Because of their commitment to autonomy, equality, and
inclusion, reformers became just as interested in securing affirmative
guarantees of social aid as they were in negative protections from state
harm. But winning recognition of welfare rights would be far more difficult than it had been for patients' rights. Indeed, the story of SSI's enact-

48. Burke, "On the Rights Track," 256–59, 270–71; see also Bagenstos, "Americans
with Disabilities Act as Welfare Reform," 995–96, and Bagenstos, "Future of Disability
Law," 3–83.

ment illustrated that reformers were fighting an uphill battle. SSI eventually became a cornerstone of the social safety net reformers wanted to erect. But their advocacy efforts had nothing to do with its creation. In fact, as I will explore in chapter 3, at the very moment that Congress endorsed the new program, it rejected an attempt by antipoverty advocates to secure for all impoverished families this same entitlement to assistance. SSI became law precisely because its proponents did not cast it as a rights issue and did not draw attention to the large numbers of disabled people the program would serve. Though it sped the movement of people with mental disorders from asylums to community settings, because SSI was not designed around the needs of severely ill mental patients, it did not patch the problems with deinstitutionalization that had emerged by the mid 1970s.

3

SSI and the New Social Safety Net

When Congress created the Supplemental Security Income program in late 1972, it ushered in a new way of thinking about welfare. By setting a nationally uniform income floor, SSI made available for the first time a minimum level of assistance to people in need regardless of their place of residence or family circumstance. The federal government administered SSI, and as a result, benefit levels and eligibility rules did not vary from state to state, as had been the case with the traditional public assistance programs that the states ran. Moreover, SSI did away with the punitive measures the states had used to deter people from applying for public assistance. Recipients enrolled in the new program no longer had to beg their relatives for help, sign their homes away to the state welfare office, or abide by work requirements or tests of moral character in order to qualify for help. SSI, in short, was the sort of entitlement program that liberal reformers had long sought but frequently failed to obtain from Congress. Yet few watershed moments in social welfare politics have occasioned as little controversy as SSI's inception. Few Americans, even few disability advocates paid any attention to the program despite the fact that, eventually, it would become a vital thread in the social safety net for people with disabilities, especially people with mental disorders.

That this far-reaching innovation in social welfare policy took place at all is remarkable. Lawmakers had long harbored doubts about assistance for the disabled, and as the debate over the Nixon administration's Family Assistance Plan (FAP) made clear, they were not amenable to claims that the poor had a right to societal help. Submitted to Congress in 1969, the

FAP, like SSI, was a radical proposal that would have entitled all poor families, even two-parent households, to some degree of income support. Congress debated the FAP for three years and ultimately rejected it in 1972. It was from the ashes of this failed endeavor that SSI came to pass. Created when Congress nationalized the state-run public assistance programs for aged, blind, and disabled adults, SSI gave to the aged and disabled poor the same right to welfare that the FAP would have given needy families. Nevertheless, SSI came into being precisely because its supporters did not call attention to its revolutionary nature, framing it neither as a right nor as a bold expansion of Social Security. Instead, they first passed it off as a way of improving wayward state public assistance programs. Then once support for the FAP had dissipated, they repackaged SSI as a way to strengthen Social Security's Old Age Insurance program and help the elderly. Practically no attention was given to disability issues. By directing attention away from poverty and disability, SSI's proponents downplayed the groundbreaking features of the new program. And because lawmakers sandwiched SSI between reform of family assistance and OAI, they failed to see that they were laying the foundations for the community-based safety net advocates desired. They also failed to see that by creating a broad income support program for the disabled, they were opening Social Security to the administrative problems that had long plagued disability benefit programs, no matter how strictly drawn.

Where Did SSI Come From?

The passage of SSI had almost nothing to do with the disabled. The program instead grew out of two shortcomings with American social welfare policy that had become evident by the late 1960s. The first was the prevailing state-run system for administering income support programs for the poor. Conservatives in Congress had long stood in the way of liberal plans to have the federal government run public assistance programs. But by 1968, many prominent conservatives in Congress were alarmed by rapidly increasing assistance rolls and studies suggesting that Aid to Families with Dependent Children, the primary income support program for poor families, encouraged family breakup and undermined employment. Blaming the states for these ills, conservatives revisited plans to nationalize public assistance. Although the ire focused on family assistance, the adult programs for the aged, blind, and disabled were brought along as well in the push for increased federal control. Nationalizing welfare, however, was deeply divisive. By the end of 1972, the drive behind the FAP had disintegrated amid acrimonious bickering. SSI, however, became law because it had been transformed into the chosen solution to a second policy quandary, the desire to provide a decent postretirement income to the nation's elderly without undermining the core principle of equity that buttressed social insurance. The equity principle demanded that Social Security beneficiaries be paid what they "deserved" based on prior payroll contributions to the Social Security trust fund, not necessarily what they needed to live adequately. Executive officials promised lawmakers that with SSI, Congress could do both: pay the elderly adequate benefits and still retain equitable payments. The disabled were never mentioned.

The Campaign to Nationalize Public Assistance

SSI was born of bipartisan efforts in the late 1960s and early 1970s to solve the "welfare mess." This mess, in turn, was rooted in the two-tiered welfare state created by the Social Security Act of 1935. The act set up two social insurance programs—Old Age Insurance and Unemployment Insurance—as well as three matching-grant public assistance programs: Aid to Families with Dependent Children, Old Age Assistance (OAA), and Aid to the Blind (AB). Aid to the Permanently and Totally Disabled (APTD) was added in 1950. Under these matching-grant programs, the federal government pledged to match state expenditures dollar-for-dollar up to a prescribed level in order to encourage states to offer as adequate a benefit as resources would allow. But states retained a role as well. Unlike Old Age Insurance, which was run by a federal agency according to rules that applied uniformly nationwide, the matching-grant arrangement left states in charge of administering public assistance. The programs had a few stipulations that banned waiting lists and overly long state residency requirements. States also had to give applicants the chance to appeal denials and had to make benefits available to residents in every county of the state. But Congress refrained from telling the states how to run their programs. The Social Security Act defined the aged to be those age sixty-five and older, but it did not spell out the meaning of blindness or, later, disability, leaving this matter to state governments. Moreover, the act did not require the states to pay an adequate benefit to poor recipients. Conservative lawmakers had deleted provisions in the original draft of the Social Security Act that had required the two public assistance programs, OAA and AFDC, to provide "a reasonable subsistence compatible with decency and health." In their place, the act simply stated that aid should be offered only "as far as practicable under the circumstances of such

State."[1] The matching-fund arrangement, therefore, did not create an individual entitlement to aid. The promise of assistance was to the states, which, in turn, distributed the money among the poor according to the guidelines of their plans. Simply put, the entitlement belonged, not to the poor, but to the states.

To liberals, the matching grant arrangement was emblematic of America's half-hearted commitment to the poor. Few states paid benefits adequate to meet the needs of their recipients, and many states were downright punitive toward the poor, appending to their programs harsh rules requiring work and dictating proper moral conduct. Southern states used these rules in a discriminatory manner to exclude most African-Americans families. But because conservative southern Democrats, who dominated positions of power in Congress, closely guarded state autonomy in welfare matters, liberals had little prospect of bringing about either greater federal control over public assistance or national uniformity. Their only hope, as voiced in 1949 by Arthur Altmeyer, the first commissioner of the Social Security Administration, was that the matching-grant programs would be rendered obsolete. Once Social Security became "a comprehensive contributory social-insurance system covering all these economic hazards to which people are exposed" and once all citizens were brought under its protective umbrella, Altmeyer argued, poverty would be reduced to such a miniscule level that matching-grant programs would "wither away" and the federal government could stop subsidizing state welfare efforts.[2] Thus, New Deal liberals, in particular SSA officials, focused their energies on expanding Old Age Insurance, not AFDC or Old Age Assistance.[3]

By the late 1960s, however, it became clear that public assistance was not going to "wither away" as had been predicted. In fact, it was growing faster than ever, and AFDC, the most unpopular of welfare programs, was growing the fastest.[4] Because they had trusted the states to hold the line on welfare expenditures, conservatives were rattled by these trends, and they too came to question the joint federal-state administrative

1. 42 U.S.C. sections 301, 201, and 1351.

2. U.S. House of Representatives, Committee on Ways and Means, *Social Security Amendments of 1949*, 81st Congress, 1st Session, 1949, 103.

3. Jerry R. Cates, *Insuring Inequality: Administrative Leadership in Social Security, 1935–1954* (Ann Arbor: University of Michigan Press, 1983).

4. The number of individuals receiving family support rose from 900,000 in 1946, to 3.5 million in 1961, to 4.4 million in 1965. By 1970, AFDC recipients numbered 7.9 million and comprised three-quarters of all individuals enrolled in state-federal assistance programs. Gilbert Y. Steiner, *The State of Welfare* (Washington, DC: Brookings Institution Press, 1971), table 1, 77–78.

arrangements that liberals had always disliked. Indeed, by 1968, Wilbur Mills, the chairman of the powerful House Ways and Means Committee, and Republican John Byrnes, the ranking member, had become convinced that the states were not carefully managing their programs. Because the federal government covered half the costs of the welfare checks regardless of how many people the states enrolled, this essentially forced Congress to pick up the tab for the ineligible families that the states were admitting. Looking at trends in AFDC, Mills complained, "Any time you have a government program that each year doubles in cost you know there is something wrong—it isn't being administered properly."[5] To compound the dilemma, because of the discretion given the states, there was little Congress could do under the matching-grant framework to rein in the states. Mills, in fact, likened the federal government's lack of control over the states to the situation of "the fellow who has the bear by the tail going downhill."[6] Voicing similar frustration, Byrnes called the existing matching-grant arrangement a "blank check," in which the "Congress and the Federal Government are completely at the mercy of the states."[7] In this sense, conservatives agreed with liberals that the states were hopelessly outdated and sought instead to circumvent them altogether in favor of administration by federal agencies. But they did so not out of a concern for fairness or adequacy but because they wanted to rationalize public assistance and control costs.

The drive to nationalize welfare took off in 1969 when President Richard Nixon responded to growing welfare rolls and demands for fiscal relief from the states with a proposal to convert AFDC into the Family Assistance Plan. An amalgamation of liberal and conservative goals, the FAP would have created a nationally uniform family assistance program by extending eligibility to all poor families with young children. In the past, states had decided on their own whether to include families with male breadwinners in AFDC, and most limited eligibility to single mothers. The FAP also would have set an income floor instead of letting states decide how much aid to give. Under the proposal Nixon sent to Congress, the new welfare program would have provided a minimum benefit level of $1,600 annually for a family of four, in effect raising benefits substantially in the South, where the poorest of the poor lived, to match more closely the payment levels prevailing in northern states. Higher

5. Quoted in Kenneth M. Bowler, *The Nixon Guaranteed Income Proposal: Substance and Process in Policy Change* (Cambridge, MA: Ballinger, 1974), 109.

6. Quoted in R. Shep Melnick, *Between the Lines: Interpreting Welfare Rights* (Washington, DC: Brookings Institution Press, 1994), 116.

7. Quoted in Bowler, *Nixon Guaranteed Income Proposal,* 112.

benefits, national uniformity, and extension of aid to all poor families had all been long-standing goals of liberals.

Yet conservative motivations drove Nixon as well. As a variant of the negative income tax, the FAP worked through a sliding scale of payments that, beyond the income floor, ensured that it would always be more profitable for recipients to work than rely solely on welfare. And since the program did not reduce benefits or end eligibility for married couples, as AFDC did, the incentive for family dissolution inherent in the prevailing version of the program would be removed. Nixon argued that moral behavior and personal responsibility would automatically follow financial inducements, allowing him to "get rid" of "snooping" social workers, many of whom had entered government following the enactment of the social rehabilitation measures that formed the core of President Johnson's War on Poverty.[8] Moreover, to placate conservatives further, the FAP included a relatively low income floor, which served as the incentive for recipients to supplement their incomes through employment, and a rule requiring adults enrolled in the program to work in order for the family to receive its full benefit amount.[9]

SSI got its start when, as an afterthought, the president's FAP taskforce headed by White House official Richard Nathan extended the idea of an income floor to the adult public assistance programs—OAA, AB, and APTD—even though they were not seen as part of the welfare crisis.[10] In August 1969, the White House sent a bill containing both the FAP and a related provision dealing with what would become SSI to Congress. As the House Ways and Means Committee debated reform of public assistance in 1970 and 1971, the FAP and SSI evolved from straightforward

8. Quoted in Vincent J. Burke and Vee Burke, *Nixon's Good Deed: Welfare Reform* (New York: Columbia University Press, 1974), 67, 90.

9. The Nixon administration proposed paying $1,600 per year for a family of four—$500 for the first two members plus $300 for each additional member. The working poor would be able to supplement the minimum with earnings up to a cutoff of $3,920.

10. The White House initially conceived of the FAP and SSI as simple plans to increase federal financial assistance to the states for the maintenance of their public assistance programs for families and the aged, blind, and disabled, also called the adult categories. For the adult categories, the White House proposed providing a minimum monthly income of $780 with the federal government paying one-quarter of the benefit thereafter up to a maximum to be set by the secretary of HEW. States would retain responsibility for administering the programs but could opt for federal administration, in which case the federal government would assume administrative costs as well. But as the legislative planning progressed, SSI and the FAP evolved into programs that would be paid for and run almost entirely by the federal government. Robert M. Ball, "Social Security Amendments of 1972: Summary and Legislative History," *Social Security Bulletin* 36 (1973): 7–8.

income floors that were still run by the states into programs run almost entirely from Washington, DC. Federal control, members of the Ways and Means Committee believed, would rein in wasteful spending on ineligible beneficiaries. In addition, committee members agreed that the SSA should be the agency that ran the new nationalized public assistance programs. As one SSA official explained, not only did the agency already have a strong reputation for professionalism and responsiveness to Congress, but in the case of the programs for the aged, blind, and disabled, it also already had a network of field offices and the bureaucratic and technical apparatus in place to "assure the maintenance and integrity of the program."[11] Families would be more difficult for the agency to integrate into its existing operations, but members of the Ways and Means Committee believed that the SSA was up to the task. Thus, throughout the debate in the House, SSI was a postscript to the real action centered on the FAP. Changes made to family assistance were simply added to the adult programs because the White House had included SSI in its initial welfare reform bill.

The FAP and SSI sailed through the House of Representatives in both 1970 and 1971. But each time, the FAP stalled in the Senate. There, the plan to nationalize and expand AFDC split the Finance Committee along ideological lines. SSI remained largely in the background and, in the end, benefited from this obscurity. Within the Senate Finance Committee, dissatisfaction with state control of welfare was not enough to overcome deep differences between liberals and conservatives as well as the implacable opposition of its Democratic committee chair, Russell Long of Louisiana. Unlike the Ways and Means Committee, where Democrats and Republicans enjoyed a collegial working relationship fostered by the cordiality between Mills and Byrnes, the Finance Committee was dominated by conservatives from western and southern states with only a handful of liberal members.[12] Neither side could find common ground on welfare reform. Liberals vehemently objected to the low income floor and work requirements. Senator Abraham Ribicoff of Connecticut referred to them as "slavefare" while the National Welfare Rights Organization (NWRO) denounced them as "an act of political repression."

11. Sumner G. Whittier, Memo to James E. Marquis, "Paper Rebutting Arguments for State Administration of the Adult Categories," March 27, 1972, SSA Archives, Office of the Historian, Social Security Administration, Baltimore, Maryland, 3. See also Renato A. DiPentima, "The Supplemental Security Income Program: A Study of Implementation," Ph.D. diss., University of Maryland, 1984, 61–62, 146–49.

12. John Manley, "Wilbur D. Mills: A Study in Congressional Influence," *American Political Science Review* 63, 2 (1969): 442–64.

The NWRO demanded an annual minimum of $6,500 for a family of four regardless of whether the family head worked.[13] Conservatives meanwhile adamantly opposed the idea of a guaranteed minimum income. Making no effort to hide his disdain for the plan, Long disparaged the FAP as "a guaranteed wage for nothing" since welfare mothers could still receive some "money without doing any work at all."[14] Though described as "flighty," "erratic," and "unpredictable," Senator Long was also an exceedingly shrewd manipulator of the legislative process.[15] Between 1970 and the summer of 1972, he used his political acumen to keep the FAP, and with it SSI, bottled up in his committee. As it stood, there seemed little hope that either program would ever see the light of day again.

The Struggle to Balance Equity and Adequacy in Social Security

With the FAP stalled in the Senate, SSI moved from welfare reform to Social Security reform. The reason lies in another policy quandary Congress confronted in the late 1960s, which was the need to reconcile two principles that guided debate over the level of Social Security benefits: equity (what one deserves to get based on prior contributions) and adequacy (what one needs to support oneself). In 1971, the House Ways and Means Committee began discussing SSI as part of an omnibus Social Security bill. Sensing an opportunity to reframe the debate over welfare reform, executive branch officials supportive of SSI decided to present the program as a way to preserve Social Security's balance between equity and adequacy and to provide dignified treatment to the poorest of Social Security's beneficiaries. This small circle of executive branch officials included SSA Commissioner Robert Ball; HEW Secretary Robert Finch; his undersecretary, John Veneman; and Veneman's deputy, Thomas Joe. These officials portrayed SSI as an incremental adjustment to the current system of social insurance rather than as an expansion of welfare, allowing the program to slip through Congress despite the fact that lawmakers were deeply divided on the question of increasing assistance to the poor.

The tension between equity and adequacy is rooted in the fact that in the 1930s supporters of Social Security's Old Age Insurance had compared the novel program to private insurance plans for retirement. Beneficiaries qualified for coverage through wage contributions, a payroll tax

13. Burke and Burke, *Nixon's Good Deed*, 135, 138.
14. Ibid., 177.
15. Richard F. Fenno, *Congressmen in Committees* (London: Little, Brown, 1973), 183–84.

that was comparable to a compulsory premium, and the amount of the past wage contribution partially determined the generosity of the benefits paid on retirement. This was known as the equity principle; how much money a beneficiary received depended on how much he had contributed to the program or, in other words, how much coverage he had "purchased" with his "premium." As a result, in absolute dollars, the affluent worker received higher payments than the low-income worker simply because he had contributed more over his working lifetime. The equity principle enhanced the political popularity of Social Security. Because workers had to pay into the system to receive payments on retirement or—once Disability Insurance was added—on disability, they regarded benefits as an "earned right," not a handout. Nevertheless, even though Social Security had been structured to resemble private insurance, it also served an important collective purpose that made it different from private insurance: it sought to provide an adequate postretirement income for low-income workers. Thus, even though the low-income worker received a lower benefit payment in absolute dollars, in relation to what he paid into the system, he received a better return on his contributions than the affluent worker. The fact that Social Security was disproportionately generous to low-income workers meant that the program played a small redistributive role.[16]

Over the years, Social Security administrators and congressional overseers had struggled to reconcile the need for equity with the demand for adequacy. In keeping with Altmeyer's recommendation in 1949 that liberals concentrate on expanding Social Security and allow welfare to wither away, Congress during the Kennedy and Johnson administrations had repeatedly enacted increases to Social Security benefits. Yet by the end of the Johnson presidency, policymakers realized that Social Security could not continue as the sole vehicle for fighting poverty. Indeed, two problems became apparent.

First, Congress was committed to ensuring that benefits were distributed equitably.[17] Maintaining an equitable benefit scale, however, meant that every time lawmakers raised the minimum monthly benefit, the payment made to those who had contributed the smallest allowable amount of payroll taxes, they also had to raise benefits for all workers, not just the bottom rung. This translated into an inefficient and expensive way of attacking poverty. The benefit increases Congress enacted between 1965

16. Martha Derthick, *Policymaking for Social Security* (Washington, DC: Brookings Institution Press, 1979), 252–70.

17. Ibid., 213–27.

and 1972 had raised the real value of OAI payments by 83 percent. But a study conducted by the Office of Economic Opportunity found that only 14 cents of every dollar from a 35 percent increase in Social Security payments went to the poor; the remaining 86 cents went to individuals whose incomes were already sufficient to meet their needs.[18] And still, lawmakers found the push for adequacy hard to resist. As senior citizens became increasingly organized and vocal on Social Security matters, higher minimum benefit payments became ever more politically alluring. Between 1968 and 1972, Congress effectively doubled the minimum benefit from $44 to $84.50 per month.[19] Yet by 1970, payments levels were still hardly adequate for those workers who had made only marginal contributions to the trust fund. For many policymakers, it seemed unfair that a worker should contribute payroll taxes for years, as was asked of him, but still receive benefits insufficient to attain a decent postretirement standard of living. Congress clearly could not continue fighting poverty among the elderly with Social Security without eroding the link between payroll contributions and benefit payments that was the core of the program's political identity. SSA Commissioner Robert Ball cautioned lawmakers that giving the same amount of benefits to the worker who had contributed "regularly and substantially" and to the worker "who had worked in covered employment very little, or not at all, and had paid practically nothing toward his insurance" undermined the very concept of social insurance.[20]

Second, increases in OAI payments did not necessarily raise the incomes of the poorest Social Security beneficiaries since states could negate the effects of these increases. This was because the neediest Social Security beneficiaries, the ones lawmakers wanted to help, supplemented their incomes with Old Age Assistance, the state-run, matching grant program created with OAI as part of the 1935 Social Security Act. The states had been granted wide discretion in determining benefit levels for their public assistance programs, and most of them reduced an individual's payment from the state's Old Age Assistance program by a dollar for every additional dollar he received from Social Security's Old Age Insurance. As a result, increases in OAI payments did not translate into a net gain in income for beneficiaries poor enough to receive OAA as well. Benefit increases instead created a fiscal windfall for the states by shifting a greater proportion of the costs of an individual's total welfare payment

18. Burke and Burke, *Nixon's Good Deed*, 14–16.
19. Ibid., 199.
20. Quoted in ibid., 200.

from state OAA rolls to OAI. In a perverse twist, one consequence of this move was to tilt the burden of fighting poverty from general revenues, which were funded by the progressive income tax, to the Social Security payroll tax, which was regressive. In effect, this meant that the anti-poverty effort fell heaviest on low- and middle-income workers, those whom Social Security was specifically designed to help.[21]

As the FAP foundered in the Senate, supporters of SSI in the House, HEW, and the SSA seized on the program as a solution to the problem of poverty among the aged. During closed hearings of the House Ways and Means Committee, SSA Commissioner Robert Ball explained that there were limits as to how far Congress "could go in making Social Security a complete replacement for an income-determined or means-tested welfare benefit" without imperiling the wage-related and contributory nature of the system.[22] The solution to the dilemma, Ball proposed, was "to meet the full need of all people . . . through a last-resort, income-tested program which guarantees a minimum level of living."[23] This new "last-resort" program was SSI. With SSI, beneficiaries would no longer be expected to live adequately solely on their meager Social Security checks. They would now have a supplemental check that would raise their incomes to an adequate level without imperiling Social Security's emphasis on equity. And because the federal government rather than the states would be administering SSI, assistance checks would not be lowered with increases in OAI benefits, as was currently state practice under OAA.

SSI then became part of a large omnibus Social Security bill winding its way through Congress. As the House Ways and Means Committee

---

21. The payroll tax is regressive because only wages up to a certain amount are taxed; taxable wages are the wage base. Wages above the wage base are not taxed. Therefore, the poor and working- and middle-class workers have a larger proportion of their income taxed than the affluent worker. The payroll tax is also more burdensome on multi-earner families since each working individual's earnings, not overall family income, is taxed. Thus, the family with two earners making a combined income of $60,000 pays a greater share of its income in payroll taxes than the family with one earner making $60,000. See Derthick, *Policymaking for Social Security*, 229–37, 283–85, for a discussion of the payroll tax and the wage base.

22. Quoted in Burke and Burke, *Nixon's Good Deed*, 199–200. Martha Derthick reconstructed Ball's testimony during the Ways and Means Committee's closed hearings using his notes. See Martha Derthick, *Agency under Stress: The Social Security Administration in American Government* (Washington, DC: Brookings Institution Press, 1990), 99–100, 100 n. 15. Vincent Burke, a journalist covering the debate over the FAP and SSI, also described the events of the hearing in Burke and Burke, *Nixon's Good Deed*, 198–202.

23. Robert M. Ball, *Social Security Today and Tomorrow* (New York: Columbia University Press, 1978), 34–35.

fleshed out the details of the new SSI program, it became clear that it would look very much like Social Security but it would be targeted specifically at the poor. Unlike Social Security, it did not provide benefits to dependents; nor did claimants have to demonstrate a history of prior employment or payroll contributions. Instead, SSI would be funded through general revenues and would be open to people who met both the means test and the categorical tests for age or disability used by Old Age Insurance and Disability Insurance. To qualify under the means test, applicants had to have income less than the program's monthly benefit, which was indexed to increase with inflation, and assets of less than $2,000 for an individual and $3,000 for a couple. Despite the fact that SSI emerged from congressional discussions over how to provide adequate incomes to the elderly poor, SSI benefits equaled only 70 to 80 percent of the poverty threshold and remained much lower than DI or OAI payments. Thus, in 2004, the average monthly benefit for disabled workers was $868 compared to only $426 for SSI recipients.[24]

Once separated from the FAP and linked to OAI, SSI was no longer caught up in the Finance Committee's protracted and heated debate over welfare reform, which allowed it to garner support from both the Left and the Right. The association with social insurance gave SSI political leverage in three crucial ways. First, the association concealed the fact that SSI represented an enormous policy shift. As John Kingdon reminds us, lawmakers generally eschew the uncertainty of bold policy steps. Because decision makers prefer to "take what they are currently doing as given, and make small incremental adjustments in that current behavior," modest proposals often fare better in the legislative process than radical schemes that promise to remake policy wholesale.[25] The FAP would revolutionize family assistance, but SSI looked like only one in a long line of incremental adjustments that Congress had made to Social Security during the postwar years. And, according to Martha Derthick, because lawmakers regarded Social Security as "thoroughly familiar and superficially mundane," incremental expansions to it were relatively easy to enact.[26] This was important political cover that the FAP did not enjoy. While the

24. Author's calculations from U.S. Social Security Administration, "OASDI Monthly Statistics, 2005," table 5, http://www.ssa.gov/policy/docs/statcomps/oasdi_monthly/2005–01/table5.pdf, and U.S. Social Security Administration, "SSI Monthly Statistics, 2005," table 1, http://www.ssa.gov/policy/docs/statcomps/ssi_monthly/2005–01/table1.pdf.
25. John W. Kingdon, *Agendas, Alternatives, and Public Policies*, 2d ed. (New York: Harper Collins, 1995), 79.
26. Derthick, *Policymaking for Social Security*, 364–65.

policy implications of the FAP were clear to lawmakers, SSI was cast as a simple extension of something that the SSA was already doing quite well (paying benefits to the aged). This made its innovative nature (the establishment of an income floor for poor people, many of whom had been excluded from state programs) difficult for lawmakers to comprehend. Reflecting on this years later, SSA commissioner Robert Ball explained that members of Congress "thought they were just taking over the existing state programs" when what they were really voting for "represented a considerably liberalized version."[27]

Second, tying SSI to Social Security allowed the new program to tap into the political clout of middle-class retirees and hid the fact that it was also a welfare program for people with disabilities. For example, after the program's passage, Senator Abraham Ribicoff lauded "what was achieved with the aged." Senator Russell Long boasted that SSI "took most of the aged in America out of poverty" while Mills noted that enactment of the program "assured that virtually no aged person will have to live below the poverty level."[28] No one mentioned the disabled. In addition, because lawmakers did not regard SSI as welfare, the program did not conjure up the images of waste, fraud, and abuse associated with AFDC. Senator Long, for example, told his colleagues that he was not worried about "increasing payments for the aged people in this country" because "there is not much abuse" in OAA.[29] Congress even went out of its way to distance SSI from the negative connotations of "welfare." During Senate debate, HEW undersecretary John Veneman suggested calling the program "Supplemental Security Income," a name that reinforced the program's ties to the social insurance system and obscured its identity as public assistance. The Finance Committee liked the idea because, according to one staff member, "it didn't want SSI called welfare."[30] So thorough was the blurring of the line between SSI and Social Security that Senator Abraham Ribicoff mistakenly praised SSI for taking the aged "off welfare."[31]

27. Quoted in Jim Haner and John B. O'Donnell, "Nixon Scheme Backfires as Democrats Trump Him," *Baltimore Sun*, Special Reprint of 4-part series, January 22–25, 1995, 9.

28. Abraham Ribicoff, quoted in Burke and Burke, *Nixon's Good Deed*, 196; Russell Long, quoted in Robert T. Mann, *Legacy to Power: Senator Russell Long of Louisiana* (New York: Paragon House, 1992), 305; and Wilbur Mills, quoted in Burke and Burke, *Nixon's Good Deed*, 197.

29. U.S. Senate, Committee on Finance, *Hearings before the Committee on Finance on H.R. 1*, 92nd Congress, 1st Session, 1971, 270.

30. Burke and Burke, *Nixon's Good Deed*, 197.

31. Quoted in ibid., 196.

Third, because lawmakers viewed SSI as a program for the aged, they paid little heed to signs that might have given lawmakers an inkling of the administrative difficulties that would plague SSI. Lawmakers had assumed that implementing SSI would be relatively easy because there would be a great deal of overlap between the clientele of Social Security and SSI, meaning that most of the people who would be eligible for SSI were already in the SSA's records. Moreover, since very few individuals would rely on SSI entirely, the program would only need to supplement incomes up to the income floor, leaving additional program costs small.[32] The overlap, however, was less substantial for the disabled than for the aged. While the SSA's estimates showed that almost all recipients of OAA were already receiving Social Security checks, only one in six or perhaps one in five APTD recipients were also Social Security beneficiaries.[33] For many of the disabled, SSI would be more than a supplement to Social Security; it would be their sole means of support.

Had lawmakers realized the SSI would be a major source of income support for the disabled, they might have paused, for disability benefit programs were administratively complex. Yet executive officials, who were in the best position to recognize the potentially expansive nature of SSI, only reinforced Congress's belief that the program would entail little administrative difficulty. In testimony before the House Ways and Means Committee in 1969, for instance, HEW Secretary Robert Finch noted that, in contrast to the surge in AFDC participation, for the adult assistance categories "the situation is a relatively stable one."[34] Considering the adult programs in the aggregate, however, masked the trends in state disability programs. For example, enrollment in OAA had been steadily declining since 1950 as Social Security coverage became broader and more generous while the number of blind recipients had remained fairly constant. APTD, on the other hand, had experienced exceptional growth since it was enacted in 1950. From an initial caseload of only 69,000 recipients in 1950, it had grown thirteenfold to well over 935,000 recipi-

32. U.S. House of Representatives, Committee on Ways and Means, *The Social Security Amendments of 1971*, H. Rept. 92–231, 92nd Congress, 2nd Session, 1971, 147 (hereafter House Ways and Means, *1971 Social Security Amendments*).

33. Arthur Hess, "A Federal Assistance Program for Adult Categories—March 4, 1971," draft paper submitted to Jack S. Futterman, 3–4, in the SSA Archives, Office of the Historian, Social Security Administration, Baltimore, Maryland.

34. U.S. House of Representatives, Committee on Ways and Means, *Written Statements Submitted by Administration Witnesses Appearing before the Committee on Ways and Means at Hearings on Social Security and Welfare Proposals*, 91st Congress, 1st Session, 1969, 7.

ents by 1970, and reached almost 1.3 million by 1973. Between 1965 and 1970, enrollment in disability assistance programs increased by an average of 11 percent each year.[35] In stark contrast to aid for the aged and blind, disability assistance was growing very fast. Yet the problems with disability benefits were never mentioned, and lawmakers scarcely discussed SSI as a disability program. The disabled were merely towed along in the wake of Congress's desire to help the elderly.

Tying SSI to Social Security reform broke the deadlock in the Senate. In the summer of 1972, after keeping the FAP and SSI bogged down in the Finance Committee for months, Senator Long reversed course. He threw his weight behind SSI, allowing it but not the FAP to finally leave the committee. Asked by his biographer some years later to explain why he had backed SSI after stalling it and the FAP in his committee for so long, the senator described an interesting ploy that showed off both his legislative skill and his deep distaste for the FAP. Recalling his frustration with White House officials for having backed the FAP, Long said proudly, "To keep them from coming back with something that was going to make the whole nation into a welfare state, I felt that the way to spike their guns on that would be take all the money they estimated on spending on this family program and apply that to the aged."[36] Of course, the demise of the FAP had little to do with fiscal constraints; each successive version of the FAP that the House had passed in 1970 and 1971 had raised the income floor. But because Senator Long believed that costs mattered, he agreed to support SSI despite his misgivings about the program. This cleared the way for policymakers to add SSI onto a package of amendments to Social Security that were working their way through the tax committees at the same time.

Over one hectic weekend in late 1972, members of the conference committee met to iron out the differences between the House and Senate versions of the FAP, SSI, and Social Security reform. On the table were hundreds of provisions relating to taxes, Old Age Insurance, Disability Insurance, AFDC, and Medicare. When the conference committee reported the bill, the FAP had been largely stripped from it, but SSI had been bundled along with several historic changes to Social Security, including an increase in benefits for widows and widowers, a plan to index benefits to wage increases, and an extension of Medicare coverage to dis-

35. U.S. Social Security Administration, *Annual Statistical Supplement*, 1973, table 142, 157.

36. Mann, *Legacy to Power*, 305.

abled workers. With major changes to more high-profile programs crowding the conference committee's agenda, there was practically no mention of SSI during conference negotiations. Congress then approved the 1972 Social Security Amendments, which contained the provisions nationalizing the adult programs, but left out the income guarantee for families. SSI had become law with hardly anyone noticing it.

How SSI Opened Federal Assistance to a New Class of Disabilities

In many ways, the enactment of SSI was a campaign of stealth, so to speak. Not a single disability interest group testified or lobbied on behalf of the program, and few journalists covered its enactment. Discussion of the program never reached beyond the handful of lawmakers on the House Ways and Means Committee and the Senate Finance Committee and a few executive officials at HEW and the SSA. Given their intimate knowledge of Old Age Insurance, Disability Insurance, OAA, and APTD, these officials were in the best position to understand that SSI was not just an add-on to OAI and DI but something quite new. Yet Finch, Veneman, Joe, and Ball did not bring attention to the program's innovative nature. Perhaps they did not anticipate the extent to which SSI would later cause the SSA a number of bureaucratic headaches. Up until that point, Congress's main concerns had been ensuring that eligible applicants were not unfairly denied and that workers received their benefits in a prompt and timely manner.[37] Or perhaps executive officials at HEW and SSA believed that the need for the program overrode the problems it might entail. As Robert Ball explained, "You can't stop a program on the ground that the agency will have difficulty. You have to be able to cope with it."[38] And if lawmakers were not aware of the potential trouble, perhaps officials did not see it as their job to point it out to them. Looking back on the episode, Veneman's deputy, Thomas Joe commented, "It was a rare opportunity to completely change a huge segment of national welfare policy, and we seized it. It was all there in black and white. If they didn't read it, whose problem is that? It wasn't like we sneaked it by them."[39] Of course, two journalists covering the debate over the FAP and SSI begged to differ. They captured the

37. U.S. House of Representatives, Committee on Ways and Means, Subcommittee on the Administration of the Social Security Laws, *Administration of Social Security Disability Insurance Program: Preliminary Report*, 86th Congress, 2nd Session, 1960.
38. Derthick, *Agency under Stress*, 99.
39. Quoted in Haner and O'Donnell, "Nixon Scheme Backfires," 9.

furtiveness behind the creation of SSI by calling its inception a "quiet revolution."[40]

What made SSI revolutionary was its open-ended view of disability. Even though it had been patterned after Old Age and Disability Insurance and had been framed as a mere extension of these two programs to the poor, SSI was profoundly different from social insurance. It would be both more prone to expansion and more trouble to administer. There were two key differences between SSI and DI that made the former expansive and problematic. First, SSI served the poor, which was a significant challenge in and of itself. Experience had taught policymakers that programs for the poor were notoriously difficult to administer. Financial need had to be reassessed periodically to ensure that recipients met income guidelines, but such reassessments—the gathering of information and the judgment of hardship—had to be conducted quickly since claimants were needy at the moment of application. Also even though medical reports were a central component of the disability certification process, many of the records that administrators relied on to make their decisions were not available in the case of the poor. Poor people simply did not visit the physician's office all that often. Administrators could ask for an examination from an independent physician, but this provided only a snapshot rather than a medical history, which would have given a more accurate picture of the claimant's condition. Consequently, it is no surprise that, through the years, the administrative costs and error rates for SSI have been much higher than those for Old Age or Disability Insurance.[41]

Second, although SSI and DI shared the same statutory and administrative definition of disability, SSI recipients proved to be more than just poorer versions of DI beneficiaries. Indeed, because it was a program for the poor, for all practical purposes, SSI created an inherently expansive understanding of disability by severing the connection between benefits and employment. In order to qualify for Disability Insurance, an applicant must demonstrate a history of sustained and recent workforce attachment, during which time the applicant has paid payroll taxes. Currently DI calls for a qualified applicant to have been employed for several years prior to

40. Burke and Burke, *Nixon's Good Deed*, 204.

41. U.S. Social Security Advisory Board, *2000 SSI Annual Report*, http://www.ssa.gov/OACT/SSIR/SSI00/AdvBrdStatement.html. According to the report, federal administrative costs for SSI were $2.3 billion, or 7 percent of the program's federal benefit outlays, while for OASDI, the figure is $3.5 billion, or less than 1 percent of outlays. SSI accounts for 7 percent of the SSA's benefit spending but 36 percent of its administrative budget, an increase from 27 percent in 1980.

the onset of the disabling impairment.[42] With SSI, however, applicants did not have to satisfy the work history requirement; poverty, not prior employment or payroll contributions, served as the qualifying bar. The fact that the program did not require claimants to show a history of work complicated administration. With a record of regular employment, adjudicators had a "before/after" scenario against which to judge the effect of a claimant's impairment. One psychiatrist familiar with Social Security disability policy explained the problem this way: "People on DI—they used to work. They had functional skills and then they lost them. You could interview an employer who could say, 'Yeah, Howard was a great employee. He was very motivated, but then he got depressed, then went into the hospital and hasn't been the same since.' How do you figure that out for someone who's never had a work history?"[43] In these cases, determining work capacity would be a purely theoretical exercise.

Moreover, even though DI and SSI used the same disability rules and tests, SSI opened the federal disability rolls to an entirely new class of recipients, people with relatively little or no experience in the labor market and who in the past would have had to rely on help from family or, as a last resort, state governments. This included people with congenital disorders, those who had been impaired early in life, or those who had spent their whole lives in residential hospitals or mental asylums. Many of these new SSI recipients were the former mental patients that advocates were trying to integrate into community settings, but they were also a class of recipients with needs that the SSA was largely unfamiliar with. Complicating matters even further was the fact that SSI also brought into its fold children with disabilities, addicts, and people with social instead of purely medical handicaps—all groups with controversial and poorly understood impairments. Thus, an all-encompassing view of disability made SSI crucial to advocates' vision of a social safety net in the community, but it also contained the seeds of the program's future polit-

42. For older workers, the DI program requires twenty quarters of calendar coverage out of the forty calendar quarters ending in the quarter in which the worker becomes disabled. Five of those calendar quarters must have been in the ten calendar quarters before the application for benefits. For younger workers, those disabled before age thirty-one must have coverage of half the calendar quarters after reaching age twenty-one, up to and including the quarter in which the disability occurs. There is a minimum requirement of six quarters of coverage. Any worker who becomes disabled before age twenty-four needs at least six quarters, fulfilled within the thirteen calendar quarters before the onset of the disability.

43. Howard H. Goldman, professor of psychiatry at the University of Maryland School of Medicine and a participant in the 1983–85 workgroup to rewrite the adult mental disorders Listings, phone interview with author, February 26, 2000.

ical troubles. The victory won by SSA and HEW officials in sneaking SSI past Congress was soon tempered by the problems the program engendered as the SSA struggled to fit children, addicts, and social handicaps into a policy framework that had been designed for adults and based on the assumptions of the medical model.

Children with Disabilities

With the creation of SSI, children were added to the federal disability rolls, giving financially stressed families the option of caring for their disabled children in their own homes rather than sending them state institutions. Nevertheless, since Disability Insurance had been designed for adults, the move not only brought many incongruities but also had the potential to vastly expand the Social Security disability rolls, a potential that advocates exploited in the early 1990s. HEW official Thomas Joe acknowledged that he anticipated as much. Joe was the one who during congressional debate in 1971 had slipped into the legislation the clause that made children eligible for SSI. Congress then approved the provision when it enacted the 1972 amendments. Thus, according to the Social Security Act, children could receive SSI benefits if they were judged to have an impairment of "comparable severity" to one that would disable an adult. Years later, when asked why he came up with the comparable severity measure, Joe confessed to an interviewer that he had hoped to cover "as many poor people as possible" through "a welfare program disguised as disability assistance." He intentionally did not ask the conference committee to clarify the clause because, he explained, "I was afraid too many people were going to discover this and it would be a big controversy."[44]

The purpose of the children's program, however, was never clear. According to Joe, the mishmash of state programs required some sort of rationalization. As he explained to an interviewer in 1995, "Under the state programs, blind individuals were eligible at age 16, while other persons with disabilities weren't eligible until age 18. State rehabilitation programs had a third age standard—their age criterion was 14. Younger children . . . would have been eligible under the family program. These age limits were completely arbitrary."[45] Still, given the large role that

44. Bob Woodward and Benjamin Weiser, "Costs Soar for Children's Disability Program: How 26 Words Cost the Taxpayers Billions in New Entitlement Payments," *Washington Post*, February 4, 1994, A1.
45. Quoted in National Commission on Childhood Disability, *Supplemental Security Income for Children with Disabilities* (Washington, DC: National Commissioner on Childhood Disability, 1995), 14.

states play in most programs for the poor, the lack of uniformity is the hallmark of public assistance in the United States. There is no reason why variation by itself would motivate reform. Confusion about SSI's mission persisted well into the 1990s. In 1995, a special commission studying the children's program suggested that one of the many possible purposes of SSI children's benefits was to offset the wages lost when a parent took time off to care for a disabled child.[46] But this was a justification after the fact; no lawmaker voiced this reasoning in 1972. Instead, during debate over SSI, the House voiced another concern. The 1971 House report on the amendments argued that disabled children should qualify for aid under SSI rather than AFDC because "their needs are often greater than those of nondisabled children."[47] But the Senate Finance Committee disputed this logic. It countered that only the "health care expenses" of disabled children were greater than that of able-bodied children, and these expenses were largely covered under Medicaid. "Disabled children's need for food, clothing, and shelter," the committee concluded, "are usually no greater than the needs of nondisabled children" and thus should be covered by AFDC, not SSI.[48] Congress did not settle this dispute. Instead, when the conference committee hammered out House and Senate differences over the 1972 Social Security amendments, it simply accepted the House's "comparable severity" standard without bothering to explain what it meant, why the children's program existed, or how childhood disability should be measured.

From the beginning, the SSA was at a loss to define and implement comparable severity. OAI and DI were designed to compensate adults for earnings lost because of old age or disability, and as a result, its disability standard was related to work capacity: claimants were considered disabled if they could not work. Under this framework, however, it was unclear what specific steps should be taken to evaluate childhood disability. Because children are not expected to work, the SSA could not directly

---

46. Ibid., 40.

47. House Ways and Means, *1971 Social Security Amendments*, 603.

48. U.S. Senate, Committee on Finance, *Social Security Amendments of 1972*, 92nd Congress, 2nd Session, 1972, 385 (hereafter Senate Committee on Finance, *Social Security Amendments of 1972*). The Finance Committee was mistaken. At the time, most disabled children were institutionalized with the states picking up the costs of their care. While Medicaid did cover some medical expenses, in the early 1970s, Medicaid was in its infancy, and its provisions for disabled children were far from adequate. The financial burden of caring for a disabled child was alleviated somewhat by the expansion of the Medicaid program in the late 1980s and the passage of the Education for All Handicapped Children Act in 1975, which required states to provide a "free and appropriate public education" to disabled children and pay for all "related services."

determine if a child claimant's impairment was "comparable" to one that would disable an adult. Any standard the SSA used would be arbitrarily chosen. Nevertheless, though comparable severity could be construed either restrictively or expansively depending on the specific rules the SSA devised, there would be pressure to adopt an expansive interpretation because disabilities in children are profoundly different from disabilities in adults. Many common childhood disorders, such as learning disabilities and conduct disorders, are diagnosed through clinical observations of the child's behavior rather than through evidence of anatomical or physiological defects. Many of these disorders are not well understood but involve behaviors, such as temper tantrums, that while "quite normal at one age but suggest mental illness at another age," complicating efforts to make sharp distinctions between medically "normal" and "abnormal" childhood behavior.[49] As a result, clinicians accept the fact that many childhood mental disorders are not pathological illnesses but marked deviations from statistical norms of "cognitive, social, and emotional development."[50] As a consequence of this clinical viewpoint, childhood disabilities could include inappropriate behaviors that perhaps stemmed from a troubled home, poverty, or other social problems rather than from disease or injury. Therefore, as Thomas Joe anticipated, SSI had the potential to vastly expand assistance to at-risk children.

Alcoholics

Alcoholics and drug addicts would also find it easier to enroll in SSI than in DI, a fact that contributed to the controversy that engulfed SSI in the early 1990s. Although alcoholics were eligible to receive benefits under DI too, their presence on the program was not so controversial since the work history requirement tended to keep the number of alcoholics small—that is, even if the alcoholics on DI had a drinking problem, they were alcoholics that at least had the wherewithal to maintain employment. Moreover, to the extent that they had paid their payroll taxes before becoming disabled, these alcoholics had "earned" their benefits. None of this could be said of the addicts enrolled in SSI.

49. U.S. Department of Health and Human Services, Public Health Service, *Mental Health: A Report of the Surgeon General*, 2000, 46, 48, 123–24.

50. Ibid., 137–38, 123–24. For examples of the lack of medical knowledge concerning specific childhood disorders, see Lexie Vernon, "Help for Puzzling Developmental Problems: Sensory Disorders Can Be Treated," *Washington Post*, November 6, 1990, Sec. Z, 10; and Geoffrey Cowley, "Understanding Autism," *Newsweek*, July 31, 2000, 46–54.

During congressional debate in 1972, the Senate Finance Committee argued that alcoholics living in poverty should not be permitted to receive cash payments but instead should be placed into a treatment program. The question was not whether severe addiction counted as a legitimate disability—legislators all agreed on that point—but whether cash benefits were the proper manner of aiding alcoholics who were already troubled enough that they could not maintain a steady job. When the House and Senate went to conference over the 1972 amendments, alcoholics, like the rest of SSI, were low on the priority list. From the negotiations emerged a compromise proposal in which drug and alcohol addicts were entitled to SSI as long as they participated in a treatment program, if one were readily available, and were monitored by a "representative payee," a person or organization that supervised the claimant's spending to make sure that the checks did not support the addiction.[51]

This compromise, however, left unresolved doubts about providing cash benefits to alcoholics. Shortly after SSI became policy, professionals working with people with mental illness and addiction problems voiced concern that the new program was so generous that it would undermine treatment efforts. Their fear was that, with SSI available, former mental patients and addicts living in the community might come to believe that they no longer needed the support of their case workers and physicians.[52] Moreover, ensuring alcoholics received treatment, as the Senate wished, was not an easy proposition. Congress never clarified how the SSA was supposed to pay for the services that alcoholics were to receive at treatment facilities (which in the 1970s were few and far between anyway), much less monitor their compliance with treatment. Nor had Congress set up a way for the SSA to ensure that representative payees properly supervised the addicts placed in their charge. All these activities extended beyond the reach of the SSA's narrow mission. The SSA had no experience with drug or alcohol counseling, and, as officials familiar with the addicts' program stressed, it was not in the business of providing social services.[53]

51. Senate Committee on Finance, *Social Security Amendments of 1972*, 395–96. See also Sharon R. Hunt, "Drug Addiction and Alcoholism as Qualifying Impairments for Social Security Disability Benefits: The History, Controversies, and Congressional Response," Ph.D. diss., Brandeis University, 2000, 27–29.

52. Martha N. Ozawa and Duncan Lindsey, "Is SSI Too Supportive of the Mentally Ill?" *Public Welfare* 35, 4 (1977): 48–52, and Richard H. Lamb and Alexander S. Roawski, "Supplemental Security Income and the Sick Role," *American Journal of Psychiatry* 135, 10 (1978): 1221–24.

53. John Ritter, former executive program policy officer for the Office of Disability, Social Security Administration, interview in the Oral History Collection, August 16, 1995, transcripts in the SSA Archives, Office of the Historian, Social Security Administration, Baltimore, Maryland.

Rather than establish from scratch a system for overseeing treatment programs and representative payees—something it did not know how to do, the SSA instead simply tried to keep the number of alcoholics on its SSI rolls small so that it would not have to worry about providing social services in the first place. The Office of Disability adopted for SSI the same restrictive rules it used to evaluate addicts who applied for Disability Insurance. Under these rules, alcoholics could receive SSI only if they showed "irreversible organ damage" from drinking. It was supposed to be the organ damage, not the drinking that established eligibility. The move had an unintended effect, however. Since Congress designed SSI as a supplement to Social Security, disabled addicts could enroll in both programs and "top off" a meager DI payment with SSI. This created an incentive for alcoholics and drug addicts with weak work histories to apply for concurrent DI and SSI benefits. By the 1990s, so many addicts were applying for both programs that applications overwhelmed the SSA. Instead of going through the hassle of carefully developing evidence so that a denial of benefits could stand on appeal, field offices simply approved applications, leading to a lax attitude toward addiction-related disabilities. Ironically, then, rather than keep SSI small, the restrictive DI rules when applied to SSI created pressure for administrators to interpret disability loosely and led to "a back-door liberalization of the way alcoholics and addicts" entered both the DI and SSI rolls. As one SSA official ruefully admitted years later, the inclusion of addicts under SSI turned congressional intention on its head: not only did treatment rarely occur but SSI loosened the agency's overall approach to addiction.[54]

People with Social Instead of Medical Handicaps

Children and addicts brought to light a recurring problem with SSI, the difficulty of separating medical impairments from handicaps that are largely social in nature. Even though SSI used the same definition of disability as Disability Insurance, because it served the poor, for SSI, non-medical or social factors could play a larger role in both the applicant's inability to find work and thus in findings of disability than is the case with Disability Insurance. Although inability to work was supposed to be primarily the consequence of a severe medical impairment, when making determinations of disability, the SSA also took into consideration social

54. Mary Ross, former career SSA official, Social Security Administration, interview in the Oral History Collection, October 26, 1995, and February 13, 1996, transcripts in the SSA Archives, Office of the Historian, Social Security Administration, Baltimore, Maryland.

factors, such as the individual's age, education, and work experience. This allowed the agency to provide an individually tailored and realistic evaluation of work ability in addition to its examination of the medical impairment. It was unclear, however, what the SSA should do when faced with a person in need who was unemployed for societal or personal reasons as well as medical ones, a dilemma that would arise repeatedly with SSI.

The SSA was well aware of this dilemma given its previous research on the adult assistance programs SSI replaced. A 1970 study, for instance, found that APTD recipients were less educated, less trained, and less skilled than insured disabled workers. They were also likely to face additional handicaps, including deficient language skills, emotional and familial problems, and illiteracy. As a result, even a moderate disability could be enough to prevent a poor person from finding or keeping a well-paying job. The outlook was even worse if the individual was a minority, a woman, or a single mother.[55] Put simply, poor people with disabilities tended to be individuals whose personal attributes and circumstances made them less desirable job candidates. When they did hold jobs, these jobs offered few opportunities for skill development and training and less occupational security than the typical jobs of the middle-class workers who ended up on DI. Yet their disadvantages in the job market stemmed not only from their medical condition but also from the very factors that disadvantaged all poor people in the world of work.

This situation created a predicament for administrators. Disability Insurance was premised on a medical understanding of disability, but SSI brought to the SSA many impoverished people whose handicap was largely social or economic. Even if the medical reasons for unemployment could be teased apart from the social ones, insisting on a medical definition meant turning a blind eye to need. Early debate over proposals to liberalize the SSI definition of disability touched on this tension. In 1974, the American Public Welfare Association (APWA) argued that applying Social Security's definition of disability to the poor was overly restrictive. If the goal was to provide a reasonable safety net for the disabled, the APWA argued, then the definition should be looser. It recommended that during determinations of disability, an individual's actual ability to function and social factors be weighed equally or heavier than the medical condition. The APWA also suggested that, for SSI, the required length of time a medical impairment had to last be dropped from twelve to six months and that, when determining if an applicant

55. Henry Brehm, "The Disabled on Public Assistance," *Social Security Bulletin* 33, 10 (1970): 29.

could find a job, the labor conditions of the local economy, not the national economy, be considered. This would have brought SSI closer to the model of an unemployment program for the temporarily disabled.[56]

In response, SSA official Sam Crouch posed the real question concerning SSI. It was "whether a disability 'oriented' approach is really the way to deal with the underlying problem" of social and economic disadvantage. Crouch explained,

> Is the basic problem facing SSI-disability-denied applicants that of an unrealistic assessment of their medical conditions and the effect on their lives, or is it more basically the fact that there are a group of socially disadvantaged or disoriented people who . . . find themselves in a state of dependency which must be dealt with as a matter of public policy? If . . . it is really the latter situation which prevails, then isn't trying to bring these people under the umbrella of a "disability" program really attempting to solve a problem with the wrong tool and shouldn't efforts be made to deal with the problem more directly?[57]

While a social as opposed to a medical definition of disability might be acceptable for older individuals, for younger persons, Crouch noted, "there should be better and more socially acceptable alternatives, whether these be in terms of re-education, re-training, vocational rehabilitation, [or] public service employment." Otherwise, he asked, "Is society really ready to take people at a young age and perhaps put them on a benefit roll for the balance of their lives when their handicaps are basically social handicaps?"[58] Policymakers never considered this central question as long as they viewed SSI as nothing more than a supplement for impoverished retirees.

How SSI Abetted Deinstitutionalization but Did Not Solve Its Problems

Because it took an open-ended view of disability, bringing into its fold many people who never would have qualified for DI, SSI had the

56. U.S. Social Security Administration, "Meeting Report, American Public Welfare Association Meeting with the SSA, Washington, D.C.," November 7, 1974, 1–3, in the SSA Archives, Office of the Historian, Social Security Administration, Baltimore, Maryland.

57. Samuel E. Crouch, "Alternative Definition of Disability for Title XVI," November 8, 1974, 12, in the SSA Archives, Office of the Historian, Social Security Administration, Baltimore, Maryland.

58. Ibid., 13.

inadvertent consequence of speeding the pace of deinstitutionalization. The program was part of a significant expansion in federal social
welfare spending that took place in the late 1960s and early 1970s.
Even though advocates had not specifically lobbied for this expansion
and none of the programs had been tailored around the needs of mental patients, many antipoverty programs, including AFDC, Food
Stamps, housing assistance, Medicaid, and SSI, grew to form a semblance of a social safety net for disabled people living outside medical
institutions. Between 1970 and 1975, as Congress increased social welfare expenditures and the federal courts enhanced the legal rights of
mental patients, the number of patients housed in state institutions
dropped rapidly, by 11 percent each year, compared to a decline of less
than 2 percent annually between 1955 and 1965.[59] SSI, in particular,
was a major force driving the transition away from institutionalized
care. The new program created two powerful financial incentives for
states to discharge patients. First, in the 1972 amendments to Social
Security, Congress required the SSA to "grandfather" into SSI anyone
who was enrolled in the state adult assistance programs when the
agency assumed control of them in January 1974. Second, SSI practically invited states to discharge mental patients by providing payments
to disabled people living in the community but barring coverage of patients who resided in public hospitals or groups homes. Given these financial inducements, rather than renovate deteriorating asylums to
meet court-mandated reforms, several states in anticipation of SSI's
1974 debut raced to release patients from state asylums and place them
on APTD, knowing that they would be automatically transferred to
SSI within a couple of years. As a result, the years between 1972 and
1974 marked both the most rapid declines in the in-patient populations of state mental hospitals and the most rapid increases in APTD
enrollments.[60]

However, SSI had not been designed with the needs of mental patients
in mind. It was by sheer accident that it and the other social welfare programs became part of the advocates' "new asylum of the community."
This pointed to a larger difficulty with the move to deinstitutionalization. Although the growth of social welfare spending facilitated deinstitutionalization, it perhaps also encouraged the shift to community mental health care to proceed too quickly, long before policymakers had

59. Rael Jean Isaac and Virginia C. Armat, *Madness in the Streets: How Psychiatry and the Law Abandoned the Mentally Ill* (New York: Free Press, 1990), 102.

60. David Mechanic and David Rochefort, "Deinstitutionalization: An Appraisal of Reform," *Annual Review of Sociology* 16 (1990): 308–9.

sufficient time to orient programs to address the specific challenges that former mental patients would encounter in the community. By the early 1970s, despite increases in mental health spending, the establishment of SSI, and the growth of many existing antipoverty programs, it was clear that the transition from deinstitutionalization to community mental health care had gone awry. Far from being comprehensive, community mental health care was rife with problems. Fewer than half of the projected two thousand community mental health centers had been built. Those that were on hand were often unprepared to serve the needs of severely disturbed mental patients. Some facilities lacked a qualified professional staff while others refused to accept ex-patients, preferring instead to concentrate on prevention and less severe maladies like marital discord and juvenile delinquency—what some critics regarded as the common troubles of everyday life.[61]

Furthermore, problems coordinating community mental health programs with existing welfare programs plagued policymakers at every turn. Like the rest of the War on Poverty, the new mental health centers were locally run, bypassing state mental health authorities, which lawmakers viewed as reactionary and antiquated, in favor of community empowerment. But this fragmentation of responsibility made it difficult to ensure both uniformity of care from locality to locality and a smooth transition from the hospital to the community. Social services programs were scattered between many federal, state, and local agencies. Because there were few efforts to coordinate existing social services with hospital release programs, once patients left the doors of the hospital, they were left to navigate the welfare bureaucracy on their own. Local residents, too, fought efforts to locate community mental health centers or halfway homes for the mentally ill in their neighborhoods, frustrating hopes of integrating the mentally disabled into the fabric of community life. With nowhere to go and no access to community-based services, many patients were not really deinstitutionalized, but "transinstitutionalized"—that is, moved from state hospitals into community board-and-care facilities, nursing homes, or group homes that offered services reimbursed by Medicaid. Ill-equipped to provide the transitional help former patients sorely needed, these residences were often no better than the asylums the

61. Leona L. Bachrach, "Disability among the Homeless Mentally Ill," in *Psychiatric Disability: Clinical, Legal, and Administrative Dimensions*, ed. Arthur T. Meyerson and Theodora Fine, eds. (Washington, DC: American Psychiatry Association, 1987), 198; Isaac and Armat, *Madness in the Streets*, 67–83; and U.S. General Accounting Office, *Community-Based Care Increases for People with Serious Mental Illness*, GAO-01-224, 2000, 6.

patients had just left—only smaller.[62] Summing up the problem, two mental health experts David Rochefort and David Mechanic argued that deinstitutionalization "was never a planned and coherent national strategy." There were no checks in place to ensure that community mental health centers served people with severe illness or that the proliferating social welfare programs were coordinated with one another. With in-patient populations dropping rapidly, advocates were literally threading the social safety net at the same time that many disabled people were falling through. As a result, the shift away from the asylum was "a nonlinear, disjointed process featuring a 'loose coupling' of policy and results."[63]

As central as it was to the new social safety net for the disabled, SSI did not solve the difficulties associated with deinstitutionalization. Quite the contrary, isolated to a small circle of legislative and executive Social Security insiders and far removed from the concerns of the disability rights and patients' rights groups, the politics of its enactment was emblematic of them. To make matters worse for the advocates, the period of social welfare expansion that they had enjoyed was quickly coming to an end. Retrenchment was on the horizon. Over the next several years, advocates would struggle simply to defend what gains they had recently made.

62. M. Gregg Bloche and Francine Cournos, "Mental Health Policy for the 1990s: Tinkering in the Interstices," in *Health Policy and the Disadvantaged*, ed. Lawrence D. Brown (Durham, NC: Duke University Press, 1991), 146–49, and the Mental Health Law Project, "Mental Health Law Project, 1972–1992: Twentieth Anniversary Report," 1993, 10–11.

63. David Mechanic and David A. Rochefort, "A Policy of Inclusion for the Mentally Ill," *Health Affairs* 11, 1 (1992): 137.

4

The Advocates
Face Retrenchment

Initially, supporters of community mental health care optimistically proclaimed that, to borrow the words of advocates David and Sheila Rothman, "the cost of delivering community care is no more expensive than . . . running bad institutions."[1] But this was misleading. It was not only a matter of how much community care would cost but also who would pay for it. During the late 1970s and early 1980s, the federal government reconsidered the expansion of social welfare assistance it had undertaken in the late 1960s and early 1970s. After decades of nationalizing the fight against poverty, President Ronald Reagan, promoting a package of reforms under the banner of "New Federalism," tried to return responsibility for social welfare and mental health to the private sector and the states. It was a policy reversal that had grave consequences for deinstitutionalization and disability rights.

The move toward retrenchment, however, began not with Reagan but with Jimmy Carter and was initially greeted with complacency by disability advocates. During the early 1970s, advocates were well aware that the transition to community mental health care would not have been possible were it not for mainstream social welfare programs like SSI. Yet lobbying on behalf of these programs was far down on their priority list. Nevertheless, even as the disability rights movement gathered steam, growing more vocal and well-organized through the mid and late 1970s, the social safety net that many people with disabilities relied on was coming undone.

1. David J. Rothman and Sheila M. Rothman, quoted in Fred Pelka, *The ABC-CLIO Companion to the Disability Rights Movement* (Santa Barbara, CA: ABC-CLIO, 1997), 328.

Between 1978 and 1980, Congress and the SSA closed the door on the easy access to Disability Insurance that advocates had once taken for granted. It was not until 1980, however, that advocates protested. The election of Ronald Reagan that year served as a wake-up call to the advocacy groups. When Reagan moved to cut drastically both mental health spending and Social Security disability benefits, the advocates were galvanized.

Retrenchment Begins

The difficulty that advocates would face in expanding social welfare supports for the disabled became apparent during the Carter years. On the one hand, President Carter was a strong proponent of community mental health care. He convened the President's Commission on Mental Health, a task force charged with exploring ways to improve community mental health care. Later he endorsed the Mental Health Systems Act of 1980, legislation that included many of the commission's recommendations and increased spending for community mental health care centers. On the other hand, Carter refused to support more far-reaching recommendations contained in a report entitled *Toward a National Plan for the Chronically Mentally Ill*. Drafted by a planning committee within Department of Health and Human Services (HHS) to serve as a companion piece to the Mental Health Systems Act, the *National Plan* focused on all social welfare programs, not just the smaller community mental health grants. Noting that existing income support and health care provisions had not been specifically created with deinstitutionalized patients in mind, the report suggested ways that the programs could be modified so that they could better address the needs of people with chronic mental illnesses. For example, the *National Plan* suggested liberalizing the definition of mental disability used by DI and SSI, expanding Medicare and Medicaid coverage of mental health services, creating trial work programs for the disabled under DI and SSI, and setting up a "prerelease program" that allowed patients discharged from mental institutions to qualify automatically for DI or SSI benefits. These reforms were expensive, however. They far outstripped the costs of the Mental Health Systems Act, and the White House was already struggling to contain skyrocketing entitlement expenditures. Thus, at the same time that Carter steered the Mental Health Systems Act through Congress, he also threw his weight behind the Social Security Disability Benefits Reform Act of 1980 (1980 DBRA), a controversial bill to curtail growth in spending for

DI. Not surprisingly, then, the administration was decidedly unenthusiastic about the *National Plan*. It delayed releasing the report for over a year, and when it finally did publish the findings in December 1980, it did so with little fanfare, having lost the election and lacking the political clout to bring about the suggested reforms anyway.[2]

Nevertheless, the Carter administration's failure to endorse the *National Plan* did not trouble advocacy groups much. As far as they were concerned, social welfare programs, despite their shortcomings, were still fairly accessible to people with mental disorders. Leonard Rubenstein, a former attorney for the MHLP, explained that in the 1970s, "Social Security wasn't on anybody's screen. . . . The rolls were really going up. The eligibility criteria were pretty liberal when they were applied. . . . People were getting on disability."[3] Nevertheless, even as advocates concentrated on securing community mental health grants, changes occurring in Social Security policy and the economy threatened to curtail the system of support they were struggling to build.

During the late 1970s, the nation's economic situation worsened. As a result of the programmatic expansions during the 1960s and early 1970s, Social Security had grown into a mature program with more commitments to pay benefits than money available. Shortfalls in the trust funds that financed Old Age Insurance and Disability Insurance became more common as economic growth slowed and the budget deficit ballooned. Thereafter, talk of program crisis and cost containment rather than expansion dominated policy debate. Retrenchment of the Social Security disability programs began with the spectacular growth in Disability Insurance between 1970 and 1975. In 1965, the SSA received 532,900 applications for DI benefits and made roughly 253,500 awards, which translated into about 4.7 awards for every 1,000 covered workers. By comparison, in 1975, when applications and award levels peaked, the agency processed nearly 1.3 million disability applications and granted benefits in 592,000 cases. This represented 7.1 awards per 1,000 workers,

---

2. Chris Koyanagi and Howard H. Goldman, "The Quiet Success of the National Plan for the Chronically Mentally Ill," *Hospital and Community Psychiatry* 42, 9 (1991): 899–905.

3. Leonard Rubenstein, former chief litigator and director of the Bazelon Center for Mental Health Law, interview with author, January 21, 2000, Washington, DC. Rhoda Davis, a former SSA official, confirms this. In an interview with the SSA historian, she notes that that in the late 1970s "the advocacy organizations were not organized around the disability adjudication issues." Rhoda Davis, former associate commissioner of the Office of Supplemental Security Income, Social Security Administration, interview in the Oral History Collection, February 5, 1996, transcripts in the SSA Archives, Office of the Historian, Social Security Administration, Baltimore, Maryland.

a record high.[4] As the awards rate climbed, the surge in enrollment threatened to bankrupt the program.

The growth of DI had many possible sources. Some analysts blamed the declining stigma attached to disability and welfare dependency while others argued that by 1975 DI benefits had become so generous relative to employment that any rational individual would apply. Less sinister explanations included the aging of the population, the slowing of economic growth, and rising unemployment.[5] Whatever the cause, many analysts also pointed to the fact that disability certification was no longer the deliberate and careful screening process that lawmakers expected. Administrative deterioration also seemed to be part of the problem.

Many experts traced this decline to the SSA's implementation of SSI in 1972–74 and the Black Lung program, a disability benefit plan for miners enacted in 1969. Both programs taxed the capacities of the SSA's field offices and state disability determination agencies. The problem was too much to do with too few resources and too little time. According to Ed Tall, an agency employee familiar with Black Lung, the SSA had three weeks between the time that SSA officials first heard that Congress was going to give them responsibility for the program and the time that miners and their families became eligible to file for benefits. During those three weeks, Tall recounted, "we were busier than a hound dog with fleas" as "miners and survivors started trooping in to the District Offices and the claims started to pile up all over the place." Describing the scene at these offices, Tall noted that SSA adjudicators were inundated as "the claims folders just stacked up in the aisles, on the floors, everywhere." In fact, some district offices in Kentucky, West Virginia, and Pennsylvania received more Black Lung claims in the first two months of the program than they had received for all other claims—OAI, DI, or survivor benefits—in the past year.[6] The situation worsened when the SSA unveiled SSI four years later. Capturing the chaos that erupted as SSI applications came pouring in, Martha Derthick described a desperate situation of backlogged files, failing computer networks, overwhelmed staff, and

4. U.S. House of Representatives, Committee on Ways and Means, *Background Material and Data on Programs within the Jurisdiction of the Committee on Ways and Means,* 100th Congress, 1st Session, 1987, table 7, 44.

5. Mordechai E. Lando and Aaron Krute, "Disability Insurance: Program Issues and Research," *Social Security Bulletin* 39, 10 (1976): 3–17.

6. Ed Tall, former policy officer, Division of Disability Policy, Social Security Administration, interview in the Oral History Collection, October 24, 1995, transcripts in the SSA Archives, Office of the Historian, Social Security Administration, Baltimore, Maryland.

many errors, not only in SSI but in the other programs the SSA ran as well.[7]

Throughout the early 1970s, the employees staffing the SSA's district offices and the state offices that conducted the disability examinations were stretched thin by the need to process millions of Black Lung and SSI applications, leading to problems that spilled over into DI. As disability applications for all programs became backlogged, the time between application and an answer from SSA increased, prompting constituents to complain to their congressional representatives. To relieve the pressure of mounting claims, many analysts believed, SSA examiners made decisions hastily and carelessly, allotting little time to dissect each file or maintain tough disability standards. Meanwhile, lacking sufficient staff, the SSA's central office in Baltimore cut back on the number of state-level decisions that internal auditors reviewed. To make matters worse, at the same time that frontline examiners approved more claims, agency hearing officers, also known as administrative law judges (ALJs), and federal judges aggressively second-guessed claims that had been turned down, reversing an increasing number of denials on appeal. As a result, decisions varied greatly from state to state and from one level of decision making to the next. In fact, most observers believed that state examiners, ALJs, and federal judges were all operating under different disability standards and different rules. This inconsistency called into question the validity of decisions made at all levels; lawmakers doubted there could be a firm standard of disability with so many adjudicators coming to different conclusions. Calling DI a "caricature of bureaucratic complexity," HEW Secretary Joseph Califano called for the program to undergo "fundamental reassessment and overhaul."[8]

With DI expenditures seemingly out of control and program administration clearly in disarray, Carter backed comprehensive legislation that would rein in spending. Written by the House Subcommittee on Social Security, the Disability Benefits Reform Act of 1980 sought to reduce the incentive to apply for DI and to encourage employment, especially among the young. It capped benefit payments for families and altered the formula used to calculate payments so that benefits represented a smaller share of a worker's predisability earnings. The bill also allowed disabled beneficiaries who returned to work to remain eligible for Medicare for up to four years and to deduct the costs of hiring personal attendants

7. Martha Derthick, *Agency under Stress: The Social Security Administration in American Government* (Washington, DC: Brookings Institution Press, 1990), 25–31.

8. Edward D. Berkowitz, *Disabled Policy: America's Programs for the Handicapped* (Cambridge: Cambridge University Press, 1987), 106.

from their earnings. Only after this deduction would the SSA determine whether the beneficiary earned too much to qualify for DI, thus allowing individuals with high attendant care expenses to continue receiving benefits even if they continued working. These measures, lawmakers believed, would make DI less attractive to applicants relative to employment.

The 1980 disability amendments halted the growth in DI awards and alleviated the shortfall in the trust fund, placing the program on sound financial footing. But the slowdown in disability awards was not just the result of legislation. At the same time that Congress debated the provisions of what became the 1980 DBRA, the SSA engaged in its own retrenchment initiative, quietly and discreetly tightening the administrative rules that governed how disability was evaluated. The effect of the 1980 disability amendments and this administrative tightening was a one-two punch that ended the period of easy access that advocates had assumed would always be there.

The Administrative Tightening of DI and SSI

In order to bring DI enrollment and spending in line, the SSA's Office of Disability began in the late 1970s an effort to assert a more restrictive interpretation of disability. This new "clinical" interpretation of disability placed overriding emphasis during the disability examination on the medical aspects of an impairment that could be objectively verified, and it downplayed both nonmedical reasons for incapacity as well as those factors that were not subject to objective verification. Under the clinical approach, for instance, the disability examiner looked primarily for laboratory test results or visible anatomical or physiological abnormalities. Evidence that was more subjective, such as a treating physician's opinions or observations of functioning, carried less weight.

Of course, the SSA's process for evaluating disabilities had always paid attention to the objective and subjective aspects of disability. During debate over the creation of Disability Insurance, members of Congress were adamant that the program should be reserved for workers with a medical condition that destroyed their employment prospects; they did not want it to become a general unemployment compensation program. If at all possible, claimants had to verify their medical condition with clinical evidence. But lawmakers recognized too that unemployment also was the result of individual characteristics (motivation, age, job skills, education, race, gender, and family situation, to name a few) as well as larger social factors (including employer attitudes, the state of the economy, and the match between individual job skills and the jobs available).[9] Lawmakers wanted to compensate the medical reasons for unemployment, but they also wanted disability certification to measure an individual's ability to actually get and hold a job, which was a reflection of medical, individual, and social circumstances. Lawmakers, moreover, wanted certification to be "simple and objective," but they rejected standardized methods, like tables or rating schedules, that made it difficult to consider an individual's specific social and vocational characteristics.[10]

The SSA attempted to reconcile the tensions between medical, social, and individual factors by creating a disability certification process that could weigh all of these.[11] Though this is a simplified version, in practice, the evaluation for both DI and SSI disability benefits worked like this:

At the first stage examiners compared the claimant's medical condition to the SSA's Listings of Medical Impairments, a catalog of over one hundred physical and mental impairments that the SSA's medical staff presumed were incapacitating enough to justify a prima facie finding of disability. This was the standardized portion of the examination.

Next, if the claimant failed to satisfy the clinical criteria contained in the Listings, the examiner moved on to an individually tailored test of the claimant's specific functional and vocational capacities. At this stage, the examiner measured the claimant's residual functional limitations (that is, what he could do despite his impairment). He then decided whether the claimant could return to his previous line of work, or if not, given his age, education, and work experience, whether he could do any other work in the national economy. This was when social factors and individual circumstances were taken into account.

9. Deborah A. Stone, *The Disabled State* (Philadelphia: Temple University Press, 1984) is a marvelous account of policymakers' struggle to contain and objectify the inherently subjective nature of disability.
10. Ibid., 82–84.
11. Social Security Act, Title II, Section 223(d)(2) [42 U.S.C. 423] and see 20 C.F.R. 404.1520–404.1521 and 20 C.F.R. 416.920–416.921 (1998). This is a simplification of what the SSA calls its five-step sequential evaluation process. For the sake of clarity and brevity, I have shortened it to a two-step process, though the essential features remain the same. Under the five-step process, the SSA determines: 1) Does the claimant have a "severe" impairment? 2) Does it meet the criteria in the Listings of Medical Impairments? 3) Does it equal the criteria in the Listings of Medical Impairments? 4) Does the claimant have the residual functional capacity to perform his previous job? 5) Does the claimant, considering his age, education, and work experience, have the capacity to perform any other job in the national economy?

For the purpose of illustrating how this process worked, consider the case of a claimant with mental retardation. If the claimant exhibited the severe clinical signs contained in the Listings—that is, if he scored a 70 or lower on a test of intelligence—then he "met" the Medical Listings. If his condition was judged to be comparable in severity and duration, then he "equaled" the Listings. In both cases, the claimant was eligible for payments for medical reasons. If the claimant had an IQ higher than 70, then the clinical criteria were not met, and the examiner looked at the claimant's functional limitations and vocational attributes.

Nevertheless, whether examiners should place more weight on the standardized, medical stage of the process or the individualized assessment of functional and vocational characteristics remained unclear. One high-ranking official, Herbert Borgen, explained to an early meeting of administrators in the Office of Disability that "to the fullest extent . . . emphasis should be placed on the medical aspects" of the disability and on "the inherent nature and severity of any given impairment."[12] However, Arthur Hess, another SSA official who helped plan Disability Insurance claimed some years later that the Listings were only meant to separate cut-and-dried cases of disability from ones that necessitated a more thorough examination.[13] Initially, the SSA adopted this more lax approach to disability certification. Capturing the mood in the early years of DI, Robert Ball in 1957 advised his staff at the Division of Disability Operations, "Where there is a reasonable doubt in a close case, the disabled individual should be given the benefit of the doubt."[14]

As DI matured, though, the SSA moved in the direction of ever more standardization. In part, this was a response to increasing congressional concern that the agency's disability criteria remained vague. In fact, as early as 1960, lawmakers sitting on the Harrison Subcommittee, a special congressional committee studying Disability Insurance, worried that if the SSA could not formulate precise rules to govern disability determinations, there was the "distinct possibility that . . . the courts rather than the Department [of Health, Education, and Welfare] or Congress will set

12. Quoted in Arthur Hess, "Summary Report: Medical Advisory Committee Meeting," February 9 and 10, 1955, 3, in the SSA Archives, Office of the Historian, Social Security Administration, Baltimore, Maryland.

13. Arthur Hess in transcripts of Arthur Hess and Alvin David, "The Disability Program: Its Origins—Our Heritage, Its Future—Our Challenge," presentation at the Savannah Disability Symposium, Savannah, GA, January 21, 1993, http://www.ssa.gov/history/dibforum93.html.

14. Quoted in Martha Derthick, *Policymaking for Social Security* (Washington, DC: Brookings Institution Press, 1979), 310.

the standards."[15] Yet this move toward standardization took on a new life in the late 1970s as the SSA tried to regain control over its disordered disability determination process. Looking back at the way that examiners evaluated disability in the late 1960s, one former SSA employee noted that in the past adjudicators had stressed the "whole person concept"— that is, they were allowed "to exercise sound judgment" and "take into account everything" instead of simply referring to grids or tables that "place[d] people in boxes" in order to decide whether they were disabled.[16] But by the late 1970s, the SSA's Office of Disability wanted to root out judgment and elevate objectivity. The medical model, insofar as it assumed that medical impairments were, by their nature, incapacitating, aligned closely with the clinical approach to disability determination that the office adopted. The office, however, took the medical model one step further, by placing primary emphasis on those medical impairments that could be verified through quantitative measures or laboratory tests. Aspects of disability evaluation that could not be independently and objectively verified or that were open to manipulation by the claimant—vocational and functional tests, testimony from treating physicians, and statements from family and friends—were all minimized.

The effect of this transition to objectivity can be seen in the changes the office made to several categories of impairments. In the case of circulatory impairments, for instance, the Office of Disability made it more difficult for claimants to qualify under the Medical Listings by raising the qualifying bar that had to be met in clinical tests. Also, the Office of Disability expected applicants claiming to experience debilitating pain to have the clinical signs of a medical condition that could serve as the basis of the pain; subjective allegations of pain alone were not enough to justify an award. And it did away with the medical improvement requirement. Used when the SSA was determining whether a current beneficiary remained disabled enough to stay on the rolls, the medical improvement rule had required adjudicators to show that the beneficiary's medical condition had gotten better before finding him "no longer disabled" and ending benefits. In 1977, the Office of Disability replaced medical improvement with a rule requiring adjudicators to base their decisions of initial and continuing eligibility on the most recent clinical evidence and the disability standards currently in place. The

    15. U.S. House of Representatives, Ways and Means Committee, Subcommittee on the Administration of Social Security Laws, *Hearings on Social Security Amendments of 1960*, 86th Congress, 2nd Session, March 11, 1960, quoted in Stone, *Disabled State*, 84, 85.
    16. Ed Tall, SSA interview.

move was a reaction to the harried years of 1970–75. With the medical improvement rule on the books, it would have been difficult for the SSA to revisit these cases and rectify erroneous awards. But by doing away with the rule, examiners would not be judging beneficiaries by the standards used when they entered the programs. They would instead apply the newly tightened clinical criteria to people who had been on the rolls for years.[17]

The impact of these seemingly minor administrative changes can be seen in the case of a fifty-one-year-old man interviewed by congressional investigators at the General Accounting Office (GAO). After having had a heart attack and experiencing continued chest discomfort, the man qualified under the Listings in 1975, and began receiving DI benefits. But by 1982, the SSA had refined its Listings for circulatory impairments so that they now called for claimants to meet specific exercise test results or readings from a resting electrocardiogram. Using these new standards, examiners found the man was no longer disabled despite the fact that his resting EKGs from 1975 and 1982 were the same and the man continued to have chest discomfort.[18] Without the medical improvement rule, the SSA could strike the man from its rolls even though it was the disability standards, not the man, that had changed.

Because they were more complicated to evaluate than physical impairments, mental impairments posed an especially daunting challenge to the SSA's efforts to make disability determination more objective and exacting. Many mental disorders lack observable anatomical or physiological signs, and psychiatry during the 1970s was underdeveloped relative to other medical specialties. As a result, as one high-ranking SSA official explained to Congress in 1983, there were few widely accepted tests for evaluating the severity of a mental disorder, and "it [was] often difficult to obtain a consistent prognosis from mental health practitioners." Thus, state examiners were forced to make decisions "based on findings which do not always agree."[19] Of course, the architects of Social Security were well aware of the problems posed by mental disorders. Early drafts of

17. U.S. House of Representatives, Committee on Ways and Means, Subcommittee on Social Security, *Social Security Disability Insurance*, 98th Congress, 1st Session, June 30, 1983, 121 (hereafter House Subcommittee on Social Security, *SSDI*).

18. U.S. Senate, Committee on Finance, *Social Security Disability Insurance Program*, 97th Congress, 2nd Session, 1982, 214. For a brief history of the medical improvement standard, see prepared statement of House Subcommittee on Social Security, *SSDI*, 127–29.

19. U.S. Senate, Special Committee on Aging, *Social Security Reviews of the Mentally Disabled*, 98th Congress, 1st Session, 1983, 118 (hereafter Senate Special Committee on Aging, *Mentally Disabled*).

Disability Insurance proposed not covering the mentally ill because the Advisory Council believed that the condition was too difficult to determine objectively and because most people with mental illness were already supported by public funds as residents of state-run asylums and hospitals.[20] Though mental disorders were eventually included, the Listings released by the Office of Disability made qualification extremely difficult. They required "manifest persistence" of the clinical signs and symptoms of a disorder. In other words, hallucinations, delusions, compulsive behavior, agitation, depression, whatever the indicator of the illness was, had to be present at the moment of examination. And they precluded eligibility if the claimant showed interest in any activity or was in any way capable of caring for himself, performing acts of daily living, or socializing with other people.[21]

Still, the SSA in the late 1970s singled out mental disorders for further tightening. Kurt Nussbaum, the chief psychiatrist for the Office of Disability, hoped to find some way "that psychiatric impairment . . . [could] be assessed or evaluated according to a medical model in the same manner as can a physical impairment."[22] His goal was to ground assessments of mental disorders on "quantifiable building stones rather than 'gut feeling.'"[23] To this end, Nussbaum devised the Psychiatric Review Form (PRF), a rating technique that assigned numerical scores to clinical symptoms, like depression, hyperactivity, phobias, or hallucinations. Using the contents of the claimant's medical file, disability examiners gave high scores to individuals with the most severe symptoms, those that they thought were serious enough to meet or equal the Medical Listings, while less severe disorders received a lower score. Examiners then consulted various tables that calculated the scores and determined whether the claimant qualified. Much to their delight, the medical staff

20. Berkowitz, *Disabled Policy*, 47–48.
21. See 20 C.F.R. 404, Appendix I, Subpart P, Section 12.00 (1979).
22. Kurt Nussbaum, "Objective Assessment of Degree of Psychiatric Impairment: Is It Possible?" *The Johns Hopkins Medical Journal* 133 (1973), 30.
23. Kurt Nussbaum, "Four Plus Four Equals Five: An Equation for Psychiatric Assessment," *Maryland State Medical Journal* 68 (1978): 69. For more details on the rating system, see Kurt Nussbaum, Abraham M. Schneidmuhl, and John W. Schaffer, "Psychiatric Evidence Needed in Social Security Disability Evaluation," *Journal of the Indiana State Medical Association* 61, 3 (1968): 370–72; Kurt Nussbaum, Abraham M. Schneidmuhl, and John W. Schaffer, "Psychiatric Assessment in the Social Security Program of Disability Insurance," *American Journal of Psychiatry* 126, 6 (1969): 165–67; Nussbaum, "Objective Assessment," 30–37; John W. Schaffer, Kurt Nussbaum, and Sophie M. Lewis, "Psychiatric Assessment from Documentary Evidence," *Comprehensive Psychiatry* 12 (1971): 564–71; Kurt Nussbaum, "Four Plus Four Equals Five," 67–70.

found that, when using the scale, agreement among examiners was as high in evaluations of mental disorders as in evaluations dealing with physical impairments.[24] For an area of decision making that had been plagued with uncertainty, the rating scale appeared a huge step forward in disability evaluation. Indeed, Nussbaum proudly proclaimed that the reliability of the rating scale would finally elevate psychiatry to the status of a "true science" and enhance public confidence in the judgments of its practitioners.[25]

At the same time that the medical staff tried to reinforce the quantitative and ostensibly objective underpinnings of evaluations of mental disability, it also moved to eliminate its subjective elements by deemphasizing tests of functioning and vocational factors, which posed all sorts of problems. In its tests of functioning, the SSA had to define the physical and mental demands of work so that it could assess whether the claimant had the capacity to meet those demands. In the case of physical impairments, the SSA examined the claimant's ability to lift, bend, and move. But mental impairments were more troublesome. In 1980, the Office of Disability defined the mental demands of work as the ability "to understand, to carry out and remember instructions, and to respond appropriately to supervision, co-workers, and work pressures in a work setting."[26] But determining whether the claimant satisfied these demands, by its very nature, required disability examiners to exercise a great deal of judgment.[27] Thus, in its campaign to root out subjectivity, the Office of Disability in 1979 virtually eliminated the consideration of functioning and vocational factors in the case of any claimant under the age of fifty alleging a mental impairment. If a younger claimant did not meet or equal the Medical Listings, examiners were told to assume that he was capable of performing "unskilled work" and deny benefits. As a member of the SSA medical staff explained in a policy directive to state disability determina-

24. Nussbaum, "Objective Assessment," 34.

25. Nussbaum, "Four Plus Four Equals Five," 69, and Schaffer et al., "Psychiatric Assessment from Documentary Evidence," 570.

26. 20 C.F.R. 404.1545(c) and 416.945(c) (1980).

27. A few years later, the Office of Disability attempted to refine the standards to offer more precision. It defined seven mental activities including understanding instructions, interacting with supervisors and co-workers, and maintaining concentration, and told examiners to rate the claimant's abilities in each area as either "limited" or "unlimited." But this was unsatisfactory too since the meaning of "limited" and "unlimited" abilities was unclear, and much of the evidence in medical files did not provide enough information for examiners to make firm judgments. See *City of New York v. Heckler*, 578 F. Supp. 1109, 1113 (E.D.N.Y 1984).

tion offices, "where the PRF is properly employed, a separate [rating of functional capacity] would be redundant."[28] Instead, the findings of the rating scale were to be used as the sole predictor of an individual's work capacity.

Like the administrative changes made to pain and circulatory impairments, efforts to quantify disability significantly restricted the ability of people with mental disorders to access DI and SSI benefits. One physician working for the SSA objected that the new rules made it "practically impossible . . . for any individual whose thought processes are not completely disorganized, is not blatantly psychotic, or is not having a psychiatric emergency requiring immediate hospitalization" to qualify.[29] Some offices in New York state, in fact, reported that after the new rules were put in place in 1978, the number of mentally ill applicants who were approved for benefits dropped by more than half.[30] Not surprisingly, then, the move proved controversial within the agency, especially among those that had direct contact with applicants. A disability examiner in New York, for instance, noted that while it was "sound practice" to require "objective, as opposed to subjective, medical documentation," the SSA was carrying "its emphasis on objective data to extremes."[31] Another complained that the evaluation of mental impairments unavoidably involved "subjective overtones" that placed "the evaluation in a grayer area than the 'typical' physical impairment, which can be seen, measured, and manipulated."[32] Yet it was precisely these "subjective overtones" that the SSA wanted to eliminate.

The SSA's subterranean tightening of DI and SSI might have continued indefinitely, without anyone noticing, had President Reagan not launched a very visible and very controversial assault on Disability Insurance in 1981. Thus, the Reagan Revolution brought the SSA's restrictive clinical approach to disability into a headlong conflict with the expansive goals of advocates committed to deinstitutionalization and community mental health. Reagan's efforts to purge the disability rolls brought the SSA's retrenchment to light and infuriated the advocates.

28. Jose Puig, the SSA's acting chief consultant in psychiatry and Nussbaum's eventual successor, quoted in *City of New York*, 578 F. Supp. at 1116.

29. *Mental Health Association of Minnesota v. Schweiker*, 554 F. Supp. 157, 162 (D. Minn. 1982).

30. *City of New York*, 578 F. Supp. at 1116.

31. U.S. House of Representative, Select Committee on Aging, *Social Security Disability Insurance Program: Cessations and Denials*, 97th Congress, 2nd Session, 1982, 111 (hereafter House Select Committee on Aging, *Cessations and Denials*).

32. Senate Special Committee on Aging, *Mentally Disabled*, 275.

The Reagan Revolution Threatens the Social Safety Net

Reagan entered office determined to cut taxes dramatically, slash federal spending for social welfare programs, reduce government oversight of business, and increase military expenditures. To trim the federal budget, the president hoped to turn back responsibility for some assistance programs over to the states and, for others, tighten income criteria so that benefits went only to the poorest of the poor.[33] But according to budget director David Stockman, given the administration's ambitious tax cut proposals, to keep the federal budget balanced, Reagan also needed to cull savings from large and generally popular middle-class entitlements.[34] To trim spending from Social Security's Disability Insurance program, the White House suggested applying a "medical only" definition of disability, barring any consideration of vocational factors, and increasing the length of time that an impairment had to last—from twelve to twenty-four months. When Congress rejected these plans, White House officials used an alternative means of retrenchment, a large-scale review of the Disability Insurance rolls designed to root out anyone who did not meet the program's disability criteria. In the absence of congressional support for the president's legislative plans, the reviews became "the principle vehicle for restricting access" to Social Security.[35]

There were two reasons Reagan pursued this administrative approach to retrenchment. First, it was politically tenable. Proposals to cut Social Security arouse widespread public opposition, but few would quibble with efforts to rid social welfare programs of fraudulent cases or well-to-do recipients and target aid at those who were the most needy. Thus, in almost every income support program, Reagan moved to tighten eligibility standards to eliminate recipients who were working or who were low-

33. For an overview of Reagan's social welfare strategy, see Kenneth W. Clarkson, "The Safety Net from the Reagan Administration's Perspective," in *Maintaining the Safety Net*, ed. John C. Weicher (Washington, DC: American Enterprise Institute, 1984), 169–88, and D. Lee Bawden and John L. Palmer, "Social Policy: Challenging the Welfare State," in *The Reagan Record: An Assessment of America's Changing Domestic Priorities*, ed. John L. Palmer and Isabel V. Sawhill (Cambridge, MA: Ballinger, 1984), 117–215.

34. David A. Stockman, *The Triumph of Politics: How the Reagan Revolution Failed* (New York: Harper and Row, 1986), 181.

35. Patricia Dilley, "Social Security Disability: Political Philosophy and History," in *Psychiatric Disability: Clinical, Legal, and Administrative Dimensions*, ed. Arthur T. Meyerson and Theodora Fine (Washington, DC: American Psychiatric Association, 1987), 397.

income but not poor. Having used a similar strategy to trim welfare spending when he was governor of California, Reagan called this process "purifying."[36] And indeed, the evidence indicated that Disability Insurance was sorely in need of purification. In two pilot studies conducted in the late 1970s, the SSA found that perhaps 20 to 26 percent of workers currently receiving benefits did not meet program criteria. Extrapolating from those figures, the General Accounting Office contended that as many as 584,000 individuals were erroneously receiving disability checks, costing taxpayers over $2 billion a year. David Swope and John Svahn, members of the president's transition team who would soon assume positions in the Department of Health and Human Services, seized on the GAO report as a rationale for scaling back federal disability spending.[37] Claiming that "misdirected benefits" were costing taxpayers $2 billion annually, Reagan pledged to begin "tightening administration . . . to insure that only the truly disabled receive benefits."[38]

Second, the reviews appeared to have bipartisan sanction. A legislative mandate for the reviews came from a little noted provision that Democrats in Congress and President Carter had approved as part of the 1980 DRBA. The provision required the SSA to examine every beneficiary who was not permanently disabled at least once every three years to ensure that he continued to meet the program's disability standards. The SSA had carried out these "continuing disability investigations" in the past as time and resources permitted.[39] Yet this system of internal checks had broken down in the mid 1970s. With its state disability determination offices overwhelmed with SSI applications, the SSA stopped requiring them to process the investigations of continuing disability as well. During debate over the 1980 DBRA, members of the Social Security Subcommittee and its staff were troubled by the fact that once a person got on the disability rolls, he was basically there for life. Thus, by requiring the SSA to conduct a minimum number of reviews each year, the provision mandating the continuing disability investigations was intended to reassert the vigilance over the disability rolls that had existed before the 1970s. Compared to the family cap and the change to the benefit formula, which were quite controversial and occupied most of the

36. Berkowitz, *Disabled Policy*, 124–25.
37. Ibid., 124–26.
38. House Subcommittee on Social Security, *SSDI*, 58.
39. A complete discussion of the 1980 disability amendments is beyond the scope of this book, but for further reading on the amendments and the reviews, see Berkowitz, *Disabled Policy*, 111–51; Derthick, *Agency under Stress*; and Dilley, "Social Security Disability."

congressional debate, the continuing disability investigations were scarcely noticed.

What Congress had approved in principle, however, was not what occurred in practice. The lawmakers who voted for the continuing disability investigations in 1980 had expected little in the way of budget savings. In fact, they expected the reviews to cost more than they saved, at least initially, since the SSA would need to hire and train additional personnel. Congress had projected that the reviews would not save money until 1984, at which point expenditures would begin to register a modest net gain of $10 million over four years. In the hands of Reagan administration officials, though, what looked like a "good government" initiative became a budget-cutting maneuver. Instead of beginning the reviews in 1982, as Congress had planned, they wanted to start a year early and pull a larger number of files for reexamination. By accelerating the investigations, the White House projected that it would save a whopping $3.4 billion between 1981 and 1986.[40] In this manner, the president could simultaneously argue that he supported the "preservation of the safety net" while also pushing for sweeping cuts in social welfare spending.[41]

In April 1981, the SSA launched an aggressive review of DI to weed out individuals whom it determined were "no longer disabled." From the start, however, the accelerated reviews were a disaster. Neither the statutory language of the 1980 amendments or the committee reports gave any guidance as to how they should be implemented or the standards that should be used to assess continuing eligibility.[42] In the face of legislative silence, the SSA used its current disability standards, which it had quietly been tightening over several years. With the onset of the reviews, those new restrictive standards would be applied not just to individuals applying for benefits for the first time but also to beneficiaries who had been on the rolls for years without ever once having been reevaluated. Most were taken by complete surprise, and in a handful of extreme but well-publicized cases, beneficiaries were so distraught over losing their benefits that their health deteriorated. Some died as a result, and a few committed suicide. Moreover, the scale of the reviews overwhelmed the administrative capacities of the state disability determination offices, which had received little time to prepare. Seen from an historical perspective, the reviews represented a staggering workload. In 1980, the SSA performed fewer than 100,000 continuing disability investigations. But the following year, it increased that number to 169,000, and by 1983,

40. Derthick, *Agency Under Stress*, 36.
41. John C. Weicher, "Introduction," in *Maintaining the Safety Net*, ed. Weicher, 1–2.
42. House Subcommittee on Social Security, *SSDI*, 61.

more than 435,000 cases were pulled. The proportion of beneficiaries reviewed grew nearly fivefold from 3 percent of the rolls in 1979 to almost 14 percent in 1983.[43] Files rained down on state disability determination offices, which had not had the time to hire more staff to handle the onslaught. According to one high-ranking SSA official, state examiners felt intense pressure to dispose of cases quickly yet also root out the large number of ineligible beneficiaries that were supposedly on the rolls. The only way for them to "relieve the pressure," she lamented, "was to terminate people from the rolls" after only a cursory evaluation.[44] Between 1981, when the SSA began the first continuing disability investigations, to 1984, when the agency suspended them in the face of widespread criticism, more than 1.1 million individuals were pulled for reexamination; over half were dropped from Social Security.[45]

Even though the SSA soon realized it had a problem, with the reviews up and running, officials found themselves helpless to remedy the situation. According to an SSA official, they simply "couldn't get a handle on the policy issues fast enough."[46] The disability reviews quickly led to a political and administrative meltdown. Media outlets ran numerous "horror stories" of individuals whose lives were ruined after the SSA cut off their benefits after seemingly perfunctory examinations. The reviews were deeply unpopular among the SSA's own field and regional officers as well.[47] One agency official later told an interviewer, "I would really have to say, if there is one period of time when I don't think Headquarters listened to what was going on out in the field, it was during that time."[48] The other components of the agency's disability determination process felt the same way. Within two years, the lower federal courts and the SSA became locked in a visible and acrimonious dispute over which institution had the final say in setting the administrative standards that governed the disability programs. ALJs hearing appeals of denied or terminated claims reversed the SSA's decision in 41 percent of the cases, 91

43. U. S. House of Representative, Committee on Ways and Means, *Background Material and Data on Programs within the Jurisdiction of the Committee on Ways and Means* (Washington, DC: Government Printing Office, 1985), 111 (hereafter House Committee on Ways and Means, *1985 Green Book*).

44. Rhoda Davis, SSA interview.

45. Author's calculations from House Committee on Ways and Means, *1985 Green Book*, 111.

46. Rhoda Davis, SSA interview.

47. John Ritter, former executive program policy officer for the Office of Disability, Social Security Administration, interview in the Oral History Collection, August 16, 1995, transcripts in the SSA Archives, Office of the Historian, Social Security Administration, Baltimore, Maryland.

48. Ibid.

percent of the time if the decision involved mental impairments. And judges issued hundreds of contempt of court citations against the SSA when it refused to abide by court-ordered policy changes.[49] By 1983, the disability determination offices in several states were operating under court-imposed rules, and in many of the states in which courts had not yet intervened, governors or other high-ranking state officials had ordered the offices in their states to stop conducting reviews. Social Security disability policy was in utter turmoil.

The Reviews Galvanize the Advocates

The disability reviews caught the advocacy community by surprise. The Mental Health Law Project was less than a decade old when the reviews began, and its attorneys knew very little about either DI or SSI.[50] They had paid the two programs little attention, but the election of Reagan forced the MHLP and other advocates to reassess their strategy of building a social safety net for people with disabilities. Among the first of Reagan's acts on assuming the presidency was the repeal of the 1980 Mental Health Systems Act, Carter's planned increase in community mental health spending. Reagan's 1981 budget drastically reduced funds for community mental health centers and rolled them into a consolidated alcohol, drug abuse, and mental health block grant. With categorical funding of community mental health centers slashed, advocates could no longer afford complacency. Advocacy on behalf of mainstream social welfare programs became an imperative.

Yet at the same time the White House slashed expenditures for community mental health care, it also went after the mainstream social welfares programs that advocates had long taken for granted. Indeed, the Social Security disability reviews had an especially devastating effect on people with mental disorders. The number of mentally disabled individuals who lost their benefits was larger than for any other impairment category. Though they comprised only 11 percent of the Disability Insurance rolls, people with mental disorders were 28 percent of the cases pulled for review and 26 percent of the terminations.[51] Even though SSA concentrated its efforts on DI, the reviews pulled into its dragnet the needy recipients of SSI as well since the two programs shared the same definition of disability and some individuals relied on both for support.

49. House Subcommittee on Social, *SSDI*, 1, and Senate Special Committee on Aging, *Mentally Disabled*, 8, 14.

50. Leonard S. Rubenstein, interview with author.

51. Senate Special Committee on Aging, *Mentally Disabled*, 164–65.

The disproportionately adverse impact the reviews had on the mentally ill was not necessarily intentional; instead it stemmed from deep-seated flaws in the way the SSA evaluated mental disorders. One high-ranking SSA official at the time explained, "Until we started terminating large numbers of people, we never understood—I don't think any of my predecessors understood—the weaknesses in the policy."[52]

Two problems with mental disability certification became apparent. First, the SSA simply was not prepared to handle the administrative workload that resulted from the huge surge in files. Even under perfect circumstances evaluations of mental disability were difficult and time-intensive. But with the accelerated schedule, the situation was far from perfect, and as a result, the SSA's jerry-rigged system for certifying mental impairments collapsed. Facing intense pressures to dispose of cases, examiners could not adequately develop assessments of a claimant's medical history or functional capacity. No one visited claimants in person to make sure the information in the files was accurate, and most state offices lacked psychiatric resources that could have provided a second opinion in complicated cases.[53] Second, during the reviews, the SSA applied the more restrictive rating scale developed by the medical staff in the late 1970s to mentally ill individuals who had entered under the more permissive climate that prevailed in previous years. But it was one thing to employ tough disability standards for individuals applying for the first time, quite another to apply them to people had been on the rolls for years and who had expected to spend the rest of their lives on DI or SSI. Hundreds of thousands of current beneficiaries were treated as if they were first-time applicants, and many fell short. The suddenness of the terminations appeared callous and unfair. As a spokeswoman for the Arc pointed out, "People affected will not be quite so aware of something that they never got, rather than something that was taken away from them."[54]

As the number of mentally disabled beneficiaries dropped from the DI and SSI rolls mounted throughout 1981 and early 1982, advocates were enraged. They accused the SSA of deliberately singling out the mentally ill for review because, given their mental state, they were the least able to appeal their denials, and they mobilized to stop the benefit terminations.[55] Soon advocacy groups for people with mental disorders joined a broad coalition of disability and antipoverty organizations to fight the re-

52. Rhoda Davis, SSA interview.

53. Senate Special Committee on Aging, *Mentally Disabled*, 14, 18.

54. House Subcommittee on Social Security, *SSDI*, 171.

55. Arthur T. Meyerson, retired professor of psychiatry at the Mt. Sinai School of Medicine and a participant in the 1983–85 workgroup to rewrite the adult mental disorders Listings, phone interview with author, March 13, 2000.

views. This coalition represented practically every type of impairment, but advocates for the mentally disabled were by far the most vocal and organized. According to Patricia Owens, who headed the Office of Disability for most of the Reagan years, though there were "pockets of spokespersons for other disabilities," no other disability group presented the same "concerted effort" that they did.[56] This was perhaps because mental health advocates realized that patients' rights would be meaningless without social welfare programs available to ex-patients. Perhaps, it was also because advocates recognized that the controversial nature of the reviews offered the opportunity to forge a "new alliance . . . among lawyers, patients, and health professionals" behind community mental health ideals.[57] As Leonard Rubenstein, the MHLP's chief litigator during the reviews, explained, because it had undermined the overriding authority of psychiatrists and condemned states for their woeful neglect of the patients, the struggle for patients' rights had pitted patients and their attorneys against medical professionals and state governments. The reviews, however, bridged this divide, as all groups fought to prevent the Reagan administration from shifting responsibility for the mentally ill from the federal government back to states and localities. Between 1981 and 1984, the MHLP served as the central clearinghouse for mental health activism on Social Security matters, coordinating the lobbying and litigation activities of Legal Services attorneys, medical and rehabilitation experts, and state and local government officials.[58] Long after the reviews had subsided, the MHLP maintained its interest in Social Security disability policy, carrying its advocacy on behalf of mental illness and mental retardation to issues pertaining to childhood disability and addiction.

An Alternative Approach to Measuring Disability

During debate over the disability reviews, advocates advanced an alternative to the SSA's restrictive clinical approach to determining disability. Theirs was a functional approach that, they argued, would provide a more accurate assessment of a person's actual ability to find and keep a job. Recent transformations in the norms and standards that governed the medical profession, in particular psychiatry, pediatrics, and psychoso-

56. Patricia Owens, former deputy commissioner for the Office of Disability, Social Security Administration, phone interview with author, April 25, 2000.

57. Leonard S. Rubenstein and Jane Yohalem Bloom, "The Courts and Psychiatric Disability," in *Psychiatric Disability*, ed. Meyerson and Fine, 437–38.

58. For an example of the hostility between doctors and lawyers, see Darold A. Treffert, "Dying with their Rights On," *American Journal of Psychiatry* 130 (1973): 1041.

cial rehabilitation, informed this functional approach. Taken together, these new professional norms viewed illness and the resulting disability as a phenomenon that needed to be considered holistically. They moved beyond isolated attention to abnormal anatomical structures or physiological processes and instead tried to assess illness and disability by considering how well an individual functioned in her larger social and physical environment. Looking further than clinical measures of objective impairment, this model of illness and disability recognized that some impairments were real even if they were not objectively verifiable, and it took a step in the direction of the social model's contention that disability was the consequence of a mismatch between a person's physical or mental capacities and the arrangement of society's organizations and structures.

Part of the functional approach rested on the revisions that the American Psychiatric Association (APA) made to its *Diagnostic and Statistical Manual*, the official handbook for recognizing and diagnosing mental disorders. In the late 1970s, psychiatry was a field under siege: patients' rights advocates attacked the authority of doctors, sociologists argued that mental illness was nothing more than a social label, and third-party insurers complained about the difficulty of compensating for mental disorders when different clinicians examining the same patient disagreed about the proper diagnosis and course of treatment. These troubles cut to the heart of psychiatry's place as a medical specialty. Stuart Kirk and Herb Kutchins pointed out that "a profession whose sole mission is understanding and treating a particular form of illness must show convincingly that it can describe and recognize the illness when it occurs."[59] Thus, in 1974, at the urging of Robert Spitzer, a well-respected and outspoken psychiatrist, APA officials decided to revise its diagnostic manual to provide clinicians with more guidance on what constituted a mental disorder and in the process, they hoped, shore up the profession's identity as a medical science. For six years, a team of top psychiatric researchers led by Spitzer labored to rewrite the diagnostic criteria for virtually every malady known to psychiatry. In 1980, the APA released the much-anticipated third edition of its *Diagnostic and Statistical Manual* (DSM-III), a lengthy tome that fundamentally restructured the standards used to identify and classify mental disorders. DSM-III represented two significant departures from previous editions. First, the manual broadened the array of conditions considered mental disorders. Whereas the preceding manual, DSM-II, listed 182 disorders, DSM-III contained

59. Stuart A. Kirk and Herb Kutchins, *The Selling of DSM: The Rhetoric of Science in Psychiatry* (New York: Aldine de Gruyter, 1992), 24.

265, and subsequent editions have added more still. Many of the new entries were created by splitting apart broad disease categories into more specific conditions. But there were also conditions that appeared for the first time, including post-traumatic stress disorder, attention deficit disorder, and many new childhood illnesses. Second, DMS-III expanded the descriptive criteria used to make a diagnosis. Whereas DSM-II contained only brief and vague narratives about each of the mental disorders, its successor featured detailed descriptions of the symptoms, sensations, emotions, and behaviors associated with each disorder. For instance, in DSM-II, the criteria for making a diagnosis of schizophrenia were contained in a few brief paragraphs that spanned a mere three pages. But DSM-III took more than a dozen pages to describe schizophrenia and its various subtypes, and each description included information about the age at which the disorder would appear, its complications, its predisposing factors, its prevalence, its gender and familial patterns, the effect of stress on the patient, secondary medical problems related to the primary mental disorder, and ways that the clinician could evaluate the patient's level of adaptive functioning.[60] With such elaborate descriptive criteria in place, the authors of DSM-III hoped that a clinician would now be less likely to misdiagnose or even miss diagnosing a disorder.

The new definition of mental illness that emerged from DSM-III was both expansive and contentious, features that would also characterize the advocates' functional approach to disability. DSM-III liberalized the clinical understanding of mental illness by broadening the range of dysfunctions considered illnesses and making clinical observations of a patient's behavior and subjective experience the primary means for diagnosing this wider array of illnesses. In addition, even though it was supposed to be a manual of mental illness, DSM-III did not provide a theory of illness. There was no attempt to explain what agent caused mental disorders, whether they were the result of biology or environment or some combination of both, or which forms of treatment best arrested the pathological development of these disorders and why. Instead, DSM-III dealt only with the outward manifestations of a mental disorder. Thus, clinicians did not have to agree on the causes and treatment of mental illness so long as they agreed that a particular condition, having satisfied the manual's detailed descriptive criteria, deserved the diagnosis of an "illness."

This was a development fraught with controversy. Without a theoretical understanding of mental illness, various factions within the APA

60. Ibid., 116–19.

butted heads over what specifically constituted a mental illness. Feminists, for example, objected to Spitzer's efforts to add masochistic personality disorder (a label that feminists feared would be widely applied to
women in abusive relationships) to DSM-III's long list of dysfunctions,
and they suggested a counterpart, delusional dominating personality disorder, which could be applied to aggressive and chauvinistic men. Meanwhile, Spitzer fought to keep post-traumatic stress disorder out of the
manual and homosexuality in; he lost on both counts.[61] What is more,
the controversy persisted long after the APA ratified DSM-III. To critics
of the new manual and its subsequent revisions, the expanded diagnostic
categories brought individual idiosyncrasies, behavior that deviated from
the statistical norms, or simple bad behavior under the therapeutic umbrella of medicine. Detractors scoffed that under DSM-III, childhood
aggression had become oppositional defiance disorder; churlishness, borderline personality disorder; shyness, social anxiety disorder; and inatten-
tiveness, attention deficit disorder.[62]

Nevertheless, the APA had good reason to use functioning and behavioral descriptions to arrive at a clinical diagnosis. First, psychiatry needed
some sort of mechanism for classifying and organizing knowledge, and
although the science was not perfect, clinicians simply could not sit
around and wait for more research before attending to the needs of their
patients. The therapeutic ethos that drove the diagnostic revision ap-
pears clearly in one doctor's defense of DSM-III. He admitted that
"DSM is fraught with inconsistencies and the potential for misuse and
abuse" and that "it is certainly unsatisfying as a philosophical document."
But he affirmed its usefulness for "those of us who were more interested
in helping suffering patients than in new philosophies of the mind." Another physician, writing in the same vein, aptly characterized DSM-III as
"a humble effort to alleviate pain and suffering in the face of incomplete
knowledge."[63]

Moreover, psychiatrists were not the only ones redefining illness and
disability along functional lines. In fact, during the postwar years, pediatrics also called for increased attention to an individual's functional abil-

61. These disputes are described in Herb Kutchins and Stuart A. Kirk, *Making Us
Crazy: DSM: The Psychiatric Bible and the Creation of Mental Disorders* (New York: Free
Press, 1997), 53–175.

62. Kirk and Kutchins, *Selling of DSM*, 111–16; Kutchins and Kirk, *Making Us
Crazy*, 21–54; and Patrick R. McHugh, "How Psychiatry Lost Its Way," *Commentary*
108, 5 (1999): 32–38.

63. Roderick Shaner, Letter to the Editor, *Commentary* 109, 3 (2000), 5, and Gary N.
Cohen, Letter to the Editor, *Commentary* 109, 3 (2000): 6.

ities and the larger social context in which dysfunction occurred. According to historian Dorothy Pawluch, as medical science made headway in preventing and treating major childhood illnesses, like diphtheria, measles, and whooping cough, children's doctors faced elimination of their livelihood. To remain relevant, they turned their therapeutic powers toward helping parents deal with more mundane dysfunctions: unsuitable conduct, temper tantrums, shyness, academic difficulties, and aggression. The shift in the pediatric perspective was profound. "Conditions once attributed to random variation in character, aptitude, . . . or to 'normal' teenage rebelliousness," Pawluch argues, "we now understand within a medical frame of reference. . . . Behaviors that we once punished, are now referred to pediatricians and other doctors or experts."[64] It was no surprise, then, that the APA responded to this growing interest in the developmental and behavioral problems of children by adding diagnostic criteria for many new childhood mental disorders to DSM-III.[65]

Experts in rehabilitation, too, called for more attention to individual behavior and functioning, particularly functioning in a work environment. Rehabilitation studies in the 1970s found that the clinical signs of a disorder were a much poorer predictor of work capacity than an individual's prior work history and assessments of his ability to socialize. According to the research, the severity of an individual's symptoms had little bearing at all on his actual ability to be successful in the job market because those measures were so detached from the real-world social settings that he would have to navigate in order to find and hold employment.[66] Even assessments of isolated tasks were not enough. Some experts noted that there was a "lack of correlation between an ability of a mentally ill person to perform daily activities such as household chores and the ability to cope in a work environment."[67] The research suggested that if what disability examiners really cared about was determining whether a person could work, then "assessments of work behavior in a simulated work setting" were "more predictive than psychological test scores or mental status examinations," the very features of an impairment on which the SSA based its decision making.[68]

DSM-III, the transformation of pediatrics, and the new rehabilitation

64. Dorothy Pawluch, *The New Pediatrics: A Profession in Transition* (New York: Aldine de Gruyter, 1996), 1–2.
65. Kirk and Kutchins, *Selling of DSM*, 118.
66. William A. Anthony and Mary A. Jansen, "Predicting the Vocational Capacity of the Chronically Mentally Ill: Research and Policy Implications," *American Psychologist* 39, 5 (1984): 537–44.
67. *City of New York v. Heckler*, 578 F. Supp. at 1115.
68. Anthony and Jansen, "Predicting the Vocational Capacity," 542.

research—none of these changes had been motivated by a concern for social justice. The drive to revise DSM-III, for example, had been led by doctors who cared about psychiatry's status as a science, not psychiatry's obligations to the poor. However, because it took a broad view of mental illness, DSM-III became the intellectual staging ground for the advocates' efforts to reform how the SSA evaluated mental and childhood disorders. The emerging functional emphasis in rehabilitation and pediatrics only added to the advocates' argument that the SSA's restrictive clinical approach to disability was outmoded and out of touch with real-world medicine. Whereas the SSA had elevated objective clinical measures, medical experts suggested a comprehensive look at how an individual functioned overall in relation to her physical and social environment. This functional approach was an expansive interpretation of disability ideally suited to the policy goals of the advocacy groups. It became problematic, however, when policymakers applied the wide-ranging diagnostic criteria used for therapeutic purposes to benefit programs premised on the narrow view of disability that informed the medical model.

Strategies and Tactics

Despite the fact that they lacked both vast financial resources and a large membership base, the advocacy groups were able to convince judges, lawmakers, and ultimately SSA officials to adopt the liberal functional understanding of disability that they favored. Their success was a testament to their sophisticated litigation and lobbying approach. Shortly after the reviews, Leonard Rubenstein and several of his fellow mental health advocates wrote a series of articles in which they described the strategy used to reform DI and SSI in hopes of replicating in other policy areas the success they had enjoyed with Social Security. Three features were evident.[69]

69. Five articles by Leonard S. Rubenstein, Howard H. Goldman, and their colleagues provide useful insight into the struggle over Social Security disability reviews and strategies and tactics of the advocates. See Leonard S. Rubenstein, "Science, Law, and Psychiatric Disability," *Psychosocial Rehabilitation Journal* 9, 1 (1985): 7–21; Leonard S. Rubenstein, "Treatment of the Mentally Ill: Legal Advocacy Enters the Second Generation," *American Journal of Psychiatry* 143, 10 (1986): 1264–69; Howard H. Goldman and Antoinette A. Gattozzi, "Balance of Power: Social Security and the Mentally Disabled, 1980–1985," *Milbank Quarterly* 66, 3 (1988): 531–51; Leonard S. Rubenstein, Antoinette A. Gattozzi, and Howard H. Goldman, "Protecting the Entitlements of the Mentally Disabled: The SSDI/SSI Legal Battles of the 1980s," *International Journal of Law and Psychiatry* 11 (1988): 269–78; and Howard H. Goldman and Antoinette A. Gattozzi, "Murder in the Cathedral Revisited: President Reagan and the Mentally Disabled," *Hospital and Community Psychiatry* 39, 3 (1988): 505–9.

First, from the very beginning, advocates understood that they "needed to reinforce . . . the legal argument with medical evidence."[70] As Rubenstein explained, the Social Security Act had little to say on what constituted a disability, what constituted ability to work, and what process the SSA should use to answer these questions. At the same time, however, the law contained "specific statutory requirements which keyed benefits to ability to work."[71] With benefits pegged to the standard of work capacity, the question then became: What was the best method for determining which claimants met this standard? In the late 1970s, with its move to tighten the standard of disability, the SSA had adopted a clinical approach to measuring work capacity: claimants had to meet certain clinical tests or show certain clinical signs or symptoms; otherwise they were presumed capable of work. Advocates, however, advanced a functional approach to disability evaluation, which, they argued, could determine a person's ability to work more accurately than the SSA's heavy reliance on clinical evidence. Rather than rest on clinical tests or symptoms, this functional approach to disability determination placed its emphasis on an individual's behavior, his ability to function in a workplace setting, and his capacity to actually find and keep a job.[72] But it was also difficult for judges and lawmakers, who were largely unapprenticed in the nuances of disability determination, to understand the differences between the two approaches. Rubenstein noted that while the published rules governing certification clearly stated that individual functioning, age, education, and work experience were to be part of the process of determining disability, how those rules were applied in practice "wasn't that black and white." "There was no rule that said skip" the tests of functional capacity and vocational factors, he argued, but when the SSA focused primarily on clinical signs, this is, in practice, what occurred. Advocates feared that because they possessed only the most general knowledge of the complex legal and medical issues involved in disability determination, judges and lawmakers would be inclined to defer to the decisions SSA officials made. Thus, the advocates believed that it was imperative that they ground their arguments, not just on legal rules, but also on the findings from the latest medical and rehabilitation research. As MHLP attorney Leonard Rubenstein explained, countering SSA's arguments with medical evidence of their own would lead policymakers to conclude that "the Social Security Administration was scientifically way

70. Leonard S. Rubenstein, interview with author.
71. Rubenstein and Bloom, "Courts and the Psychiatric Disabled," 447.
72. Rubenstein et al., "Protecting the Entitlements of the Mentally Disabled," 269, 271, and Rubenstein, "Science, Law, and Psychiatric Disability," 7–21.

off base" and this would "make the violations of the regulations more compelling."[73]

Second, advocates enlisted the help of professional organizations, a move that they viewed as a "real coup."[74] Concerned about the well-being of deinstitutionalized patients, New York City psychiatrist Arthur Meyerson was one of the many medical professionals who signed up to help the advocates. Interested in doing more than catering to "Park Avenue clients," Meyerson had long been critical of his profession for ignoring the plight of poor people with mental illness. When the Reagan administration's reviews began, he pushed the American Psychiatric Association to establish a committee on the reviews, which he then chaired. From this vantage point, he became a vocal critic of the Reagan administration's policies.[75] By allowing respected experts to critique the SSA's certification process, Meyerson and MHLP lawyers hoped to educate policymakers on the shortcomings of the SSA's disability determination in cases of mental illness and undermine the agency's authority on matters of disability.[76] Later when advocates sought to overhaul the SSA's standards for evaluating disabled children, they again drew on the authority of medical professionals critical of the SSA's methods for evaluating childhood disability.

Finally, advocates treated litigation as one prong in a multifaceted strategy that was mindful of the importance of administrative details. Given their background in the patients' rights movement, mental health advocates were predisposed to turn to the federal courts to halt the reviews. But they were also aware of their shortcomings. Rubenstein argued that although litigation was "highly promising," favorable court decisions were the beginning rather than the end of an advocate's work. From their failed attempts to establish the right to social assistance for patients living in the community, advocates had learned that judges were often "reluctant to involve themselves in the implementation of their decisions," a process which involved making complex funding decisions that courts preferred leaving to legislatures. Because the judiciary remained "limited in its ability to effect the systematic changes necessary" to achieve meaningful community mental health care, Rubenstein encouraged advocates to take advantage of the "complex interplay among judicial decisions, legislation, and executive action."[77] Under this approach,

73. Leonard S. Rubenstein, interview with author.
74. Ibid.
75. Arthur T. Meyerson, phone interview with author.
76. Leonard S. Rubenstein, interview with author.
77. Rubenstein and Bloom, "Courts and Psychiatric Disability," 442, 447.

litigation could instigate the process of reform, as successes in the court-room were then leveraged into the desired legislative and administrative changes. Of course, this meant that advocates were often brought into the "seemingly mundane behavior of bureaucracies." But, Rubenstein argued, even incremental changes in administrative practice could translate into significant liberalizations of policy.[78]

The Decision to Launch an Advocacy Campaign on Three Political Fronts

The retrenchment battles of 1981–84 set the stage for a new way of looking at disability. On one side, there was the narrow, clinical under-standing of disability, developed when workload pressures in the late 1970s compelled the SSA to move away from "careful development and monitoring and toward expedition and productivity." Though inspired by an effort to provide a "more 'manageable' and 'objective' approach to adjudication," this clinical model of disability did not necessarily comport with "better-quality adjudication."[79] Ironically, the SSA's efforts to accen-tuate the clinical aspects of impairment took disability determinations further from the medical knowledge that was supposed to serve as the basis of decision making. One disability examiner explained, "In its overemphasis on objective results, SSA overlooks the way medicine is practiced in the real world. A physician does not evaluate a patient solely on the basis of test results. . . . Objective factors, combined with subjec-tive factors lead the doctor to form an overall judgment as to how im-paired the patient is."[80] Advocates agreed. Indeed, from their point of view, while the SSA's quest for objectivity was understandable, it became unreasonable when it prized objectivity about all else, ignoring the real-world consequences of decision making. One MHLP lawyer complained about the SSA's medical staff: "The idea of assessment had completely overtaken the question of *what* was being assessed. For Nussbaum and his colleagues, obtaining agreement on *anything* was more important than the consequences or meaning of that agreement."[81]

Thus, on the other side was the liberal approach favored by advocates, which directed the emphasis from objective clinical measures of disability to functional deficits. Though unavoidably subjective, this approach re-

78. Rubenstein, "Treatment of the Mentally Ill," 1266.
79. Jerry L. Mashaw, *Bureaucratic Justice: Managing Social Security Disability Claims* (New Haven, CT: Yale University Press, 1985), 176.
80. House Select Committee on Aging, *Cessations and Denials*, 111.
81. Rubenstein, "Science, Law, and Psychiatric Disability," 13.

tained an acute awareness of the human needs that the Social Security disability programs served. Of course, the shift from an approach that looked at objective clinical measures and one that emphasized functional deficits was so subtle that it might be tempting to regard it as a distinction without a difference. But the implications for disability certification were enormous. In a system as large as Social Security with a significant number of borderline cases, small shifts of emphasis could translate into considerable changes in the aggregate size and costs of the programs. It was the difference between, on the one hand, letting onto the disability rolls individuals who did not work *because of* a medical impairment, and on the other, granting benefits to individuals who did not work *and happened to have* a medical impairment.

Given the political animosity it engendered and the devastating effect it had on the nation's disabled, the Reagan administration's purge of the Social Security disability rolls provided the advocacy community with a renewed focus and an opportunity to advance the functional understanding of disability. Attempting first to halt the reviews and then later expand DI and SSI to excluded groups, advocates began in the federal courts. They then used these judicial victories to leverage additional gains with skeptical lawmakers and administrative officials. The following chapters trace the advocates' campaign to broaden Social Security through three political forums: the courts, Congress, and the SSA.

5

Contesting Disability in Court

Given that it was born of the litigation crusade on behalf of patients' rights, the MHLP instinctively turned to the federal courts to stop the disability reviews. But the first time that mental health lawyers tried to challenge the SSA's mental impairment policy, they were met with stinging disappointment. In 1982, a federal district court flatly dismissed their claim that the standards "[bore] no factual or rational relationship to the actual psychiatric condition and disability of the plaintiffs involved." The court refused to strike down the agency's rules simply because advocates thought them too strict.[1] Over the next several years, the situation changed dramatically. The advocates became well versed in the intricacies of both disability evaluation and psychiatric, pediatric, and rehabilitation medicine. With this knowledge in hand, they presented a compelling legal claim buttressed with a powerful medical logic. At the same time, judges became less willing to defer to the SSA's expertise and asserted their own understanding of disability, aided, of course, by the medical reasoning offered by advocates. Begun in the early 1980s as a desperate attempt to halt the Reagan revolution, by the late 1980s and the 1990s, legal challenges to the SSA's standards and rules had evolved into a full-scale effort to restructure disability policy to bring it closer to the ideal of social inclusion.

This chapter examines the litigation strategy the advocates used to

1. The case was *H.J. v. Schweiker* (1982) and is recounted in Leonard S. Rubenstein, Antoinette A. Gattozzi, and Howard H. Goldman, "Protecting the Entitlements of the Mentally Disabled: The SSDI/SSI Legal Battles of the 1980s," *International Journal of Law and Psychiatry* 11 (1988): 271.

expand the availability of DI and SSI benefits to the mentally ill, disabled children, and alcoholics. It explains how the federal courts, largely quiescent and only sporadic participants in the past, became energized by the disability reviews and emerged by the 1990s as a vigorous force in Social Security policymaking. Yet the effort to remake Social Security disability policy through the courts was not without problems. As this chapter also explains, administrative confusion and political controversy were the inadvertent consequences of judicial activism.

Given its far-reaching effects on Social Security disability policy, what is so surprising about the advocates' litigation campaign is how little public attention it received. Few of these legal challenges reached the Supreme Court; fewer still attracted any media or congressional interest. Instead, concerned with the finer points of disability certification, the court rulings would have been difficult for those unfamiliar with Social Security policy to understand. Still, their cumulative effect pushed disability determination away from the standardized clinical criteria the SSA had endorsed toward the much looser and individualized understanding of disability favored by the reformers. Reflecting on a decade of progress, one Legal Services attorney proudly declared, "[The] litigation has been more successful than could have possibly been imagined."[2] This was no exaggeration.

The Politicization of the Federal Courts

Because the Social Security Act allows federal judges to hear the appeals of claimants who have lost or been denied benefits, policymakers long recognized the courts as a potentially expansive force in disability benefits programs.[3] There are two reasons why courts have this tendency. First, because the Social Security Act has so little to say about what constitutes a disability, it opens the door to rival interpretations, even among well-intentioned parties using the same rules. Second, although both judges and administrators perform essentially the same function (that is, translating general statutory mandates into specific

2. Richard P. Weishaupt and Robert E. Rains, "*Sullivan v. Zebley:* The New Disability Standards for Indigent Children to Obtain Government Benefits," *St. Louis University Law Journal* 35, 3 (1991): 595. Weishaupt was one of the two lead attorneys on the case, and he argued the case before the Supreme Court.

3. Deborah A. Stone, *The Disabled State* (Philadelphia: Temple University Press, 1984), 154–55.

rules to be applied to individual claimants), their perspectives differ greatly.[4] Administrators seek to develop workable rules that street-level bureaucrats can readily apply to many cases, and ideally, they balance their humanitarian inclinations with the need for fiscal prudence. Specialists in the areas over which they have responsibility, they can appreciate the deep complexities of a specific policy issue. Judges, on the other hand, are generalists; they hear cases on a broad range of policy issues, and few specialize in any one area.[5] When presented with a case, judges see the litigant before them, not the broad class of cases she represents, the overall program, or annual expenditure levels. Those are abstract issues compared to the immediacy of the litigant's financial needs. Therefore, "judges may be more likely to award benefits in borderline cases, the kinds that get appealed."[6]

For all the worries about judicial intervention, prior to the mid 1970s, the courts had limited impact on Social Security policy. The SSA tended to fare well in appeals that came before the federal bench, and even when it did lose, the agency adopted a policy called "nonacquiescence." It followed the court's ruling in the case of the specific litigant but made little effort to align its policies with judicial precedent. With the onset of the disability reviews in 1981, however, the relationship between the court and SSA took a new and crucial turn. Legal challenges flooded the federal courts as aggrieved claimants appealed their denials and advocates bundled hundreds or thousands of individual cases into massive class action lawsuits designed to alter the rules of disability determination. By the fall of 1983, the SSA was defending itself against 34,400 lawsuits, including 95 class action cases.[7] Fearing that it would lose control of the disability programs, the SSA dug in its heels. Despite several high-profile rulings striking down the SSA's disability standards, the agency flatly refused to apply the logic of the courts except in the case of the actual litigant. Ordering SSA adjudicators to ignore adverse judicial precedent unless it was a Supreme Court decision, a high-ranking

4. Martin M. Shapiro, cited in Martha Derthick, *Agency under Stress: The Social Security Administration in American Government* (Washington, DC: Brookings Institution Press, 1990), 131.

5. Donald L. Horowitz, *The Courts and Social Policy* (Washington, DC: Brookings Institution Press, 1977), 22–67.

6. Susan Gluck Mezey, *No Longer Disabled: The Federal Courts and the Politics of Social Security Disability* (Westport, CT: Greenwood Press, 1988), 55.

7. *Newsday*, October 3, 1983, 13, cited in *DeLeon v. Secretary of Health and Human Services*, 734 F.2d 930, 931 n. 1 (2nd Cir. 1984), and Carolyn A. Kubitschek, *Social Security Disability: Law and Procedure in Federal Court* (Deerfield, IL: Clark Boardman Callaghan, 1994), 37–38.

agency official defiantly declared, "The Federal courts do not run the SSA's programs."[8]

But by refusing to treat the opinion of federal district and appellate courts as binding precedent in their respective jurisdictions, the SSA violated a deeply held legal tradition.[9] This, more than anything else, politicized the courts. Judges regarded the agency's refusal to accept the authority of the lower courts as a direct challenge to the power of the federal bench, a move that enraged them and strengthened their determination to bring the SSA into line. Between 1981 and 1984, judges issued hundreds of contempt citations against the agency, and the language they used in their opinions became increasingly bitter as the reviews progressed. One judge excoriated the SSA for taking advantage of disabled claimants who "lack[ed] the financial resources, litigational persistence, or physical or mental stamina" to seek judicial relief.[10] Another called the SSA's actions an "ill-advised policy" that "not only scoffs at the law . . . but flouted some very important principles basic to our American system of government."[11] Yet others accused the SSA of "stupidity," "extreme callousness," and "bureaucratic dishonesty."[12]

All this animosity redounded to the benefit of the advocates. Shep Melnick explains, "Judges' images of the administrative process are of the utmost importance because the central issue in administrative law is the

8. Louis Hayes, Memorandum to SSA ALJs, January 7, 1982, quoted in *Stieberger v. Heckler*, 615 F. Supp. 1315, 1351 (S.D.N.Y. 1985). The SSA's practice of "nonacquiescence" was not new. Prior to the review, the agency would follow the court's directives in the case of the specific litigant, and because the system of disability determination was such a large and complex enterprise, few noticed the SSA's disregard for precedent. But the SSA could pursue this strategy only when the number of appealed cases and the attention surrounding them was small. The disability reviews, however, quadrupled the number of cases appealed to the courts and brought thousands of aggrieved claimants before judges, making the SSA's failure to comply obvious. Jerry L. Mashaw, Charles J. Goetz, Paul R. Verkuil, Milton M. Carrow, and Warren F. Schwartz, *Social Security Hearings and Appeals: A Study of the Social Security Administration Hearing System* (Lanham, MD: Lexington Books, 1978), 140.

9. The full story behind the contest over medical improvement and nonacquiescence is beyond the scope of this book, but for an excellent analysis, see Derthick, *Agency under Stress*, 135–51.

10. *Stieberger*, 615 F. Supp. at 1363.

11. *Lopez v. Heckler*, 713 F.2d 1432, 1441 (9th Cir. 1983), Judge Harry Pregerson, concurring.

12. *Sanders v. Secretary of Health and Human Services*, 649 F. Supp. 71 (N.D. Ala. 1986); *Cannon v. Heckler*, 627 F. Supp. 1370 (D.C. N.J. 1986); and *Boyd v. Secretary of Health and Human Services*, 626 F. Supp. 1252 (W.D.N.Y. 1986). For these and additional quotations demonstrating the hostility between the judiciary and the SSA, see Kubitschek, *Social Security Disability*, 9 n. 34.

extent to which judges should defer to administrative judgment and expertise. Judges are unlikely to defer to administrators they do not trust."[13] By the time the reviews ended in 1984, few judges trusted the SSA. Surveying the situation, SSA officials themselves admitted, "The agency's credibility before the courts is at an all-time low."[14] As a result, the SSA suffered a string of humiliating defeats in court, which continued long after the reviews were over. Between 1976 and 1981, federal judges reversed only 13 to 18 percent of the SSA's decisions. But by 1984, the federal courts were reversing the SSA's decision in more than half the disability cases appealed, and this did not include the substantial number of cases the courts remanded back to the agency for further adjudication.[15] Though the number of reversals tapered off once the controversy over the disability reviews subsided, through the late 1980s, rates of reversals remained higher than what they had been during the previous decade.[16]

The demise of the SSA's standing is reflected in the contrast between two cases, *Schweiker v. Gray Panthers* from 1981 and *Sullivan v. Zebley* in 1990. In *Gray Panthers*, the Supreme Court refused a legal challenge to the income test for SSI, arguing that the SSA "rather than to the courts," should have "the primary responsibility for interpreting" legislation that was so "Byzantine" that it was "almost unintelligible to the uninitiated."[17] Nine years later, the justices were not so deferential. Striking down the SSA's childhood disability standard in *Zebley*, the court complained that the rules "make little sense." Compared to the arguments made by the many medical organizations filing amicus briefs on behalf of Brian Zebley, the SSA's line of reasoning, the court concluded, was "unconvincing" and "not persuasive."[18] The justices may have been uninitiated, but they would no longer shy away from asserting their own views of Social Security policy.

13. R. Shep Melnick, "Administrative Law and Bureaucratic Reality," *Administrative Law Review* 44 (1992): 245, 246.

14. Lou Enhoff, quoted in Edward D. Berkowitz, *Disabled Policy: America's Programs for the Handicapped* (Cambridge: Cambridge University Press, 1987), 140.

15. U.S. Congressional Research Service (CRS), prepared by David Koitz, Geoffrey Kollman, and Jennifer Neisner, *Status of the Disability Programs of the Social Security Administration*, 1992, table 88, 155.

16. Ibid., table 88, 155. See also Mashaw et al., *Social Security Hearings and Appeals*, table 5–1, 129, for figures on the early 1970s; they were not appreciably different from the 1976–81 period.

17. *Schweiker v. Gray Panthers*, 453 U.S. 34, 43 (1981).

18. *Sullivan v. Zebley*, 493 U.S. 521, 539, 541, (1990).

A New Jurisprudence of Disability

Once the appeals came flooding into the federal courts, the Reagan administration's purge of the disability rolls had few defenders. The director of a California disability determination office told Congress that she was in "personal anguish" because she could not "stop what [she] consider[ed] to be an atrocity."[19] Even White House officials recognized that the reviews had gotten out of hand. David Gergen later told an interviewer, "You could see that these people were clearly disabled. They were powerful stories and, apart from the human toll, . . . they enabled our critics to say, with some truth, that our cuts were really hurting poor, disabled people, and we didn't have much defense for that."[20] Across Pennsylvania Avenue, several congressional committees held hearings investigating the reviews, and the titles of these hearings left little doubt as to what lawmakers thought of the purge: "Social Security Disability Reviews: A Costly Constitutional Crisis," "Social Security Disability Reviews: A Federally Created State Problem," and "Social Security Disability Reviews: The Human Costs."[21] Representative Claude Pepper denounced the disability reviews as a "witch hunt" and a "cruel chapter in our nation's history" while Senator Carl Levin called disability adjudication "a system that is in shambles."[22]

The sweeping criticism emboldened the courts to remake disability determination. Two principles guided their approach. First, in keeping with their concern for the specific litigant, the courts held that determi-

19. U.S. House of Representative, Select Committee on Aging, *Social Security Disability Insurance Program: Cessations and Denials*, 97th Congress, 2nd Session, May 21, 1982, 96 (hereafter House Select Committee on Aging, *Cessations and Denials*).

20. Quoted in David Whitman, "Television and the 1981–1984 Review of the Disability Rolls," in Martin Linsky, Jonathan More, Wendy O'Donnell, and David Whitman, *How the Press Affects Federal Policymaking: Six Case Studies* (New York: W. W. Norton, 1986), 309–10.

21. U.S. House of Representatives, Select Committee on Aging, *Social Security Disability Reviews: A Costly Constitutional Crisis*, 98th Congress, 1st Session, 1984; U.S. House of Representatives, Select Committee on Aging, *Social Security Disability Reviews: A Federally Created State Problem*, 98th Congress, 1st Session, 1983; and U.S. Senate, Special Committee on Aging, *Social Security Disability Reviews: The Human Costs*, 98th Congress, 2nd Session, 1984.

22. Claude Pepper in House Select Committee on Aging, *Cessations and Denials*, 1, 3, and Carl Levin in U.S. Senate, Committee on Governmental Affairs, Subcommittee on Oversight, *Oversight of Social Security Disability Benefits Terminations*, 97th Congress, 2nd Session, 1982, 3.

nations of disability should be individually tailored. To the extent possible, they should make a case-by-case assessment of the specific limitations and obstacles that each claimant confronted rather than rely on a universal, routine set of guidelines mechanically applied to all claimants. Second, demonstrating a tendency to defer to professional expertise, the courts held that the rules and procedures that guided the certification of disability should conform to prevailing medical opinion concerning the diagnosis and treatment of injuries and disease. After all, if policymakers viewed disability as a medical phenomenon, then it was reasonable for them to expect determinations of disability to incorporate the norms and beliefs of those trained in medicine. This meant that the courts came down on the side of advocates and their allies in the medical profession who insisted on a functional rather than clinical approach to disability determination.[23]

By following these lines of reasoning, however, the courts advanced a vision of disability that weakened the boundary between sickness and bad behavior. How could examiners tell the difference between a man with a personality disorder and one who was just plain rude, between a child with a learning disorder and one who merely refused to learn? The SSA clung to a clinical interpretation of disability precisely because it was so difficult to distinguish between actions that were willful misconduct and actions that while objectionable were excusable because they were the result of an injury or illness. By insisting on a functional approach to disability determinations, the courts made it harder for the SSA to maintain this distinction.

The difficult questions raised as the courts moved from straightforward cases of disability to more subjective impairments can be seen in the progression from mental disorders, to childhood disability, to addiction. In the case of mental disorders, the courts held that in order for it to provide an accurate assessment, the SSA had to place greater emphasis on a claimant's functioning in a worklike setting as opposed to the severity of clinical symptoms. This was not terribly controversial. In the case of childhood disorders, the courts then demanded that the SSA look at a child's ability to function in an age-appropriate manner across a range of activities. The SSA, however, had difficulty applying the slippery standard of "age-appropriate behavior." Addictions raised even more problems with the SSA. Because the medical profession regarded addiction as an illness, the courts insisted that the SSA treat uncontrollable drinking

23. The need for an individualized assessment and an assessment based on medical knowledge is hinted at in *Mathews v. Eldridge*, 424 U.S. 319, 343–44 (1976).

absent any other clinical signs as a disability. Thus, inappropriate behavior itself became the equivalent of a medical impairment. At this point, the functional approach reached the limits of political acceptability. The rulings disconnected disability from Americans' everyday understanding of the concept and precipitated an administrative breakdown. Thus, as the courts turned from mental to childhood and addictive disabilities, they moved from easy, clear-cut distinctions between illness and behavior to more uncertain territory, in which it became more difficult for judges to justify their decisions based on commonsense notions of disability.

Mental Impairments: From Bureaucratic Rules to Scientific Judgment

Legal Services and MHLP attorneys brought two class action lawsuits contesting the SSA's mental impairments rules and suggesting a more "realistic" and "accurate" interpretation of disability. *Mental Health Association of Minnesota v. Schweiker* (1982) and *City of New York v. Heckler* (1984) were the first cases in which the courts endorsed the functional interpretation of disability favored by reformers.[24] In both, advocates argued that the SSA did not provide the individualized assessment envisioned in the Social Security Act because it relied so heavily on the clinical components of impairment but made little attempt to link the medical condition to an individual's actual ability to find and retain a job. In order to provide a realistic assessment of disability, advocates contended, the SSA needed to place greater emphasis on an individual's capacity to function rather than rely solely on the severity of the clinical signs and symptoms.

The strategy was a ringing success. The physicians called on to testify in the two district court cases were openly scornful of the SSA's clinical approach to disability determination. One psychiatrist dismissed it as "absolutely ludicrous" and called it "a silly notion." Even one of the SSA's own physicians claimed that he was "uncomfortable" with the agency's rigid approach to mental illness because "it did not square with what he knew as a doctor." Another SSA doctor declared that only "in the best possible world" or "some fantasyland" were the claimants who were denied benefits capable of "getting and maintaining some employment."[25] Yet another protested that the SSA was being so unreasonable that an applicant for disability benefits "may be committable due to mental illness

24. *Mental Health Association of Minnesota v. Schweiker,* 554 F. Supp. 157 (D. Minn. 1982), and *City of New York v. Heckler,* 578 F. Supp. 1109 (E.D.N.Y. 1984).
25. *City of New York,* at 1116.

according to the State's Mental Health Codes and yet found capable of 'unskilled work' utilizing our disability standards."[26]

Medical and vocational experts explained to the judges that the clinical approach was a completely unrealistic way of figuring out the ability of a person to work in a competitive situation. A person who appeared sound while taking medication or engaging in therapy, they argued, might very well deteriorate if placed in the stressful environment of a job. Indeed, even without "active delusions," experts told the judges, claimants might still be disabled since the side effects of many powerful psychotropic drugs rendered "a patient unable to work." Said one doctor, a severe mental illness is a "disorder of energy" that that created an "inability to get motivated to get started" and that left a "residual person . . . [who was] really unable to sustain . . . activity for any period of time."[27] Strict attention to clinical findings alone failed to take into account the intricacies of mental disabilities, including the episodic nature of symptoms, the ameliorative effects of medication and therapy, and the importance of longitudinal evaluations from physicians familiar with the claimant's medical history.[28]

In both cases, the judges were convinced. Citing the testimony of the medical experts at trial, the district court in *Mental Health Association of Minnesota* overturned the SSA's mental disability certification process, characterizing it as having "no medical, vocational or other empirical or scientific basis" whatsoever.[29] The court noted that in contrast to the "extensive and knowledgeable testimony" offered by the medical experts, the SSA had "conducted no studies of its own" nor presented studies of others that would support its practice of using clinical signs as the sole predictor of work capacity. Finding this unacceptable, the judge called the SSA's mental impairment rules "arbitrary, capricious, irrational, and an abuse of discretion."[30] The district court in *City of New York v. Heckler* agreed. Judge Jack Weinstein was even more biting in his rebuke of the SSA, denouncing the agency's disability determination process as nothing more than a "paper charade," in which staff physicians "completed a cursory report . . . knowing the conclusion had to be that the claimant" would be denied benefits.[31] Appalled at the "disdainful professional atti-

26. *Mental Health Association of Minnesota*, 554 F. Supp. at 162.
27. *City of New York*, 578 F. Supp. at 1115.
28. *Mental Health Association of Minnesota*, 554 F. Supp. at 162.
29. Ibid., at 163.
30. Ibid., at 166.
31. *City of New York*, 578 F. Supp. at 1124.

tude" toward the SSA's assessment practices, Weinstein excoriated the SSA for the fact that "physicians were pressured to reach 'conclusions' contrary to their own professional beliefs." From the point of view of the judges like Weinstein, the problem was not one of rival interpretations of disability. Instead, the problem was that the SSA promoted "bureaucracy over professional medical judgments" in order to meet the Reagan administration's budget projections.[32] Politics, not science, appeared to drive decision making.

In place of the SSA's disability standards, the courts substituted the remedies suggested by advocates. Both courts ordered the SSA to reopen denied claimants and redetermine eligibility using "proper standards" that were "based on a realistic assessment of the individual's remaining capacity to function in the conditions of the real world of work." This meant that, at least in the Midwest and New York regions where the two district court opinions applied, clinical symptoms were no longer the sole or even the most important factor to be weighed in the disability examination. Adjudicators were required to give consideration to each individual's ability to function, the effects of medication, the testimony of treating physicians, and the claimant's medical history when making a disability certification.[33] Advocates had succeeded in prying disability determination loose from its strict clinical moorings and edging it closer to the functional understanding of disability endorsed by the medical community.

Children's Disability

The mental disability cases represented only an opening salvo in the effort to push the SSA toward the adoption of a more individualized and functional approach to disability determination. Litigation did not conclude when the SSA halted the disability reviews in 1984, but instead continued well into the next decade. Two cases in particular, *Sullivan v. Zebley* and *Wilkerson v. Sullivan*, stand out as important in the crusade to restructure disability benefits policy. Community Legal Services (CLS) of Philadelphia, the most aggressive of the advocacy organizations, brought both. Taken together, they reflect the advocacy strategy of combining medical with legal arguments and illustrate the judicial attachment to professional judgment.

32. Ibid., at 1116, 1124.
33. Ibid., at 1125, and *Mental Health Association of Minnesota*, 554 F. Supp. at 168–69.

No single judicial decision better exemplifies the power of the reformers' litigation strategy than the case of *Sullivan v. Zebley*.[34] Born in 1978, Brian Zebley suffered from congenital brain damage, mental retardation, visual problems, developmental delays, and partial paralysis. Enrolled in SSI as a toddler, he became a casualty of the Reagan administration's purge of the disability rolls at the age of five.[35] Begun as a little noted appeal of denied benefits, *Sullivan v. Zebley* evolved into a major class action lawsuit, representing more than 300,000 children. It is one of the few Social Security cases to have ever reached the Supreme Court, and its outcome was by no means a foregone conclusion. Latecomers to disability litigation, the Supreme Court did not hear a Social Security case until 1968, and when it did, it always sided with the SSA. But in late 1990, the justices dealt the SSA a stunning blow. By a vote of 7–2, they struck down the standard that the SSA had been using for seventeen years to evaluate childhood disabilities. It was the first time the court had ever overturned an agency rule, and in one fell swoop, it threw the entire children's program into disarray.

That CLS attorneys were able to persuade a rather conservative court to accept the functional approach is a testament to their cleverness. Several early challenges to the SSA's rules for evaluating childhood disability had failed, in part because there seemed little legislative evidence that Congress had intended for the SSI children's program to be broad. When lawmakers enacted the 1972 Social Security amendments, making children eligible for SSI, they had left the details of disability determination to the SSA. The law stated that a child would qualify for benefits if she had an impairment of "comparable severity" to one that would disable an adult. But because children did not work, SSA officials were unsure about how to apply the adult definition of disability to children. The final regulations, published in 1977, revealed the SSA's preference for emphasizing the medical aspects of disability. According to rules drafted by the Office of Disability, children could qualify only if they satisfied the medical criteria contained in the Listings, the SSA's catalog of disabling conditions. Children had to meet the standards contained in either the Listings used to evaluate adults or a supplemental set of Listings drawn up specifically for childhood disorders. Unlike adults, children could not qualify under the individualized tests of functioning and vocational factors since, the Office of Disability argued, these were used to assess

34. *Sullivan v. Zebley*, 493 U.S. 521 (1990).
35. The facts of Zebley's case are described in the appellate court decision, *Zebley v. Bowen*, 855 F.2d 67, 70–71 (3rd Cir. 1988).

whether a claimant *could actually work*. And since children did not work, these tests did not apply to them. The Office of Disability insisted that because the children's Listings contained "modifications of the adult criteria . . . to take into account the different impact" that diseases had on children, this "lessen[ed] any inequity that could result because of the absence" of an individualized test of functional and vocational factors.[36] Accordingly, "comparable severity" for children did not require a disability determination process identical to that used for adults but instead one that would reach largely the same substantive results. Ultimately, SSA officials were not necessarily satisfied with what they had come up with. They realized that the approach was somewhat incoherent, but according to one official, they concluded that "it's better than nothing."[37]

By all accounts, the committees overseeing Social Security were happy with this approach. Lawmakers on the Senate Finance Committee and the House Ways and Means Committee were well aware of the fact that the SSA did not weigh the nonmedical components of a disability when the claimants were children. For instance, in its report to accompany the 1972 amendments, the House Ways and Means Committee explicitly stated that for the SSI program, the definition of disability would encompass assessments of functional and vocational characteristics for any individual "other than a child under 18."[38] Later, in reports issued in 1976 and 1977, the Finance Committee noted that the SSA did not weigh individual factors when deciding children's claims because "as a group they" do not have "enough attachment to the labor force to make application of these factors feasible."[39] Advocates and at least one member of the Finance Committee, Senator William Hathaway of Maine, suggested

36. 42 *Federal Register* 14705–14706 (1977), and 45 *Federal Register* 55566, 55570–55571 (1980).

37. Mary Ross, former career SSA official, Social Security Administration, interview in the Oral History Collection, October 26, 1995, and February 13, 1996, transcripts in the SSA Archives, Office of the Historian, Social Security Administration, Baltimore, Maryland.

38. U.S. House of Representatives, Committee on Ways and Means, *Social Security Amendments of 1971*, H. Rept. No. 92–231, 92nd Congress, 2nd Session, 1972, 147–48.

39. For instance, a 1976 Senate report observed that the SSA's process for determining disability in children required a child to meet the medical criteria contained in the Listings or, failing that, be found to have an impairment that is the medical equivalent of a listed impairment. U.S. Senate, *Unemployment Compensation Amendments of 1976*, S. Rept. No. 94–1265, 94th Congress, 2nd Session, 1976, 24. The following year, after the SSA had issued its final rules for the children's disability program, a Finance Committee staff report again noted with approval that in children's cases, the disability certification process heavily weighted the medical factors. U.S. Senate, Committee on Finance, *The Supplemental Security Income Program*, 95th Congress, 1st Session, 1977, 125.

that the SSA consider the ability of a child to function in an age-appropriate manner in the areas of learning, speaking, and socializing and that it treat education and family background as vocational factors.[40] But they failed to persuade most committee members, who never once insisted that the SSA change its administrative practices.

Given that the legislative history showed that the SSA and Congress had largely been in agreement, previous legal challenges to the SSI children's program had not fared well.[41] The CLS attorneys who brought the *Zebley* case, therefore, adopted new tactics. First, they urged the court to use a textualist reading of the statute, a method of statutory interpretation, long endorsed by conservative Supreme Court justice Antonin Scalia, in which judges ignored the legislative history and looked only at the plain words of a statute when deciphering its meaning. If the justices looked no further than the statutory language, CLS attorneys could skirt the fact that not only were the overseeing committees knowledgeable about the SSA's childhood disability determination practices but also that they had refused to heed suggestions from advocates and other lawmakers that the criteria be loosened. In fact, it was the dissenting justices, Byron White and William Rehnquist, who were left singing the praises of legislative history.

In addition, CLS attorneys needed to show why the SSA's practices did not result in comparable results and suggest an alternative procedure that would. Toward this end, they enlisted the help of a formidable coalition of professional and advocacy organizations that submitted amicus briefs backing a functional interpretation of disability. This coalition included respected groups like the American Medical Association, the American Academy of Pediatric Medicine, the American Psychiatric Association, the March of Dimes, Easter Seals, and the Arc.[42] Time and time again, the amicus briefs filed by the professional organizations gave examples of children who were disadvantaged by the use of the Listings alone. Time and time again, the briefs hammered home the point that the SSA's method of evaluating disability went against the grain of accepted medical opinion. The strategy was a ringing success. Justice Harry Blackmun

40. William D. Hathaway, 122 *Congressional Record*, S4025–34026 (September 30, 1976), and 42 *Federal Register* 14706 (1977).

41. See *Powell v. Schweiker*, 688 F.2d 1357 (11th Cir. 1982) and *Hinckley v. Secretary of Health and Human Services*, 742 F.2d 19 (1st Cir. 1984).

42. For profiles of the Community Legal Services of Philadelphia, see Allen Redlich, "Who Will Litigate Constitutional Issues for the Poor?" *Hastings Constitutional Law Quarterly* 19 (1992): 745–82, and Catherine C. Carr and Alison E. Hirschel, "The Transformation of Community Legal Services, Inc., of Philadelphia: One Program's Experience since the Federal Restrictions," *Yale Law and Policy Review* 17 (1998): 319–35.

extensively cited the amicus briefs in his majority opinion striking down the SSA's procedures for evaluating childhood disability.

According to CLS attorneys, the procedural differences between the adult and the children's certification process meant that the results were inherently not "comparable." But they did not assert that the procedural differences held all children to a higher standard than adults. In fact, children applying for SSI were actually more likely to have their claims approved than their adults.[43] Rather than challenge the overall restrictiveness of the childhood standards, Zebley's attorneys focused on certain groups of disabled children. They argued that the Listings-only evaluation process unfairly disadvantaged children with mental disorders, children with multiple or rare impairments, and infants. Infants were too young to take part in many of the clinical tests used by the Listings. And in the case of older children, because the Listings could not enumerate every possible way a child could be disabled or take into account the side effects of medication, they understated the severity of an impairment's impact. Brian Zebley, with his many medical problems, was just such a child. Even though none of the impairments on their own were severe enough to meet the standards contained in the Listings, one would find it hard to believe that a child with so many impairments was not signifi cantly limited in his activities. Although the adult Listings also did not fully index all disorders, for adults failure to satisfy the Listings was not a bar to program participation; the shortcomings were cured through individual functional and vocational tests. Yet the SSA did not afford children this opportunity, thus violating the individualized assessment called for by the Social Security Act. CLS attorneys argued that if adult determinations used individualized functional evaluations because the Listings did not always capture the actual limitations that an impairment placed on a claimant, then a comparable standard for children should include the same tests.

The SSA tried to make the case for its Listings-only approach. In its defense, the agency argued that it could evaluate children like Brian Zebley under the Listings of the most similar disorders or under combina-

43. Author's calculation based on data in tables IV.B1 and IV.B2, Social Security Advisory Board, *1998 SSI Annual Report,* http://www.ssa.gov/OACT/SSIR/SSI98/ssiIV .html. Between 1977 and 1983, the annual final awards rate for children slightly exceeded that for adults. The final award rate for children ranged between 33 and 43 percent. After 1983, the final awards rate for children hovered below that for adults until the *Zebley* decision in 1990, at which point the final awards rate surged and peaked at over 50 percent in 1991 and 1992. That surge can be attributed to the liberalization of the rules, the dispensation of the *Zebley* class, and the adjudication of retroactive claims (as required by the court in the *Zebley* settlement). It again dipped below the final awards rate for adults in 1994.

tions of several Listings. Even though it did not provide for a separate individualized test of functional capacity, the SSA explained that considerations of functioning could be written into the Listings.

The court, however, was unconvinced. In his opinion for the majority, Justice Blackmun cited testimony from medical professionals that what the SSA proposed was an impossibility. The AMA had stated in its amicus brief that it was highly unlikely "that any physician could make meaningful comparisons between extremely rare diseases and the set of clinical criteria listed" by the SSA. Blackmun doubted that lay disability examiners would be able to make such comparisons if trained physicians could not.[44] The approach, he asserted, likely understated the severity of a child's impairment because it did not fully capture all the signs that the claimant presented.[45] The problem, moreover, was widespread. Blackmun noted that the SSA lacked specific Listings for many debilitating childhood disorders, including Down syndrome, spina bifida, muscular dystrophy, fetal alcohol syndrome, infant drug dependency, autism, and AIDS, meaning that children with these disorders were not receiving adequate evaluations of their impairments.[46]

Blackmun furthermore held that any system of disability adjudication that did not take into account a child's level of functioning was out of line with the norms of the medical profession. Attention to clinical severity alone, he noted, failed to take into account the limitations imposed by the side effects of medication or medical treatment and the scientific advances that had been made in pediatric medicine. To hammer home this point, he quoted extensively from the AMA's amicus brief, which had stated that the "biological severity of an illness is an abstraction, measured only by proxies, the most familiar of which are physiological severity, functional severity, and burden of illness." Pitting its professional expertise against that of the SSA, the AMA asserted, "The view that proper study or treatment of pediatric illness or injury must include an assessment of the child's functional capacity to perform age-appropriate activities is well accepted in the medical community."[47] The implication was clear. By refusing to conduct individualized functional assessments of children, the SSA flouted accepted medical practice.

44. Quoting the American Medical Association in *Zebley*, 493 U.S. at 535, n. 17.

45. Blackmun observed that a child claimant with Down syndrome "would have to fulfill the criteria for whichever single listing his medical condition most resembled," which he found unacceptable. Quoting the National Easter Seal Society in ibid., at 531, n. 10.

46. Citing the American Medical Association, in ibid., at 534, n. 13.

47. Quoting the American Medical Association in ibid., at 541, n. 22.

In response to the SSA's assertion that it could draw up better Listings with more attention to functional impact and more cataloged disorders, the court held that no standardized approach could ever conform to congressional intent. Said Blackmun, "No decision process restricted to comparing claimants' medical evidence to a fixed, finite set of medical criteria can respond adequately to the infinite variety of medical conditions and combinations thereof, the varying impact of such conditions due to the claimant's individual characteristics, and the constant evolution of medical diagnostic techniques." Such an approach was not in keeping with "the individualized, functional analysis contemplated by the statute."[48] Although gainful employment could not be used as the yardstick to measure functioning, the court suggested that the SSA could look at a child's ability to appropriately feed herself, dress herself, learn, and play—all activities that the court deemed the "work" of children. But as I explain in chapter 7, examining functioning across so many areas and against an amorphous standard like "age-appropriateness" led to the perception that the SSA accepted children who were not severely disabled. To critics, the agency had gone from one extreme to the other, from turning away children, like Brian Zebley, who had legitimate medical impairments, to accepting children who simply misbehaved, children whom former House Speaker Newt Gingrich called "brat kids."[49]

Alcoholism and Addiction: Bad Behavior or Medical Illness?

If *Zebley* illustrated how the functional interpretation could lead to seemingly less severe impairments entering disability rolls, then *Wilkerson* shows how functionalism could virtually erase the boundary between disability and bad behavior. In *Wilkerson v. Sullivan*, CLS attorneys sought to advance an interpretation of disability that would remove the moralistic value judgments associated with addiction. The SSA had treated addiction-related disabilities with suspicion since it was difficult to disentangle medical dysfunction from destructive misbehavior. The courts, on the other hand, accepted drug addiction and alcoholism as illnesses because the medical profession saw them as such. But by insisting that the SSA treat addiction as a disease, judges impeded the agency's efforts to distinguish misconduct from medical impairments.

48. Ibid., at 539 (italics in original removed).
49. Quoted in Deborah Lutterbeck, "Government by Tantrum," *Common Cause Magazine* 21, 2 (1995): 8 (online document from Expanded Academic).

Before Congress eliminated substance addiction as a qualifying condition for Social Security benefits in 1996, the SSA had experimented with many different ways of evaluating addiction-related impairments. Taken together, these measures exemplify the SSA's conviction that addiction alone, even if severe, could not serve as the basis of an award. The addiction had to be accompanied by another underlying impairment.[50] Beginning in the 1970s, however, several district and appellate courts refused to adopt the SSA's restrictive interpretation of addiction-related disabilities. Citing a developing medical consensus, the Ninth Circuit ruled in 1975 that because the "proposition that chronic alcoholism is itself a disease . . . is hardly debatable today," the "absence of 'underlying' physical or mental impairments as accompaniments or products of the disease . . . is not controlling" for the purposes of determining disability.[51] Two years later, the Eighth Circuit in *Adams v. Weinberger* held that not only was alcoholism a disease in its own right but the proper standards for judging the severity of the impairment was whether the claimant addicted to alcohol "has lost voluntary ability to control its use."[52] Thus, as far as the courts were concerned, addiction was disabling if it was uncontrollable and it prevented the claimant from engaging in gainful employment. The claimant did not have to prove any other physiological or anatomical abnormality.

Legal challenges to the SSA's addiction standards culminated in the case of *Wilkerson v. Sullivan,* a class action lawsuit brought in 1990 in the Third Circuit. In 1985, following the passage of the 1984 Disability Benefits Reform Act, the SSA revised its rules for addiction in an effort to bring them in line with the medical profession's acceptance of addiction a disease.[53] The new rules contained references to other body-system im-

50. Sharon R. Hunt, "Drug Addiction and Alcoholism as Qualifying Impairments for Social Security Disability Benefits: The History, Controversies, and Congressional Response," Ph.D. diss., Brandeis University, 2000, 60–68, and William Bartosch, "Defining Addiction as a Disability: Congress, the Courts, and the SSA," paper delivered at the Annual Meeting of the New England Political Science Association, April 30–May 1, 1999.

51. *Griffis v. Weinberger,* 509 F.2d 837 (9th Cir. 1975). A full discussion of the many court decisions in addiction-related disabilities is beyond the scope of this book, but see Hunt, "Drug Addiction and Alcoholism"; Bartosch, "Defining Addiction as a Disability"; Nicole Fiocco, "Notes and Comments: The Unpopular Disabled: Drug Addicts and Alcoholics Lose Benefits," *Administrative Law Review* 49, 4 (1997): 1007–29; and Notes, "Alcohol Abuse and the Law," *Harvard Law Review* 94, 7 (1981): 1660–1712.

52. *Adams v. Weinberger,* 548 F.2d 239 (8th Cir. 1977).

53. Howard H. Goldman, professor of psychiatry at the University of Maryland School of Medicine and a participant in the 1983–85 workgroup to rewrite the adult mental disorders Listings, phone interview with author, February 26, 2000.

pairments, such as organic brain damage, mental impairments, liver damage, gastritis, and pancreatitis, and stated that the severity of the claimant's addiction should be measured against the referenced impairments.[54] But CLS attorneys called the new Listings a "sham."[55] In *Wilkerson*, they argued that the allusions to referenced impairments meant that the new rules still required claimants to show physical or "psychological manifestations before a substance abuse disorder can be conclusively found to be disabling." This, they contended, flew in the face of judicial rulings that stated that addiction, if uncontrollable, could constitute a claim of disability on its own.[56]

Ultimately, the Third Circuit sided with the SSA, but even in upholding the agency's rules, the court endorsed the logic of the advocates. Giving the SSA the benefit of the doubt, the court chose to view the referenced impairments as present only to help disability examiners measure the functional impact of the alcoholism on the claimant, not as an additional physical or mental impairment the claimant had to demonstrate. "In its capsule definition," the court stated, "the listing recognizes that alcoholism is a separate, valid cause of disability" that "by itself, can, if severe enough, constitute a disability."[57] Examiners who took the strict approach, it assumed, simply misunderstood prevailing policy. Addressing its opinion to Louis Sullivan, the secretary of Health and Human Services, the court urged Sullivan to "reduce the risk of further litigation" "by clarifying his listing for substance addiction and by taking steps to advise his subordinates that the former practice is no longer in accord with the law."[58]

Even in defeat, therefore, *Wilkerson* contributed to the loosening of the SSA's addition standards. As one career official explained, anytime the SSA issued a new rule or provided additional instruction, it prompted expansion, in part, because the publicity led to more applications.[59] Moreover, when the SSA attempted to explain the ramifications of the court's decision, some state disability determination offices thought that the agency was adopting a more liberalized attitude toward addiction rather

54. The Listings of Mental Disorders, 20 C.F.R. 404, Subpart P, Appendix I, section 12.09 (1985).

55. *Wilkerson v. Sullivan*, 727 F. Supp. 925, at 932 (E.D.P.A. 1989).

56. Ibid., at 932.

57. *Wilkerson v. Sullivan*, 904 F.2d 826, 845 (3rd Cir. 1990).

58. Ibid., at 850–51, 851, n. 21.

59. John Ritter, former executive program policy officer for the Office of Disability, Social Security Administration, interview in the Oral History Collection, August 16, 1995, transcripts in the SSA Archives, Office of the Historian, Social Security Administration, Baltimore, Maryland.

than simply clarifying old policy. Furthermore, by urging examiners to make sure they rendered correct decisions, the new instructions could have made adjudicators more aware of the problems of addiction and thus more willing to tip the balance in the claimant's favor.[60]

As the addiction court cases illustrate, judges insisted on removing the moral stigma associated with controversial disorders like addiction. Because they were manifestations of a disease, the courts held that these disabilities should be dealt with through humane consideration of individual needs rather than through hard-and-fast bureaucratic rules that embodied unscientific moral judgments. The Third Circuit's decision in *Wilkerson* exemplifies this viewpoint. Recounting the evolution of Social Security disability case law on addiction, the court explained that in the past it was understandable for the SSA to take a hard line on alcoholism. This approach, the court reasoned, "was arguably consistent with the formerly prevailing social and legal view that an alcoholic is simply an individual who lacks the will or moral fiber to curb his self-indulgence." But "as the medical profession, along with many segments of society, came to believe that alcoholics were victims of disease," then its "refusal to recognize alcoholism and other substance addiction disorders as independent causes of disability" became unacceptable. The court then noted that its role was to compel the SSA to accept the prevailing medical opinion.[61]

The Anomalies in the Many Meanings of Disability

Judicial activism pushed the SSA to develop a more thorough and arguably more accurate certification process. As a result of many court rulings, the SSA was driven to gather more evidence about its claimants, consider medical as well as nonmedical sources of information, and become more exacting in how it examined evidence. Perfunctory reviews that resulted in denials were no longer likely to withstand judicial scrutiny.

But by complicating administrative practices, efforts to reform Social Security disability through the courts spawned their own problems. The accumulating layers of court decisions and ad hoc administrative responses resulted in fragmented disability standards, uncertain and confusing administration, and an inherently expansive interpretation of disability. These troubles were far from trivial matters. By 1990, deterioration of

60. Hunt, "Drug Addiction and Alcoholism," 66, and Bartosch, "Defining Addiction as a Disability," 13–14.

61. *Wilkerson*, 904 F.2d at 834–35.

the SSA's administrative capacities and growing DI and SSI enrollments—both of which had been facilitated by the courts—prompted a political backlash against the expansive, functional understanding of disability that advocates had championed.

The Fragmentation of Policy

Only the decisions of the Supreme Court apply nationwide; otherwise, the legal precedent is binding only within the district or circuit in which it is issued. But courts do not always speak with one voice. As a result, if policy is not rendered uniform by a Supreme Court decision, lower court judges developing rules of disability determination on their own can splinter the nation's disability standards, turning them into a patchwork of differing rules and regulations. Indeed, fear of fragmentation is one of the reasons that the SSA strongly resisted judicial intervention despite the fact that it enraged judges and undercut the Reagan administration's disability reviews. At a practical level, tailoring practices to the controlling precedent in each region was an administrative nightmare. As Paul Simmons, the acting commissioner during the disability reviews, explained to Congress, "We would need to keep track of applicants as they move through the decision-making process, determine which circuit law should apply, and separately handle claims by jurisdiction." The task would become even more complicated if there "are conflicting decisions within a single circuit, or a claimant or beneficiary changes residence while a decision on appeal is pending."[62] Most important, in principle, fragmentation flew in the face of everything Social Security stood for. Program founders had taken great pride in the fact that Social Security, unlike public assistance, was not subject to regional disparities. Agency officials, like their predecessors, strongly believed that from the standpoint of equity, it was unfair to beneficiaries "to subject claims to different standards depending on where they reside."[63]

Nevertheless, by the early 1990s, these fears had come to pass. In 1988, under mounting political pressure, the SSA gave up its policy of nonacquiescence and agreed to apply judicial precedent within circuits.[64] Within a few years, federal courts had issued rulings that touched every

62. U.S. Senate, Committee on Finance, *Social Security Disability Insurance Program*, 98th Congress, 2nd Session, 1984, 106.

63. U.S. House of Representatives, Committee on Ways and Means, Subcommittee on Social Security, *Social Security Disability Insurance*, 98th Congress, 1st Session, 1983, 37. These points are also made in Derthick, *Agency under Stress*, 141–43.

64. 53 *Federal Register* 46628 (1988).

aspect of the disability programs. They reworked the criteria the SSA used to evaluate cardiovascular disease, AIDS and HIV, pain, diabetes, and hypertension.[65] They even contested routine administrative details, including the methods for calculating the amount of SSI payments, counting veterans' benefits, determining whether the claimant's impairment has lasted for twelve months or longer as required by law, and deciding whether a claimant's impairment was "severe" enough to warrant benefit payments.[66] In 1992, the SSA confronted forty-six threatened or pending class action lawsuits and thousands of individual lawsuits dealing with issues pertaining to its disability programs.[67] Analysts reported to Congress that the situation was so dire that the SSA's operations threatened to break under the sheer weight of litigation. "The Federal courts' influence is so extensive," they noted, "that SSA has difficulty contesting the many decisions rendered against it." As a result, "different standards are now in operation across the country depending on the judicial circuit in which someone lives."[68]

Inconsistent and Confusing Disability Rules

Extensive judicial involvement in disability adjudication also contributed to uncertainty in the disability determination process because courts within the same circuit sometimes established internally conflicting standards. For example, in the early 1980s, the Second Circuit was unable to articulate a consistent rule regarding the evaluation of pain. In 1980, it held that allegations of pain did not have to be "supported by 'objective' clinical or laboratory findings" and that "subjective pain may serve as the basis for establishing disability, even if such pain is unaccompanied" by clinical findings.[69] Three years later, however, it retreated from this position, ruling instead that "some impairment [relating to the

65. *New York v. Sullivan*, 906 F.2d 910 (2nd Cir. 1990); *Rosetti v. Sullivan*, 788 F. Supp. 1380 (E.D. Pa. 1992); *Luna v. Bowen*, 834 F.2d 161 (10th Cir. 1987); *Polaski v. Heckler*, 739 F.2d 1320 (8th Cir. 1984); and *Hyatt v. Sullivan*, 899 F.2d 329 (4th Cir. 1990).

66. *Farley v. Sullivan*, 983 F.2d 405 (2nd Cir. 1993); *White v. Shalala*, 7 F.3d 296 (2nd Cir. 1993); *Titus v. Sullivan*, 4 F.3d 590 (8th Cir. 1993); and *Bowen v. Yuckert*, 482 U.S. 137 (1987). See also *Bailey v. Sullivan*, 885 F.2d 52 (3rd Cir. 1989), and *Dixon v. Sullivan*, 729 F. Supp. 942 (S.D.N.Y. 1992).

67. CRS, *Status of the Disability Programs*, 1–2.

68. Ibid., 4–5.

69. *McLaughlin v. Secretary of Health, Education, and Welfare*, 612 F.2d 701, 704 (2nd Cir. 1980), quoting *Cuter v. Weinberger*, 516 F.2d 1282, 1286–87 (2nd Cir. 1975), and *Marcus v. Califano*, 615 F.2d 23, 27 (2nd Cir. 1979).

pain] must be medically ascertain[ed]."[70] That same year, the court changed course again, restating that pain could serve as the basis for an award even if unconfirmed by objective medical evidence.[71] To be fair, pain is one of the most complicated impairments to evaluate, but the constantly fluctuating standards created a conundrum not only for the adjudicators who ran the programs but also for claimants trying to prepare their applications.

Policy in a Vacuum

According to Donald Horowitz, litigation tends to "isolate artificially what in the real world is merged" because it presents only one aspect of a policy question that often requires comprehensive solutions.[72] Judges can only respond to the legal questions brought to them; they do not consider programs whole or revisit the results of their decisions absent a lawsuit. Since the remedies that courts provide fail to take into account the complex connections between social problems, they can result in incoherent policy at best, inadvertently detrimental outcomes at worst. In the case of Social Security, judges focused their rulings on the standards for determining disability: whether the SSA used the right rules or whether the agency had gathered appropriate evidence. But for the SSA, adjudication of initial disability claims was only one of many responsibilities that accompanied the administration of DI and SSI. The agency was also charged with conducting periodic reviews of the disability rolls to ensure that recovered claimants did not continue to receive payments, placing addicts in treatment programs, and referring younger disabled claimants to vocational rehabilitation programs. These administrative duties were not minor considerations. An intrinsic part of disability benefits policy, they existed to ensure that those individuals who received DI or SSI payments acted in a manner that lawmakers and the American public believed was responsible. As such, these duties made disability benefits to controversial groups, like addicts and young people, politically acceptable.

The numerous court decisions handed down in the early 1990s, however, severely compromised the SSA's ability to perform these functions. They bombarded the SSA with additional administrative tasks that taxed its capacity to do anything other than process the claims that the courts

70. *Gallagher v. Schweiker,* 697 F.2d 82, 84 (2nd Cir. 1983).
71. Kubitschek, *Social Security Disability,* 240–41.
72. Horowitz, *Courts and Social Policy,* 73.

pressed on the agency. As part of the settlement in *Zebley*, for instance, the Washington, DC, district court overseeing the case ordered the SSA to contact each of the approximately 450,000 children it had denied between 1980 and 1990, and offer them the opportunity to redetermine eligibility. This in and of itself was a monumental task. But the court also required the SSA to conduct a nationwide publicity campaign informing disabled children and their parents of the fact that the Supreme Court had relaxed program standards. The campaign was so successful that in 1994 alone, SSA field offices received almost a half million applications from children.[73] This amounted to four times the number of children's cases that the SSA handled in a typical year. Nor was the DC district court the only court adding administrative burdens. *New York v. Sullivan* (1990) and *Stieberger v. Sullivan* (1992) were two additional cases in which the courts ordered the SSA to reopen and readjudicate the claims of tens of thousands of class members, some with claims stretching as far back as a decade.[74] Because the SSA did not receive an increase in staff, it was ill-prepared to handle the surge in applications and readjudications.[75] Yet administrative capacity to following through on judicial holdings is not a factor that courts often consider when they hand down their decisions, and in fact, many legal scholars argue that it should not be.[76]

Nevertheless, failure to consider an agency's ability to actually carry out a judicial decree can wreak havoc on program administration and policy outcomes. As a cumulative result of *Zebley* and other lawsuits, a downturn in the economy, and increased outreach programs, congressional investigators estimated that the SSA confronted a backlog of well over 1 million disability claims by 1993—an unprecedented situation that represented four times the number of backlogged cases the SSA carried during the crisis years of 1974–75.[77] Because of these workload pressures, the SSA again diverted its resources away from its periodic reviews. Other important responsibilities, including the referral of younger applicants to rehabilitation and of addicts to treatment centers, never high

73. U.S. General Accounting Office, *Social Security: New Functional Assessments for Children Raise Eligibility Questions*, GAO/HEHS-95-66, 1995, 26–27.

74. *New York v. Sullivan*, 906 F.2d 910 (2nd Cir. 1990), and *Stieberger v. Sullivan*, 792 F. Supp. 1376 (S.D.N.Y. 1992).

75. Staff at state disability determination agencies remained fairly constant, but applications increased from about 1.2 million to close to 2 million between fiscal years 1988 and 1993. See "Notices: Process Reengineering Program; Disability Reengineering Project Plan," 59 *Federal Register* 47887, 47891, 47893–94 (1994).

76. Patricia M. Wald, "Judicial Review in a Time of Cholera," *Administrative Law Review* 49 (1997): 659–70.

77. CRS, *Status of the Disability Programs*, 17–18, 60.

priorities of the agency in the first place, also fell by the wayside.[78] This disjointed approach to disability—in which awards were divorced from corresponding treatment, rehabilitation, and review—was not what law-makers envisioned for the Social Security disability programs. It is also likely not what judges would have wanted had they stopped to consider disability holistically.

An Expansive Reading of Disability

According to Deborah Stone, being expansionist is the only way that judges can put their stamp on the program; otherwise, since only denials are appealed, they are left simply to affirm the SSA's decisions.[79] But judges did not necessarily intend for their decisions to liberalize the disability programs. Instead, seeking to develop a more accurate and realistic certification process, the federal courts articulated an understanding of disability that was grounded on individualized treatment and professional norms. While it may not seem so on its face, this conception of disability contained an inherently expansive logic.

This was the case for two reasons. First, attention to the specific needs and circumstances of claimants inclined the courts toward a charitable reading of the disability rules. For instance, while not explicitly contradicting SSA rulings, the courts pushed the agency toward an ever more individualized approach toward addiction. In 1985, the Third Circuit held that failure to complete a treatment program could be proof of a chronic and disabling addiction.[80] But other courts ruling that same year stated that bouts of sobriety and past success in a treatment program could not be treated as indicative of an individual's ability to control his alcohol intake.[81] In short, there could be no standardized rules on treatment; whether it pointed to a disability depended on individual circumstances. The courts required the SSA to consider evidence that could help a claimant but minimized the significance of evidence that could damage an application.

---

78. See Social Security Advisory Board, *2000 SSI Annual Report*, http://www.ssa .gov/OACT/SSIR/ SSI00/ssiV_A.html, and U.S. General Accounting Office, *Effects of Budget Constraints on SSA Disability Programs*, GAO/T-HRD-88–1, 1987. For a personal account of these pressures, see John Ritter, SSA interview. Ritter worked as an executive program policy officer and chaired a task force on implementing the *Zebley* decision and the DAA treatment requirements during this time period.

79. Stone, *Disabled State*, 154–55.

80. *Purter v. Heckler*, 771 F.2d 682, 698, n.19 (3rd Cir. 1985).

81. *Burton v. Heckler*, 622 F. Supp. 1140 (D. Utah 1985), and *Simmons v. Secretary of Health and Human Services*, 621 F. Supp. 1174 (W.D.N.Y. 1985).

Second, as the courts struggled to make disability certification more accurate, more realistic, and more attentive to individual needs, they also induced decision makers to place increased emphasis on the intangible components of disability. For example, to ground determinations on something concrete, the SSA has long maintained that a claimant alleging a disability due to pain must provide evidence of a medical condition that might serve as the cause of that pain. But a district court in 1988 ruled that psychosomatic pain—that is, pain that an individual claimed to feel—could be debilitating enough to justify a claim, even if there was no objective evidence that the pain existed. "If in a person's mind, he suffers pain," the court held, "then he truly suffers whether the cause and justification are there."[82] Similarly, another court ruled that occupational stress, which the SSA defined as the "demands of work," was not the objective characteristics of the position, but rather, the claimant's subjective reactions to the job. Thus, vocational experts might not consider a particular job too stressful for a claimant with mental illness, but if the claimant believed otherwise, he could be found disabled.[83] By compelling the SSA to take into consideration the claimant's subjective reactions to his impairment and the stresses of work, the courts, no doubt, promoted a certification process that was more precise in the sense that it perhaps better predicted whether a particular claimant could, in fact, endure the pressures of a competitive workplace. But they also shifted adjudication toward matters that were within the power of the claimant to manipulate and away from tangible and objective indicators that the SSA could point to when justifying an award.

The Logic of Judicial Activism

That advocates could have mobilized the federal courts to their cause is a remarkable feat, especially considering that just a few years earlier, MHLP attorneys had found judges unreliable allies in their drive to erect the social safety net for mental patients. Perhaps in the midst of the political uproar concerning disability reviews, some judges came to share the sentiments of appellate court judge Gerald Heaney, who argued that because the "underlying purpose" of the programs was "to ease the economic dislocations and hardships that accompany disability," the Social

82. *Bolling v. Bowen*, 682 F. Supp. 864, 867 (W.D. Va. 1988).
83. *Lancellotta v. Secretary of Health and Human Services*, 806 F.2d 284, 285 (1st Cir. 1986).

Security Act "should be broadly construed and liberally applied to effec-
tuate its humanitarian goals."[84] However, other judges were perhaps also
persuaded to side with the advocates because program expansion could
be tempered by three interlocking principles: individualized assessment,
deference to professional norms, and objective decision making. Together these were the pillars of what Jerry Mashaw calls the "professional
treatment" model of justice. According to this model, "justice lies in having the appropriate professional judgment applied to one's particular situation in the context of a service relationship."[85] Judges wanted disability
determination to take into account the needs and circumstances of each
individual applicant; standardized tests or approaches were unacceptable.
They also wanted determination to be informed by the norms of medical
professionals, who could provide both disinterested objectivity and compassionate expertise. In fact, judges like Jack Weinstein could pride themselves with having elevated "science" above crass political considerations
like budget targets and partisan ideals. With decision making in the
hands of professionals, judges were not troubled by the move toward
program expansion and subjectivity, for in the professional treatment
model, "the incompleteness of facts, the singularity of individual contexts, and the ultimately intuitive nature of judgment are recognized, if
not exalted."[86] So long as the humanitarian and client-serving ethos of
the medical professions guided disability certification, judges were com-
fortable trusting "intuitive" judgment as a necessary step toward a more
accurate assessment of an individual's capacity for employment.

But despite their success in the courts, advocates found it challenging
to capitalize on these gains. Winning a favorable court ruling was a relatively easy matter compared to compelling the SSA to implement its requirements. Federal judges were sometimes willing to monitor and enforce their decisions, but others were not. Take, for instance, *Stieberger v.
Sullivan*, a class-action suit brought in the late 1980s by Legal Services
attorneys in the Second Circuit. The lawsuit sought to require the SSA to
place greater emphasis on the opinions of treating physicians.[87] As part of
the settlement in *Stieberger*, the SSA agreed to publish and distribute to

84. Gerald W. Heaney, "Why the High Rate of Reversals in Social Security Disability Cases?" *Hamline Law Review* 7, 1 (1984): 2.

85. Jerry L. Mashaw, *Bureaucratic Justice: Managing Social Security Disability Claims*
(New Haven, CT: Yale University Press, 1983), 29 (emphasis in original omitted).

86. Ibid., 27.

87. *Stieberger v. Sullivan*, 792 F. Supp. 1376 (S.D.N.Y. 1992). On the limits of
Stieberger, see Robert J. Axelrod, "The Politics of Nonacquiescence: The Legacy of
Stieberger v. Sullivan," *Brooklyn Law Review* 60 (1994): 765–829.

its state disability offices within the circuit a manual of selected Second Circuit decisions that upheld the advocates' viewpoint. Legal Services attorneys hoped that the manual would prevent the SSA from defying the rulings simply by refusing to inform its adjudicators of them. The appellate court accommodated the attorneys by directly overseeing both the writing of the manual and its distribution to state disability offices. But this was an exceedingly tedious, labor-intensive, and protracted process. The *Stieberger* case lasted ten years and consumed countless hours of legal work. Also, it relied extensively on the willingness of the court to intervene—something that advocates would not always be able to count on. In other jurisdictions where appellate courts were not so ready to involve themselves in day-to-day SSA operations, attorneys were obliged to follow a state-by-state litigation strategy, suing individual state disability agencies that, they believed, were not properly following court precedent.[88] In the end, moreover, advocates were not satisfied with simply tweaking mental disability certification in one or two circuits. They wanted the functional and individualized emphasis that the courts demanded to become nationwide policy.[89] As I show in chapters 6 and 7, litigation was only a springboard to lobby for larger victories in legislation and administrative practice.

88. See, for instance, *Samuels v. Heckler,* 668 F. Supp. 656 (W.D. Tenn. 1986); *Boring v. Sullivan,* 1989 WL 281952 (S.D. Ohio 1989); *Day v. Sullivan,* 794 F. Supp. 801 (S.D. Ohio 1991); *Goodnight v. Shalala,* 837 F. Supp. 1564 (D. Utah 1993); and *Cuffee v. Sullivan,* 842 F. Supp. 1219 (W.D. Mont. 1993).

89. "Mental Disability Law in 1984: Presentation of Programs and Struggle for Protections in State Institutions and Services in the Community," *Clearinghouse Review* 18 (1985): 1066–67.

6

From Litigation
to Legislation

Reform is often a process of two steps forward and one step back. Disability advocates in the late 1980s took many steps forward, but a giant step back as well. As they turned from litigation to lobbying, they were able not only to secure the gains they had made in the courts but also to build on them. Moreover, after the Reagan administration's disability reviews ended in 1984, liberal reformers regrouped to push anew for social welfare expansion, and the resilience, even growth, of many programs for the poor during the late 1980s is a testament to their success. On the civil rights front, disability activists in 1990 won passage of the Americans with Disabilities Act, a watershed law that provided protection against discrimination for people with disabilities. But this success was purchased at a steep price. In order to survive in a political climate in which politicians were increasingly skeptical of "big government" and apprehensive over the budget deficit, disability advocates made two crucial tactical choices. First, they downplayed the costs associated with the policy innovations they sought. Whether it was the revision of Social Security's mental disability standard or the enactment of the ADA, advocates assured lawmakers that reforms would not cost more than the nation currently spent on the disabled and might even save money. Second, some disability rights activists even went so far as to encourage lawmakers to see welfare and civil rights as two opposing policy approaches to the problem of disability. As a result, even though lawmakers came to expect the disabled to work, they did little to provide the public resources that could facilitate this. Thus, only half the equation for social inclusion was fulfilled. An emphasis on work and self-sufficiency came to dominate welfare and disability policy, but the income support and social services programs that could have served as a complement to ending the isolation of the underclass poor and the disabled were sorely lacking. This chapter explains how this bifurcation of welfare and disability rights came about.

Social Security Disability Reform in Congress

Although advocates successfully used the courts to halt the Reagan administration's purge of the DI and SSI rolls, they were not satisfied with their judicial victories. Instead, they sought to build on favorable court rulings in two ways. First, the advocates wanted to codify the holdings of advantageous rulings from cases like *Mental Health Association of Minnesota* and *City of New York* into the statutory and regulatory language of the Social Security Act. Otherwise, they feared that once the controversy surrounding the reviews had subsided, the SSA would revert back to its subterranean administrative tightening of the programs.[1] In addition, if court precedent were written into legislation, then district or circuit court opinions would apply nationwide rather than remain limited to the region in which the court had jurisdiction, and they would apply even if the judges were later inclined to change their minds. Second, for advocates, the courts did not go far enough. *Mental Health Association of Minnesota* and *City of New York* had urged the SSA to use the "proper standards" but had said little about what those proper standards were other than to make general recommendations that the SSA pay closer attention to the claimant's vocational profile and medical history. Advocates, however, wanted more than mere tinkering at the margins. Instead, they wanted to reach into the Medical Listings themselves and ingrain an emphasis on functioning. Together with a medical improvement requirement, this change in the medical rules would move a long way toward their goal of building a community-based social safety net.[2] A proper rewriting of the rules

1. See the congressional testimony of Arthur T. Meyerson with the American Psychiatric Association, in U.S. House of Representatives, Committee on Ways and Means, Subcommittee on Social Security, *Social Security Disability Insurance*, 98th Congress, 1st Session, 1983), 149, and U.S. Senate, Committee on Finance, *Social Security Disability Insurance Program*, 98th Congress, 2nd Session, 1984, 193–94, 272 (hereafter Senate Committee on Finance, *SSDI Program* [1984]), and the testimony of MHLP lobbyist Joseph Manes in ibid., 232–33.

2. Senate Committee on Finance, *SSDI Program* (1984), 270. See also "Mental Disability Law in 1984: Presentation of Programs and Struggle for Protections in State Institutions and Services in the Community," *Clearinghouse Review* 18 (1985): 1066.

would expand the eligibility for the mentally disabled while the medical improvement standard would lock these expansions in place. As one mental health advocate explained to the Senate Finance Committee, "Whether the intent is to add to the rolls or purge the rolls, claimants will be judged by ongoing statutory criteria."[3]

In this regard, the court victories were a godsend. The *Mental Health Association of Minnesota* and *City of New York* cases legitimated claims from advocacy groups that the functional interpretation of disability was more accurate than the clinical approach the SSA used. Advocates could point to the courts as proof that Reagan's budget timetables motivated the SSA more than accurate findings of disability. In hearings discussing the reviews, a senator on the Finance Committee suggested that the removal of large numbers of mentally ill beneficiaries might indicate not that the removals were biased or wrong in any way but that there were large numbers of mentally ill claimants who were not really disabled. But MHLP spokesman, Joseph Manes, replied that the "proof" of incorrect removals could surely be found in "the court actions that have almost uniformly found SSA not properly" evaluating the mentally ill.[4] Meanwhile, Arthur Meyerson, a physician for the American Psychiatric Association told lawmakers that the fact that the "federal courts have repeatedly overruled the SSA's decisions to terminate mentally ill patients' benefits" demonstrated that the current "review methods, staff, and philosophy need improvement."[5] Court victories, therefore, served as the stepping stones to a much broader effort to persuade Congress to remake Social Security disability policy.

A New Institutional Environment

The Congress that passed the 1984 Disability Benefits Reform Act (1984 DBRA) was a far cry from the one that had enacted SSI. In the political uproar that followed Reagan's disability reviews, what had once been a close alliance of SSA officials and lawmakers concerned primarily with pacing the growth of Social Security exploded into a vast constellation of public interest groups and policy entrepreneurs in Congress organized around issues of disability. Lawmakers who previously had little involvement in Social Security issues suddenly became key players in the drive toward passage of the 1984 disability amendments. Senators

3. Senate Committee on Finance, *SSDI Program* (1984), 169.
4. Ibid., 273.
5. Ibid., 192.

William Cohen and Carl Levin, for instance, used their positions on the Subcommittee on Oversight (part of the Governmental Affairs Committee) as a platform to publicize problems with the reviews. Meanwhile, John Heinz, the chair of the Senate Special Committee on Aging and a member of the Finance Committee, took a special interest in the plight of the mentally disabled, which he called "the clearest example of abuse and catastrophe."[6] When his colleagues on the Finance Committee proved reluctant to stop the reviews, he used his position on the aging committee to highlight the concerns of mental health advocates. Liberals on the House Select Committee on Aging also became vocal proponents of Social Security disability reform. The aging and government affairs committees were much more amenable to the concerns of the advocacy groups than the two tax committees with jurisdiction over Social Security. Organized around particular constituent groups, the advocacy committees were given free rein to investigate wide-ranging issues. Unlike the Ways and Means and the Finance Committees, they did not have to trouble themselves with balancing the competing interests necessary to craft legislation with a credible chance of passing. Instead they earned their accolades simply by voicing the demands of their particular constituent groups.[7]

Not surprisingly, then, these newcomers were frequently at odds with the traditional overseers of Social Security policy, who had struggled for years to contain program growth and who were not enthusiastic about making disability entitlements more widely available.[8] For instance, as the highest-ranking Democrat on the Finance Committee and, by virtue of having been present for the 1956 vote that created program, the institutional memory on DI, Senator Russell Long was an exceedingly influential voice on Social Security matters. But he remained unmoved by the many heartbreaking stories of needy individuals cut from the disability rolls, adamant as ever that, as he put it, too many beneficiaries "simply do not have the severe disabilities we had in mind when we passed" the pro-

6. Edward D. Berkowitz, *Disabled Policy: America's Programs for the Handicapped* (Cambridge: Cambridge University Press, 1987), 131–36.

7. Martha Derthick, *Agency under Stress: The Social Security Administration in American Government* (Washington, DC: Brookings Institution Press, 1990), 161–62.

8. On the outlook of members of the overseeing legislative committees, see Patricia Dilley, "Social Security Disability: Political Philosophy and History," in *Psychiatric Disability: Clinical, Legal, and Administrative Dimensions*, ed. Arthur T. Meyerson and Theodora Fine (Washington, DC: American Psychiatric Association, 1987), 399. On the difference between advocacy and legislative committees, see also Derthick, *Agency under Stress*, 161.

gram.[9] Similarly, when confronted in early 1982 with the hardship visited on the mentally disabled, Texas representative J. J. Pickle, chair of the Social Security Subcommittee, initially defended the reviews. He explained, "[My] committee feels very strongly that the requirement for a review . . . is proper." Though he admitted, "Some harshness has occurred," he stressed that "that was not the intent . . . when we call in that large a number of people, it is inevitable that that kind of result will happen."[10] In fact, having worked with President Carter to shepherd the 1980 disability amendments through his committee and Congress, Pickle was well aware of the long-standing problems that had plagued disability adjudication. As late as 1982, he was working on legislation to streamline disability evaluation and curtail the influence of the courts, measures that advocates opposed. Eventually, however, Pickle became frustrated with the Reagan administration and threw his weight behind reform.

In the past, opposition from the SSA and the legislative committees would have brought an end to advocacy measures. With the mobilization of new groups and the fragmentation of power following the congressional reforms of the 1970s, this was no longer the case. Though they lacked legislative jurisdiction over Social Security, lawmakers on the advocacy committees nonetheless used their institutional positions to advance the cause of disability reform. Senators Cohen and Levin scrutinized the SSA's conduct of the reviews during hearings of the governmental oversight committee.[11] Meanwhile, when officials for the Department of Health and Human Services and SSA signaled their opposition to disability reform legislation, Heinz threatened to "put on some kind of a road show," holding hearings hammering away at the disability reviews until the White House and Congress reached agreement on a bill.[12] Also, Senators Levin, Cohen, and Heinz twice attempted to attach Social Security disability reform measures as amendments to other pieces of legislation on the floor of the Senate, a move that Representa-

9. Quoted in Linda A. Demkovich, "Administration About-Face on Disability Could be a Political Blessing in Disguise," *National Journal* 16 (April 28, 1984): 825.

10. U.S. House of Representatives, Committee on Ways and Means, Subcommittee on Social Security, *Disability Amendments of 1982*, 97th Congress, 2nd Session, 1982, 18, 25.

11. Cohen and Levin were especially outraged by the agency's attempts to rein in administrative law judges who overturned a large proportion of denials made by state disability examiners. U.S. Senate, Committee on Governmental Affairs, Subcommittee on Oversight of Government Management, *The Role of the Administrative Law Judge in the Title II Social Security Disability Insurance Program*, 98th Congress, 1st Session, 1983.

12. Senate Committee on Finance, *SSDI Program* (1984), 149.

tive Pickle saw as a direct challenge to the institutional prerogatives of the Ways and Means and the Finance committees. The three senators were never successful, but their determination to circumvent the tax committees forced Russell Long and Robert Dole, the chair of the Finance Committee, to draw up their own reform bill, if for no other reason than to stave off efforts to bypass them.[13] This was a striking contrast with the early years when lawmakers accorded the tax committees a great deal of deference and, in the House of Representatives, debated Social Security bills under a closed rule that prohibited amendments.[14]

The Social Security Disability Benefits Reform Act of 1984

With the SSA's disability determination process on the brink of collapse in mid 1983, HHS secretary Margaret Heckler suspended further reviews. Several months later, Congress passed the Social Security Disability Benefits Reform Act of 1984. The bill attempted to resolve some of the most contentious questions that had arisen during the reviews, including how the SSA should assess pain, whether it had to abide by judicial precedent, and whether it had to show that the claimant's medical condition had improved before ending benefits. Though the 1984 amendments were an amalgamation of compromises struck between the House and the Senate, as far as mental health issues were concerned, the law gave advocates much of what they wanted.[15] Far from heralding a renewed commitment to expanding Social Security, however, these measures passed precisely because lawmakers were unaware of the true price of reform. Advocates disguised the major liberal policy innovations as cost-neutral, even cost-saving, devices that would bring outdated SSA

13. Katherine P. Collins and Anne Erfle, "Social Security Disability Benefits Reform Act of 1984: Legislative History and Summary of Provisions," *Social Security Bulletin* 48, 4 (1984): 19, 21–22, 25.

14. Martha Derthick, *Policymaking for Social Security* (Washington, DC: Brookings Institution Press, 1979), 40–42.

15. Howard H. Goldman, professor of psychiatry at the University of Maryland School of Medicine and a participant in the 1983–1985 workgroup to rewrite the adult mental disorders Listings, phone interview with author, February 26, 2000, and Carolyn L. Weaver, "Social Security Disability Policy in the 1980s and Beyond," in *Disability and the Labor Market: Economic Problems, Policies, and Programs*, ed. Monroe Berkowitz and M. Anne Hill (Ithaca, NY: ILR Press, 1986), 41. The legislation had been largely based on a draft bill written by the Arc, the American Psychiatric Association, and the Bazelon Center for Mental Health Law, and introduced by Representative Fortney "Pete" Stark, Senator Carl Levin, and Senator William Cohen, congressional allies of the disability advocates.

evaluation practices in line with current medical thinking. In addition, many of the important details of the proposed changes were devolved to the administrative level, leaving the ultimate financial costs of the proposals difficult to calculate.

To win over skeptical lawmakers, advocates went out of their way to stress the "scientific" nature of the revisions that they supported. For example, James Folsom, a representative of the American Psychiatric Association, explained to Congress in 1982 that advocates were simply asking that the SSA bring its rules into harmony with DSM-III, the APA's most current diagnostic manual, and with what psychiatrists knew about disability. Otherwise, failure to align the rules of disability determination with professional norms and practices created "confusion" and made "SSA evaluation of such disability unnecessarily difficult." Indeed, medical science called for a loosening of the SSA's disability standards. Folsom noted that "good clinical practice" indicated that the SSA expected too much of claimants. The agency required claimants to show the clinical signs of a mental disorder at the very moment of examination as well as an extremely limited ability to function across many different areas before they could qualify for DI or SSI benefits. Folsom argued, however, that such demands flew in the face of what doctors' "experience has shown," leaving out many mentally ill individuals who were utterly incapable of work.[16] Similarly, psychiatrist Arthur Meyerson denounced the conduct of the reviews of the mentally disabled as "contrary to sound medical practice and sound professional clinical practice." Furthermore, he reassured Congress that the reforms advocates endorsed were not meant to break new ground. "The goals of that [revision] should not be confused," he argued. "All we are doing is attempting to update, in light of current psychiatric knowledge and understanding of the illnesses involved, the standards that the Social Security Administration has embodied in their regulations."[17]

That advocates would appeal to the neutrality of scientific standards and medical expertise is understandable, for faith in the power of medicine to render realistic evaluations has guided disability policymaking from the beginning. So strong was Congress's conviction in the power of medicine that even in the 1950s when physicians for the American Med-

16. Letter of James Folsom, American Psychiatric Association, to John Svahn, reprinted in U.S. Senate, Committee on Finance, *Social Security Disability Insurance Program*, 97th Congress, 2nd Session, 1982, 25 (hereafter Senate Committee on Finance, *SSDI Program* [1982]).

17. Senate Committee on Finance, *SSDI Program* (1984), 162, 272.

ical Association denied that accurate determinations were possible, law-makers refused to listen. By contrast, in 1982–84, advocates and the physicians allied with them claimed that not only was it possible for med-icine to play the verifying role that Congress envisioned but that they could show the SSA the way to do this properly. This temptation was dif-ficult for lawmakers to resist.

An additional reason reform was possible is because advocates could hide the costs associated with expansion. They suggested that a disability standard that conformed to "good clinical practice" would not only ren-der disability determination more accurate but also cost little more than current spending levels. In fact, advocates argued, better standards, even if slightly liberalized, might actually result in budget savings since indi-viduals dropped from DI and SSI often ended up reinstitutionalized. One APA psychiatrist emphatically explained to Congress, "State hospitaliza-tion for a year or two costs the taxpayers a hell of a lot more money than maintaining somebody in the community on one of these programs."[18] Another expert noted that even if the federal government ended up sav-ing money, the reviews actually cost American taxpayers more once poli-cymakers included the added costs of shifting the disabled from federal programs to state general assistance programs, appealing Social Security denied claims, and caring for the disabled in local institutions, such as jails, prisons, and outpatient clinics. As he explained, without DI or SSI, "there is a high probability" of a mental patient "moving from a $15,000 per year program in the community to a $35,000 per year program in an institution."[19]

To be sure, pessimists counseled Congress to proceed cautiously. One expert on disability who worked for private insurance companies warned lawmakers that simply revising the Medical Listings to conform to the professional diagnostic norms would not necessarily make disability ad-judication any easier or more objective. He told members of the Senate Finance Committee, "Distinguishing between unemployment and un-employability due to mental problems is extraordinarily difficult. . . . I really doubt that the Secretary and the advisory council together can write regulations that can objectively determine the existence or nonex-

18. Ibid., 276.
19. U.S. House of Representative, Select Committee on Aging, *Social Security Dis-ability Insurance Program: Cessations and Denials*, 97th Congress, 2nd Session, 1982, 207. William Copeland's findings were confirmed by Courtney Peterson and Eric Kingston, "The Effect of Changes in the Federal Disability Programs on State and Local General Assistance Programs," *Journal of Sociology and Social Welfare* 14 (1987): 95–115.

istence of an emotional disability on a consistent and uniform basis." He went on to characterize the efforts as "pretty much wishful thinking."[20]

The reform argument was difficult for conservatives to rebut, however. As Congress wrapped up debate of the 1984 amendments, the SSA, bowing to political pressure, convened a work group of mental health advocates, outside physicians, and its own officials to negotiate revisions to the Medical Listings for mental disorders. The Social Security disability reform bill that finally passed Congress in late 1984 endorsed both the deliberations of the SSA work group and the advocates' contention that the SSA's medical standards were sorely outdated. Noting that "serious questions" had been "raised by the old listings," the amendments required the SSA to rewrite its mental disorders rules so that they reflected current medical thinking and provided a realistic standard of disability. Lawmakers, though, could not predict ahead of time what those rules would look like or how expensive they would be. Thus, they made no attempt to estimate the ultimate cost of the revised Listings, leaving the issues entirely up to the SSA work group and robbing opponents of expansion a palpable budget target. Compared to the heated disagreement surrounding the other issues the reviews raised, including medical improvement and determinations of pain, the provision concerning mental impairments caused hardly a stir. The only difference between the House and Senate on the issue pertained to how soon the SSA would have to publish its new regulations and how far back the redeterminations under the new Listings would reach.[21]

As I explain in chapter 7, the revisions to administrative standards and practices that eventually emerged from the work group were far from incremental updates. By pegging the disability criteria to evolving psychiatric and rehabilitation norms, the new rules ingrained into administrative routine the functional model's emphasis on individual limitations

20. Senate Committee on Finance, *SSDI Program* (1984), 280.

21. U.S. House of Representatives, *Social Security Disability Benefits Reform Act of 1984*, Conference Report to accompany H.R. 3755, Report No. 98–1039, 98th Congress, 2nd Session, 1984, 30–31. The House version would have required the SSA to redetermine the eligibility of mentally disabled persons terminated or denied after March 1, 1981, when the reviews officially began, while the Senate, hoping to save money, would have required the SSA to reach back only as far as June 7, 1983, the date HHS Secretary Heckler announced a moratorium on reviews of the mentally ill. The final law required the SSA to publish new regulations within 120 days and to redetermine the eligibility of terminated and denied mentally impaired individuals who had been cut off since the initiation of the reviews. Mental health advocates pressed for the short time frame, fearing that the SSA would stall until the fervor over the reviews died down and ultimately leave the Listings unchanged.

and social disadvantage. The 1984 disability reform law, therefore, marked not a new consensus in favor of expanding Social Security, but the appeal of grounding policy on the supposed objectivity of professional expertise and medical science.

From the Reagan Revolution to a Kinder, Gentler Social Welfare Policy

After 1984, it was clear that the Reagan Revolution had run out of steam. The American public was increasingly apprehensive over the sluggish economy, which pushed more people into poverty, and statistics showing deepening income disparity. Having cheered the president's determination to scale back the federal government's social welfare and regulatory commitments, Republicans became sensitive to the charge that low-income families and the deserving poor had unfairly lost out under Reagan. Signaling a break with his predecessor, President George H. W. Bush pledged to take what he characterized as a "kinder, gentler" approach. During these years, liberals were eager to make up for lost ground. Because control over the federal government was divided, with the White House in the hands of Republicans and Congress run by Democrats, liberals did all they could to force conservatives into uncomfortable positions by presenting sympathetic and deserving causes. But they found themselves hampered by a tight fiscal environment, the product of large budget deficits created by the tax cuts of Reagan's first term and the failure to trim entitlement spending accordingly.[22] The budget deficit did not foreclose liberal policy innovation, but it certainly channeled it in particular directions.[23]

Throughout the late 1980s, SSI and many other means-tested programs that had been squeezed during the first half of Reagan's tenure rebounded and began growing once again.[24] Others became easy casualties

22. James T. Patterson, *America's Struggle against Poverty in the Twentieth Century* (Cambridge: Harvard University Press, 2000), 217–33. Also David A. Stockman, *The Triumph of Politics: How the Reagan Revolution Failed* (New York: Harper and Row, 1986), 303–14. On difference between programmatic and systemic retrenchment, see Paul Pierson, *Dismantling the Welfare State? Reagan, Thatcher, and the Politics of Retrenchment* (Cambridge: Cambridge University Press, 1994), 15–17.

23. Paul Pierson, "The Deficit and the Politics of Domestic Reform," in *The Social Divide: Political Parties and the Future of Activist Government*, ed. Margaret Weir (Washington, DC: Brookings Institution Press, 1998), 126–27.

24. Robert Greenstein, "Universal and Targeted Approaches to Relieving Poverty: An Alternative View," in *The Urban Underclass*, ed. Christopher Jencks and Paul E. Petersen (Washington, DC: Brookings Institution Press, 1991), 437–59.

of the budget-cutter's axe. According to Aaron Wildavsky, each program had a unique reason for its resilience or lack thereof, and these reasons were related to the institutional structure of the program and public attitudes toward it. In general, though, entitlements tended to fare better than discretionary spending programs. Also, programs that served worthy causes, in particular those programs that rewarded work and protected deserving groups, prospered while unpopular programs like AFDC did not.[25] Indeed, the two themes of work and moral worth surfaced repeatedly during debate over social welfare policy in the late 1980s and early 1990s. On the one hand, lawmakers believed, as Bill Clinton so aptly stated in 1992, that people "who work hard and play by the rules" should not be needy. Thus, Congress expanded the Earned Income Tax Credit (EITC) to alleviate the hardships of low-income working families.[26] The emphasis on work can also be seen in AFDC. In 1988, lawmakers passed the Family Support Act, which balanced a work requirement for welfare recipients with increased funds for job training and child care (though the financial commitment never matched the ambitious rhetoric). This law became the precursor for President Clinton's welfare reform proposals. On the other hand, at the same time that lawmakers ingrained the value of work into programs for the able-bodied, they expanded assistance to impoverished individuals who were not expected to work, the so-called deserving poor. Policy followed what former HHS official and antipoverty advocate Peter Edelman dubbed "the children's strategy" because it focused on groups whose claim was impossible to resist. In the area of health care, for instance, Representative Henry Waxman spearheaded legislation that extended Medicaid coverage for young children and pregnant women.[27] Similarly, in the Senate, Republicans John Chafee and John Heinz explored legislation to extend SSI and public health care benefits to more needy children and their families.[28] The homeless, the mentally ill, the disabled, the aged, and children became the targets of various legislative efforts.

25. Aaron Wildavsky, "The Politics of the Entitlement Process," in *The New Politics of Public Policy*, ed. Marc K. Landy and Martin A. Levin (Baltimore: Johns Hopkins University Press, 1995), 143–46, and Greenstein, "Universal and Targeted Approaches," 437–59.

26. Christopher Howard, *The Hidden Welfare State* (Princeton: Princeton University Press, 1997), 145–56.

27. On the strategy and success of Edelman and Waxman, see Dan Morgan, "Medicaid Costs Balloon into Fiscal 'Time Bomb,'" *Washington Post*, January 30, 1994, A1.

28. Rachelle Lombardi, "The Evaluation of Children's Impairments in Determining Disability under the Supplemental Security Income Program," *Fordham Law Review* 57 (1989): 1107.

In this respect, SSI was especially blessed. Because it served people who were not expected to work, it avoided some of the perverse incentives that cropped up with AFDC. (Although as I argue later, this changed as the program expanded to include people with less severe disabilities.) And because it was an entitlement program, SSI was more difficult to rein in than discretionary spending programs. With discretionary programs, Congress could simply refuse to reauthorize spending levels to keep pace with increased needs. Few voters are likely to notice a few more students in a classroom or longer lines at the neighborhood clinic.[29] But to trim spending for an entitlement program like SSI, lawmakers would have to enact a change in the eligibility criteria or benefit levels, a very visible and controversial action. This helps explain why Reagan retreated from plans to cut Social Security disability benefits, but discretionary programs that served the disabled—vocational rehabilitation, independent living, and community mental health—were all scaled back.

SSI, the Forgotten Safety Net

Fifteen years after SSI was first implemented in 1974, liberals looked at it and saw a great deal of unrealized potential. To borrow the words of Arthur Flemming, former SSA official and head of the Save Our Social Security coalition, they sought to ensure that the "landmark legislation" that created SSI led to the "landmark results" that had been promised.[30] Because it was a program that served so many different groups of the poor, SSI was particularly attractive to antipoverty advocates. Given its open-ended definition of disability, SSI could reach many groups that fell through the cracks of social insurance. SSI thus became the centerpiece of advocacy efforts on behalf of the mentally ill, the homeless, and other marginalized groups. In the late 1980s, advocates rediscovered SSI, which had been ignored since its inception and long overshadowed by Disability Insurance. It emerged from the decade as one of the fastest growing means-tested programs and more expensive than either AFDC or the EITC.

Reform efforts centered on the House Select Committee on Aging, which was chaired for many years by Edward Roybal, and the Subcom-

29. This point about traceability and ease of retrenchment is made by Pierson, *Dismantling the Welfare State?* 19–22.
30. U.S. House, Committee on Ways and Means, Subcommittee on Human Resources, *Proposals to Improve the Supplemental Security Income Program*, 101st Congress, 1st Session, 1989, 114.

mittee on Human Resources (a subcommittee of the Ways and Means Committee), headed by Thomas Downey, who had a strong interest in children's issues. Other strong supporters of SSI expansion in the House included Harold Ford of Tennessee as well as Pete "Fortney" Stark and George Miller, both from California. Where congressional liberals were able to expand SSI and where they failed highlights the hurdles that the advocates faced in trying to reconstruct welfare programs left tattered by Reagan's retrenchment initiatives.

During the late 1980s and early 1990s, SSI was the subject of a flurry of legislative activity. Following the resolution of the debacle over Reagan's continuing disability reviews, liberals set out to make SSI and DI more accessible to deinstitutionalized patients. In 1986, Congress created an improved prerelease plan so that patients leaving state resident hospitals could quickly enroll in SSI, and a year later it extended benefits for individuals who were temporarily institutionalized. Lawmakers also enhanced Medicaid and Medicare coverage of mental health medical services and psychosocial rehabilitation. So pleased were advocates with their progress that two of them proudly claimed that the Reagan years had not been such a setback to their cause after all. Indeed, they pointed out that by 1990 advocacy groups had brought to fruition most of the bold recommendations outlined in the Carter administration's 1980 report, *Toward a National Plan for the Chronically Mentally Ill*.[31]

When homelessness emerged as an issue of public interest in the late 1980s, SSI fit into these efforts as well. Homelessness advocacy began in 1978 when a group of homeless activists occupied part of Union Station in Washington, DC, and it culminated in 1989 with a march that brought a quarter million homeless people and their advocates to the nation's capital. In response to this growing interest in homelessness, Congress passed the 1987 Stewart B. McKinney Homeless Assistance Act, the first significant piece of legislation in fifty years to address the problem of homelessness. Although Reagan was not enthusiastic about the measure, he did not oppose it. The new law appropriated increased funding for homeless services and in 1990 added programs to address the specific needs of the mentally ill and homeless children.[32] Because many homeless persons suffered from disabilities as well, Congress also urged the SSA to explore ways of making its programs easier for the homeless to

31. Chris Koynagi and Howard H. Goldman, "The Quiet Success of the National Plan for the Chronically Mentally Ill," *Hospital and Community Psychiatry* 42, 9 (1991): 900–901.

32. Kim Hopper, *Reckoning with Homelessness* (Ithaca, NY: Cornell University Press, 2003), 175–203.

obtain. In response, the agency allowed homeless individuals to use shelters as home addresses to receive their SSI checks, and it encouraged social service agencies to serve as representative payees to oversee the spending habits of homeless individuals with mental disorders.[33]

Congressional liberals had much grander visions for SSI, however. During the late 1980s, Democrats on the House Select Committee on Aging proposed changes to both the program's means test and its disability standard that would have extended reform beyond just the mentally ill and the homeless. Committee chair Edward Roybal, for example, suggested meeting the full measure of poor people's needs by raising SSI benefits from 70–80 percent of the poverty line to the poverty threshold and relaxing the means test for SSI so that it would no longer be a program of last resort. Specifically, he wanted to raise the limit on the value of assets, such as a car or house, that a claimant could possess; eliminate reductions in benefits to claimants living in the households of others; and increase the disregards for earned and unearned income. Roybal also proposed pegging to inflation the limits on assets and the disregards for earned and unearned income. The disregard is the amount of money that is not counted toward a recipient's income when the means test is conducted; essentially, it allows the recipient to keep small gifts and modest earnings. Pegging the assets limit and the disregards to inflation, Roybal hoped, would prevent SSI's means test from becoming increasingly stringent with the passage of time.[34]

Roybal also focused on SSI's disability criteria. He sponsored a plan that would have severed the program's definition of disability from the strict one used for Disability Insurance, thus allowing SSI to explicitly take into account the compounded social barriers to employment faced by some groups of poor people. The homeless, illiterate persons, retired migrant farm workers, individuals with less severe but chronic behavioral problems, addicts, long-term recipients of welfare, persons over age fifty who had not worked for five years, and infants with congenital defects—all would have automatically qualified as disabled under SSI.[35]

33. U.S. General Accounting Office, *Community-Based Care Increases for People with Serious Mental Illness*, GAO-01-224, 2000, 14.

34. U.S. House of Representatives, Select Committee on Aging, Subcommittee on Retirement Income and Employment, *Supplemental Security Income (SSI): Repairing the Safety Net*, 100th Congress, 2nd Session, 1988, 3–4 (hereafter House Subcommittee on Retirement Income and Employment, *Repairing the Safety Net*). For a list of statutory changes in eligibility criteria and benefit levels, see Social Security Advisory Board, *2000 SSI Annual Report*, Appendix A, http://www.ssa.gov/OACT/SSIR/SSI00/ssiV_A.html.

35. House Subcommittee on Retirement Income and Employment, *Repairing the Safety Net*, 3–4.

Ultimately, though, these efforts meant with little success. With the burgeoning of the budget deficit in the late 1980s, apprehension over deficit spending curbed enthusiasm for expanded social welfare initiatives.[36] In 1989, Congress increased SSI's asset limit from its 1974 level of $1,500 for an individual and $2,250 for a couple to $2,000 for an individual and $3,000 for a couple. But after that, no other changes were made to SSI's benefit levels, assets and income limits, or disregards. As a result, the program's earnings disregard stood at its 1974 level of $65. After that, every dollar earned would lead to a $0.50 reduction in SSI benefits. This meant that over time rising inflation made the means test more difficult to meet. For example, had it been indexed to inflation, in 2002, the $65 earnings disregard would have been $275, and the $2,000 limit on assets that individuals could own would have stood at $6,345. Thus, the pool of potential recipients and the real value of SSI payments are smaller today than was the case in 1974, and the people who currently qualify for SSI are poorer relative to those who qualified three decades ago. As stunning as SSI's growth has been over the past thirty years, it would have been even more pronounced had it not been for the increasing restrictiveness of the means test.[37] Similarly, Congress never seriously considered Roybal's proposals to relax the disability criteria used for SSI to include more disadvantaged groups. Unlike the expansive reforms enacted as part of the 1984 disability amendments, these measures lacked a medical logic and thus could not muster enough congressional support.

Advocates, however, were not disheartened. The Supreme Court's decision in *Zebley* quickly mitigated the legislative setback they encountered in trying to liberalize SSI. With *Zebley*, liberals received from the courts what they could not accomplish in Congress, at least with respect to children. Moreover, when their legislative reforms failed to pass, advocates turned to outreach strategies instead. Indeed, members of Congress liked outreach because they could meet the needs of many different groups of the poor without granting new entitlements. Targeted first at the elderly and moving on later to other groups, outreach efforts began in earnest in the early 1980s when advocates for the aged pointed out that enrollment of the elderly in SSI fell far short of projections made in 1972 when the program was passed. To address this shortcoming, the 1983 Social Security amendments required the SSA to inform more than 7 million elderly

36. Eugene Steuerle, "Financing the American State at the Turn of the Century," in *Funding the Modern American State, 1941–1995*, ed. W. Elliot Brownlee (Cambridge: Cambridge University Press, 1996), 404–44.

37. Mary C. Daly and Richard V. Burkhauser, "Left Behind: SSI in the Era of Welfare Reform," *Focus* 22, 3 (2003): 37.

persons that they might also be eligible for SSI. The campaign was such a success that enrollment of the aged in SSI reached an all-time high of 2.1 million individuals in September 1984.[38]

When homelessness became an issue in the late 1980s, outreach became a solution to this problem as well. Members of the House aging committee urged the SSA to address the special needs of the homeless and the homeless mentally ill. Ever accommodating of Congress, the SSA between 1987 and 1990 established contact stations in local homeless shelters, churches, mental health clinics, and social service offices so that field workers could take applications and conduct preliminary disability examinations on the spot.[39] After the initial success with the aged and homelessness campaigns, Congress pushed the SSA to take bolder steps to find potential SSI applicants, appropriating over $33 million between 1990 and 1995 for outreach campaigns.[40] Soon the SSA had created outreach programs for all manner of disadvantaged but deserving groups, including migrant farmer workers, legal immigrants, African-Americans, Native Americans, AIDS and HIV patients, and disabled children.[41] Though it is difficult to calculate the full impact of outreach, many SSA field employees clearly viewed it as a key source of program

38. U.S. House of Representatives, Committee on Ways and Means, *Background Material and Data on Programs within the Jurisdiction of the Committee on Ways and Means* (hereafter House Committee on Ways and Means, *1989 Green Book*) (Washington, DC: Government Printing Office, 1989), 686.

39. U.S. House of Representatives, Committee on Ways and Means, *Background Material and Data on Programs within the Jurisdiction of the Committee on Ways and Means* (hereafter House Committee on Ways and Means, *1994 Green Book*) (Washington, DC: Government Printing Office, 1994), 255–57. For history of congressional initiatives in the area of homelessness in the late 1980s, see Congressional Research Service, *Homelessness and the Federal Response, 1987–1990*, prepared by Ruth Ellen Wasem, June 17, 1991. On renewed concern with homelessness, see Julie Kosterlitz, "They're Everywhere," *National Journal* 19 (February 28, 1987): 492–94, and Julie Kosterlitz, "No Home, No Help," *National Journal* 22 (September 8, 1990): 2120–23.

40. Jennifer Dixon, Associated Press, "Government Spends Millions Selling Cash Benefits to the Poor," November 7, 1995, Lexis-Nexis document, no page numbers available.

41. House Committee on Ways and Means, *1994 Green Book*, 254–55. For a description of the SSA's outreach efforts, see Charles G. Scott, Ruth Ellen Mulberg, and Howard Oberheu, "SSA's Outreach Efforts to Contact Beneficiaries Eligible for SSI Payments," *Social Security Bulletin* 51, 1 (1988): 12–17. In one of its studies, the SSA suggested several reasons why people did not enroll in SSI. According to the agency, failure to enroll occurred not because people were not aware of benefits but because they did not want to take welfare. See John A. Menefee, Bea Edwards, and Sylvester J. Schieber, "Analysis of Nonparticipation in the SSI Program," *Social Security Bulletin* 44, 6 (1981): 3–21.

growth. One manager of a district office commented, "This increase in disability claims is not a great mystery to us in the field offices. Rather it is the logical outcome of this agency's goals and initiatives over the past several years."[42]

There are several reasons why outreach received broad support while other measures aimed at expanding SSI did not. First, compared to liberalizing the income and disability standards, outreach campaigns were relatively inexpensive. They were one-time allocations of money rather than lifetime grants of an entitlement to new groups of individuals. Moreover, because provisions mandating outreach were tucked into huge omnibus budget and Social Security bills, their costs paled in comparison to the enormous amount of funds being allocated to the more high-profile measures in the legislation. As one Senate staff member noted about these spending bills, there were so many provisions and programs that "in the end you couldn't tell what was paying for what."[43] Even if lawmakers chose to penny-pinch, the full budgetary impact of outreach was impossible to calculate upfront. The SSA had only limited information as to how many additional recipients its outreach activities would bring into SSI, and because costs were unknowable, deficit hawks had little to oppose. Finally, the logic of outreach was compelling. Outreach did not create new benefits for new groups of people but only sought to ensure that those who were already entitled to SSI benefits knew about them and could apply for them. This was difficult even for conservative Republicans to contest.[44]

The Continuing Disappointment of Community Mental Health

Nonetheless, despite their success in repairing the social safety net, when it came to furthering community mental health, advocates were more disappointed than ever. In 1986, the American Psychiatric Association declared that the visibility of the homeless in the streets of virtually every major American city was indicative of the nation's failure to create a mental health care system that would allow the disabled to live

42. L. Scott Mueller and Peter M. Wheeler, "The Growth in Disability Programs as Seen by SSA Field Office Managers," in *Growth in Disability Benefits*, ed. Kalman Rupp and David C. Stapleton (Kalamazoo, MI: W. E. Upjohn, 1998), 211.

43. Quoted in Morgan, "Medicaid Costs Balloon."

44. Ronald Haskins, former staff member of the U.S. House of Representatives, Committee on Ways and Means, Subcommittee on Human Resources, 1986–2000, phone interview with author, July 10, 2001.

with dignity in the community.[45] Yet advocates for the homeless and the disabled were unsure of how to proceed. They disagreed about whether homelessness should be seen through the lens of mental illness or whether the two problems should be dealt with separately. Some advocates argued that focusing on mental illness allowed policy to target the hardest-to-reach and most marginalized group of the homeless population and did much to rectify a major source of homelessness. Others contended that treating homelessness as a result of a clinical disorder individualized what was, at bottom, an economic and structural problem.[46]

In many ways, the frustrations that advocates encountered in their efforts to rectify the disadvantages created by disability, poverty, mental illness, and homelessness shared the same root cause. Kim Hopper, an advocate for the homeless, complained that homelessness crossed many different policy areas, and yet there was no way to make the voice of the homeless heard in all of them, much less coordinate policy reform across such a fragmented system. He noted that "homelessness was effectively absent from discussions of welfare changes, health care reform, and economic policy, as though decisions in those realms would have no impact on present rates or future trends" in homelessness.[47] The same telling critique could be said of disability policy, welfare policy, or mental health policy in general. Antipoverty reformers had succeeded in defending, even expanding many social welfare programs, but these existing programs were simply patched together to serve fashionable groups of the poor with little attention to overall policy coherence. Comprehensive reform of the existing structure of social welfare policy, which early patients' rights activists had envisioned, was much more difficult to bring about. Moreover, as the 1980s drew to a close, it became apparent that disability rights and the social safety net, theoretically complementary approaches to bringing about the social inclusion of the disabled, had diverged. In the drive to enact the Americans with Disability Act, activists defined disability rights as the antithesis of social welfare assistance.

45. Richard H. Lamb and John A. Talbott, "The Homeless Mentally Ill: The Perspective of the American Psychiatric Association," *Journal of the American Medical Association* 256 (1986): 498–501.

46. Irwin Garfinkel and James Wright, "Is Mental Illness a Cause of Homelessness?," in *Controversial Issues in Mental Health*, ed. Stuart A. Kirk and Susan D. Einbinder (Boston: Allyn and Bacon, 1994), 94–105, and M. Gregg Bloche and Francine Cournos, "Mental Health Policy for the 1990s: Tinkering in the Interstices," in *Health Policy and the Disadvantaged*, ed. Lawrence D. Brown (Durham, NC: Duke University Press, 1991), 145.

47. Hopper, *Reckoning with Homelessness*, 195.

The Americans with Disabilities Act as Welfare Reform

The Americans with Disabilities Act of 1990 was a landmark piece of civil rights legislation, the culmination of years of disability rights advocacy. In contrast to the narrow definition of disability used in DI and SSI, the ADA employed a broad and rather vague definition of disability and then left it to the courts to adjudicate violations on a case-by-case basis. A person was considered disabled if she had a physical or mental impairment that substantially limited a major life activity, if she had a record of such an impairment, or if she was regarded as having such an impairment even though the impairment was not necessarily incapacitating.[48] To those considered disabled, the ADA extended the guarantees of its predecessor, Section 504, to all private employers, public facilities, and state and local governments. Employers had to give "reasonable accommodation" to "otherwise qualified" disabled individuals unless doing so would prove an "undue hardship." Similarly, mass transit systems and new or renovated public buildings were to be made accessible to people with disabilities.[49] Yet in an important sense, the ADA was a pyrrhic victory. In order to secure support for the law from conservatives, disability rights activists largely jettisoned the call for a comprehensive social safety net that could facilitate community integration for people who would otherwise become institutionalized. The bifurcation of civil rights from welfare and the ensuing denigration of the latter were by no means carried out by all disability rights activists. But those who struck this chord caught the ear of policymakers. Throughout debate over the ADA, members of Congress repeatedly claimed that disability rights would make welfare obsolete.

Philosophical orientation and political strategy rooted activists' repudiation of social welfare initiatives. By the late 1980s, many of the activists at the forefront of the campaign for the ADA shared the principles of the independent living movement. Given their frustrating experiences with traditional vocational rehabilitation programs, independent living activists tended to view social welfare programs as confining and paternalistic. Some viewed welfare as a way in which society mollified disabled people so that they would focus on securing individual services rather than social change; others with a libertarian streak rejected the attitude that "society should and

48. 42 U.S.C. sections 12102(2)(A), 12102(2)(B), and 12102(2)(C), though the definition has been interpreted narrowly by the courts and so in practice the definition is not as broad as ADA proponents had hoped.
49. 42 U.S.C. sections 12112, 12132, and 12182.

can provide certain benefits to each human with no corresponding obligation on the part of the individuals." Still other activists believed that the benevolence inherent in welfare perpetuated the inequality of the disabled; to be excused from civic expectations like work also meant being excluded from the rights and privileges of full citizenship.[50]

This critique of the welfare state fit in with the "small government" zeitgeist of the Reagan years, which at first threatened many of the gains disability rights activists had made. On entering the White House, Reagan appointed his vice-president, George H. W. Bush, to chair the Task Force for Regulatory Relief. The job of this task force was to prune back governmental regulations, and among its first targets were Section 504 and the Education for All Handicapped Children Act. Disabled activists and parents of disabled children were outraged. Deluged with angry letters, the task force retreated. But disability rights advocates realized that they needed to adapt their strategies to a new political reality, one in which sweeping government regulations of the private sector would be a tough sell.[51] Thus, activist Evan Kemp gave voice to a rationale for disability rights that accorded with core conservative values. In a *New York Times* editorial in 1981, Kemp argued that the accommodations in Section 504 were not government handouts or special privileges; instead, they were key to allowing the disabled to work and become self-sufficient. Without them, societal discrimination forced the disabled out of the workplace and onto welfare programs, and according to Kemp, the costs of maintaining the disabled on these programs far outstripped the costs of complying with the equal access mandates in Section 504.[52]

The juxtaposition of welfare and disability rights continued with the National Council on the Handicapped (later renamed the National Council on Disability), a working group carried over from the Carter administration. In 1984, Congress charged the council with studying federal programs and making recommendations that would improve the quality of life of people with disabilities. The council's 1986 report, *Toward Independence*, went beyond this charge by producing draft legislation that would become the foundation for the Americans with Disabilities Act. According to Frank Burgdorf, a disability rights lawyer who worked with the council, members saw civil rights "as simply a way to get

50. Samuel R. Bagenstos, "The Future of Disability Law," *Yale Law Journal* 114 (2004), 14–17, quote on 16.

51. Joseph P. Shapiro, *No Pity: People with Disabilities Forging a New Civil Rights Movement* (New York: Times Books, 1993), 119–22.

52. Evan J. Kemp, "Aiding the Disabled: No Pity, Please," *New York Times*, September 3, 1981, A19.

from a society that takes care of people with disabilities to a society that tries to help people become productive and mainstream."[53] Their report reflected this libertarian outlook. Noting that the nation spent more than $60 billion on disability pensions, *Toward Independence* explained that "spending disability-related dollars more prudently and productively" could be accomplished by "reducing existing barriers, both structural and attitudinal," so that people with disabilities "may realize their full potential and become more independent and self-sufficient."[54] Moreover, even though early disability rights activists had compared the prejudice the disabled encountered to that suffered by African-Americans in the Jim Crow South, the council's report dropped all references to the black civil rights movement and instead called for "equality of opportunity" and "independence," terms sure to resonate with conservatives. As Thomas Burke succinctly put it, the National Council on the Handicapped "embraced the rights model's critique of dependency-inducing effects of traditional disability policy but left out its emphasis on the societal oppression of people with disabilities."[55]

Of course, disability rights activists were not completely unaware of the need for some modicum of social welfare assistance. In addition to calling for passage of the ADA, the council's report also suggested changes to DI and SSI so that people with disabilities could work and still retain their eligibility, and it recommended fuller funding of special education programs and independent living centers.[56] But lawmakers scarcely discussed these issues during the debate leading up to the passage of the ADA. If anything, policymakers expected to spend less money on welfare, not more, by enacting disability rights legislation. Indeed, in a 1983 report on the integration of people with disabilities, the Commission on Civil Rights seconded the arguments made by the National Council on the Handicapped, noting that the costs of erecting architectural barriers and other accommodations would translate into "large savings in reduced expenditures of public benefits programs, such as social security disability insurance, supplemental security income, and State welfare, home relief, and aid to families with dependent children."[57] Sim-

53. Thomas F. Burke, *Lawyers, Lawsuits, and Legal Rights: The Battle over Litigation in American Society* (Berkeley: University of California Press, 2002), 76.

54. U.S. National Council on the Handicapped, *Toward Independence* (Washington, DC: National Council on the Handicapped, 1986), vi.

55. Burke, *Lawyers, Lawsuits, and Legal Rights*, 77.

56. Ibid., 77–78.

57. U.S. Commission on Civil Rights, quoted in Samuel R. Bagenstos, "The Americans with Disabilities Act as Welfare Reform," *William and Mary Law Review* 44 (2003): 959.

ilarly, in hearing after hearing, disability rights advocates asserted that the ADA would lead to self-reliance and reduce welfare dependency. Lawmakers, too, repeatedly voiced their belief the law would save American taxpayers billions in entitlement costs.[58]

Members of Congress were receptive to the argument about fiscal prudence, especially at a time of growing unrest over the nation's budget deficit and increasing entitlement spending. By 1990, individual entitlements, which included Old Age Insurance, Disability Insurance, Medicare, and a host of smaller means-tested programs, consumed $603.5 billion, representing almost half of all government outlays and 11 percent of the nation's gross domestic product.[59] In this fiscal environment, the ADA looked promising. Senator Patrick Leahy told his colleagues, "If we remove barriers to work for the disabled, we can turn welfare payments into tax receipts."[60] Disability activists encouraged this line of reasoning. Timothy Cook went so far as to tell a Senate subcommittee, "If we get people off of public assistance and paying taxes, it is unquestionably going to bring down the deficit."[61] What made the ADA so popular, therefore, was that it allowed lawmakers to do something good for a sympathetic group without having to dip into the federal treasury. Instead, the costs of compliance were passed onto the private sector and state and local governments, which would be forced to spend their own resources to achieve compliance with the act. As far as members of Congress were concerned, the ADA cost the federal government nothing and might even end up saving money. Thus, the link between disability rights and social welfare expenditures was clear. Said Thomas Burke, "For the Reagan and Bush officials the ADA was a kind of welfare reform."[62]

Social Inclusion, Disability Rights, and Welfare

By 1990, policymakers agreed on two principles. First, if possible, all working-aged adults, including those with disabilities, should seek employment, and society should not exclude anyone because of difference. On a second point policymakers also seemed in agreement: for those who

58. For numerous illustrative quotes, see ibid., especially on 949–69.

59. Aaron Wildavsky and Naomi Caiden, *The New Politics of the Budgetary Process*, 3rd ed. (New York: Longman, 1997), table 7.3, 171.

60. Quoted in Bagenstos, "Americans with Disabilities Act as Welfare Reform," 969 n. 235.

61. Quoted in ibid., 968,

62. Burke, *Lawyers, Lawsuits, and Legal Rights*, 95.

could not work, public income support must be available so that these individuals would not become homeless or end up institutionalized, where the drain on public resources was greater. Yet commitment to this latter principle was less apparent. Both policymakers and advocates were slow to realize, or perhaps reluctant to admit, that bringing about meaningful social inclusion required a positive commitment of public resources, whether this took the form of the enforcement of equal access laws, such as Section 504 and the ADA, or the extension of social welfare benefits, such as DI, SSI, Medicare, and Medicaid.

Throughout the 1980s, therefore, welfare and disability rights policies entered separate political tracks and, as the decade progressed, diverged further from one another. As a result, the expansion of social welfare programs in the late 1980s and early 1990s, including the growth of SSI, occurred with little input from disability rights activists, aside from advocates interested in mental health and children's issues. Policymakers did not engage in any serious or in-depth discussion of how the programs could better serve the disabled community or, more importantly, how they could be coordinated with disability rights laws. One set of programs was simply layered over an older set of programs, creating a policy area in which programs and agencies lacked formal linkages and often worked at cross-purposes. In addition, as I explain in chapter 7, the expansion of DI and especially SSI to previously marginalized groups of the disabled shattered lawmakers' twin expectations: first, that disability determination had been made more accurate following passage of the 1984 disability amendments and, second, that neither the 1984 reforms nor the ADA would lead to significantly more disability spending and might even reduce it. To the contrary, by the early 1990s, it appeared that DI and SSI had expanded to encompass people with less severe disabilities, a development that undermined the work-oriented approach of the ADA. Welfare expansion, never an easy sell, was even more difficult to rationalize in a post-ADA world. By denigrating governmental activism and assuring lawmakers that integration of the disabled could be accomplished on the cheap, disability rights advocates had inadvertently undercut political backing for the kind of social safety net that could make meaningful social inclusion a reality.

7

Putting Reform into Administrative Practice

In 1982, during congressional debate over the Reagan administration's disability reviews, Senator John Heinz brought up the story of Kathleen McGovern, a woman from his home state of Pennsylvania who suffered from severe mental illness. McGovern was so distraught upon being cut from Social Security that she committed suicide. The story touched Heinz.[1] He and other lawmakers came to believe that if only the SSA used reasonable and realistic disability standards, such tragedies could be avoided. For the next several years, the SSA tinkered with the disability rules and practices, trying to arrive at that elusive goal. But by 1993, disability had a new face, and it was that of "Lisa T." Lisa T lived in an impoverished South Boston neighborhood and struggled to raise her eight-year-old son on her own. The young boy was having trouble in school. He frequently threw temper tantrums and fought with his classmates. He was also academically weak, and school officials placed him in a class for children with special needs. Despite misgivings, Lisa T applied on her son's behalf for SSI. "I don't think of him as disabled," she explained. "I just think he needs help in terms of his attitude." But she added, whatever her reservations, "We need the money." Indeed, the SSI checks Lisa T and her son began receiving amounted to $480 a month, far more than what most of the families in their neighborhood received from other welfare programs. Nevertheless, one of the boy's teachers was critical. She claimed that when calm and fo-

---

1. U.S. Senate, Committee on Finance, *Social Security Disability Insurance Program,* 97th Congress, 2nd Session, 1982, 13–15. Heinz's concern for the mentally disabled is discussed in Edward D. Berkowitz, *Disabled Policy: America's Programs for the Handicapped* (Cambridge: Cambridge University Press, 1987), 133–34.

cused, Lisa T's son was actually quite bright. The attitude problems he displayed, she believed, were attributable to the boy's troubled home environment, a situation that the disability checks did little to change. "I don't see how handing a parent a check helps her son correct his behavior," the teacher complained. "This is bad for the kids."[2]

This chapter explains how the Social Security Administration got from Kathleen McGovern to Lisa T. It begins with the waning days of the disability reviews, when a small group of MHLP lawyers, physicians, and policy officers met to discuss a thorough rewriting of the standards used to evaluate mental disorders in adults. Chastened by the reviews, the SSA emerged from the experience more aware of the inclusive ideals that motivated the disability rights activists and mental health advocates. Determined to win back the trust of the disabled community, SSA officials opened both their minds and their programs to the concerns of disability advocates. They took seriously the advocates' critique of the clinical concept and invited advocates and outside experts to help formulate a new functional interpretation of disability. Starting first with the rules that govern adult mental disorders and then proceeding to the childhood disability standards, sympathetic administrators rewrote the rules for disability determination to conform to the functional paradigm. Because of this collaborative effort, advocates were able to ingrain their expansive views of disability deep within the DI and SSI programs.

Reformers in the Social Security Administration

Prior to the Reagan administration's disability reviews, the SSA had little contact with the welfare and disability crusaders of the rights revolution. Thinking back about the officials who set program policy from their offices in the SSA headquarters in Baltimore, Rhoda Davis, previously the associate commissioner for SSI, recounted, "There was no awareness beyond Baltimore of the advocacy community," either of its existence or its ideas.[3] Leonard Rubenstein, a former MHLP attorney, painted a similar picture of the agency, noting that SSA officials in the Office of Disability "had no contact with the people whose cases were

2. Charles M. Sennott, "Disability Grants for Children Fuel Welfare Debate," *Boston Globe*, May 12, 1994, Metro Section, 1.

3. Rhoda Davis, former associate commissioner of the Office of Supplemental Security Income, Social Security Administration, interview in the Oral History Collection, February 5, 1996, transcripts in the SSA Archives, Office of the Historian, Social Security Administration, Baltimore, Maryland.

before them and no knowledge of the communal mental health system, no understanding whatsoever." As a result, the medical staff devised the rules for DI and SSI with little input from the advocacy groups that represented the disabled and with little attention to their principles of inclusion and community living. In the eyes of the advocates, this insularity was part of the problem. SSA officials, Rubenstein argued, had become so consumed with arriving at objectivity that "they lost sight of the medical and real-world issues about disability," in particular the economic hardships people with disabilities confronted.[4]

The reviews marked a significant shift within the agency from those who favored cost containment and objectivity to those who shared the concerns of the advocacy community. When Reagan entered office, his political appointees to SSA and HHS reflected his political ideology. Although Reagan's HHS secretary, Richard Schweiker, was a moderate Republican, he was generally circumvented by his conservative undersecretary, David Swoap, who had a closer relationship with the White House. Swoap, White House officials, and budget director David Stockman set policy.[5] Similarly, Reagan's appointees to the SSA were more conservative than their nominal supervisors at the Department of Health and Human Services. Both John A. Svahn, SSA commissioner until 1983, and Dorcas Hardy, his successor, had been welfare officials in California when Reagan was governor. And they shared the president's conviction that states and the private sector should bear primary responsibility for income support. This placed them at odds with Schweiker's successor, Margaret Heckler. A moderate and former member of Congress who took control of HHS in the mist of the disability reviews, Heckler intuitively understood the public outrage the reviews provoked. She entered office determined to " 'quell the fires' on the disability issue," and for her, this meant making the SSA more receptive to the demands of the advocacy organizations.[6]

To put the rancor of the reviews behind them, SSA officials did their best to mend fences with the groups they had antagonized by inviting advocates into the policymaking process. Patricia Owens, who assumed the

4. Leonard S. Rubenstein, former chief litigator and director of the Bazelon Center for Mental Health Law, interview with author, Washington, DC, January 21, 2000.

5. Linda E. Demkovich, "HHS Department: It's Humphrey's No More," *National Journal* 13 (April 25, 1981): 713–16, and Linda E. Demkovich, "Madame Figurehead?" *National Journal* 15 (January 22, 1983): 178.

6. Demkovich, "Madame Figurehead?" 178, and Linda E. Demkovich, "Margaret Heckler Shows Fighting Style, Proving She Came to Stay at HHS," *National Journal* 16 (May 19, 1984): 977–82.

head of the Office of Disability in the waning months of the review campaign, chose to accommodate the advocates, rather than fight them. She explained, "I had the opportunity to fix the disability program, which was a mess. I decided to go to the people who were the most critical of us and listen to their concerns and communicate the agency's constraints."[7] Pragmatic and sympathetic to the arguments they were making, Owens won the trust of the advocates. One even went so far as to praise her as "that wonderful woman."[8]

This spirit of accommodation continued throughout the late 1980s and early 1990s. In keeping with President George H. W. Bush's "kinder, gentler" approach to social issues, his political appointees seconded congressional interest in SSI. Whereas Reagan's SSA commissioner, Dorcas Hardy, wanted to devolve SSI to the states, Gwendolyn King, Bush's head of the SSA, was a strong supporter of the program and made outreach to hard-to-serve, impoverished groups one of her top priorities.[9] Because many district offices faced staff shortages following administrative budget cuts and could not devote as many man-hours to outreach as managers felt appropriate, local SSA offices contracted their outreach work to advocacy organizations that were already in the field and engaged in their own private campaigns to sign up the poor for SSI. By 1994, the SSA was taking part in more than eighty cooperative programs with state and local governments, related agencies of the federal government, private charities, welfare agencies, reform groups, and legal aid centers.[10] These efforts brought the agency into close contact with the vast network of mental health, poverty, and children's welfare groups that had developed an interest in SSI since the years of the disability reviews.

Moreover, under King, the SSA convened the SSI Modernization Project, a work group that solicited recommendations for improving the SSI program from disability experts and advocates. Although Congress failed to enact most of the recommendations, according to former SSA official Rhoda Davis, the effort was still constructive. She later said that

7. Patricia Owens, former deputy commissioner for the Office of Disability, Social Security Administration, phone interview with author, April 25, 2000.

8. Arthur T. Meyerson, retired professor of psychiatry at the Mt. Sinai School of Medicine and a participant in the 1983–85 workgroup to rewrite the adult mental disorders Listings, phone interview with author, March 13, 2000.

9. Julie Kosterlitz, "Where Conciliation is Producing Dividends," *National Journal* 22 (January 27, 1990): 226, and Rhoda Davis, former associate commissioner of the Office of Supplemental Security Income, interview in the Oral History Collection, February 5, 1996.

10. U.S. General Accounting Office, *Social Security: District Managers' Views on Outreach for the Supplemental Security Income Program*, HRD-91–19FS, 1990, 10–11, 15–17.

"it was very good for both people who work in the SSI program" and the advocates, who, "because of who they are and what they've done in their lives, do not understand anything about how big machine bureaucracies like ours operate." Through the experience, she explained, "We educated them a lot about SSA and corrected some of the paranoia that lingers on from the CDR [continuing disability review] debacle," and they saw "that we are honorable people trying to do the right thing." At the same time, the encounter was also beneficial for the SSA. "A whole lot of people in my office," Davis noted, "saw the program from another perspective."[11]

As the SSA opened itself to the advocates, influence within the agency shifted from those who had sought to elevate objectivity and stringency to those who favored a liberal approach. When it came to drawing up the mental and childhood disability rules, outside medical experts and representatives of advocacy organizations were invited to sit at the table with SSA policymakers as equals. By the same token, the role of the agency's in-house medical experts diminished. For example, in 1990, the Office of Disability revisited its disability certification process for children. During debates over the design of the rules, the Office of Disability overruled the objections voiced by the physicians on its medical staff, who argued that only the reports of doctors, not school officials and parents, should be included in the disability examination. Following the advice of children's advocates and pediatric experts, officials concluded that the testimony of nonmedical sources was essential to obtaining a complete picture of a child's functioning.[12] Confirming the waning influence of the medical staff, one former official reflected on the climate of the late 1970s and early 1980s. He explained, "There was a strong emphasis, I think stronger than it is today, on medical staff. There was an increased effort to make sure that the medical staff was involved more heavily in policy." Back then, "the policy making function was much more dominated by physicians than it is today."[13] In sum, in the aftermath of Reagan's disability reviews, SSA officials tried to strike a balance between their apprehension about program growth with recognition of real hardships and unmet needs that advocates brought to their attention.

11. Rhoda Davis, SSA interview.

12. James Perrin, professor of pediatrics at the Harvard University School of Medicine and participant in the 1990 workgroup to devise the Individualized Functional Assessment for children, phone interview with author, July 25, 2000.

13. John Ritter, former executive program policy officer for the Office of Disability, Social Security Administration, interview in the Oral History Collection, August 16, 1995, transcripts in the SSA Archives, Office of the Historian, Social Security Administration, Baltimore, Maryland.

Subterranean Policy Innovation

This spirit of accommodation carried over into the rule-writing process, giving advocates another opportunity to build on their successes in the courts and in Congress and embed functionalism deep into the DI and SSI programs. The new rules that emerged were subtle but far-reaching changes to the interpretation of disability and the practice of disability determination. They often went above and beyond what a strict reading of the statute or the court ruling required, and it is likely that few lawmakers were aware of, much less understood, these reforms. As a result, as the Social Security disability rolls grew and the number of mentally disabled claimants and children increased in the early 1990s, not only did the changes take lawmakers by surprise but they also proved incredibly difficult to undo.

Rewriting the Listings for Adult Mental Disorders

Following Congress's enactment of the Disability Benefits Reform Act in 1984, SSA officials revamped the Listings for adult mental disorders. By then, they were convinced that the medical rules were deeply flawed.[14] Determined to placate restive advocates and required by the 1984 amendments to align its rules with current professional thinking, SSA officials invited advocates along with representatives from the National Institute of Mental Health, the National Institute on Alcoholism and Alcohol Abuse, and the National Institute on Drug Abuse to participate in the work group charged with making the revisions. Describing the atmosphere of the talks, one participant noted that advocates "had already won the war; this was simply a matter of determining the terms of the armistice."[15]

In 1985, the SSA released a new set of Listings for adult mental disorders that reflected the work group's deliberations. The emphasis on functioning unmistakable, the new Listings liberalized the standards for mental disability in three ways. First, they replicated the changes that psychiatric professionals had made to their diagnostic handbook in 1980. Like DSM-III, the revised Listings of Medical Impairments greatly expanded the number of mental disorders. While the previous Listings had

14. Patricia Owens, phone interview with author.
15. Howard H. Goldman, professor of psychiatry at the University of Maryland School of Medicine and a participant in the 1983–85 workgroup to rewrite the adult mental disorders Listings, phone interview with author, February 26, 2000.

been brief and perfunctory, the new ones went into great detail about the behaviors that someone with a disorder would exhibit. Just as DSM-III had provided clinicians with a more refined set of diagnostic criteria to make sure that clinicians did not inadvertently miss diagnosing a disorder, the new disability rules were designed to minimize the chances that a symptom would not be counted because an examiner did not realize it was indicative of an impairment.

Illustrating these changes, table 7.1 shows the old and new Listings for affective disorders, such as bipolar disorder. The criteria are more specific and thorough in the revised set of Listings, and because more signs and symptoms were listed, in effect, the claimant had more chances to qualify. For instance, under the old Listings, a person with bipolar disorder had to show that she suffered one of the following bizarre behaviors: depression or elation, agitation, psychomotor disturbances, hallucinations, autistic behavior, or illogical association of ideas. Under the new Listings, however, the claimant was evaluated under a more detailed description of affective disorders that counted symptoms such as disturbances in eating or sleeping habits, decreased energy, thoughts of suicide, hyperactivity, erratic ideas, risky behaviors, inflated self-esteem, and distractibility—signs that an examiner using the old set of Medical Listings might have ignored since they were not specifically mentioned.

Second, the previous Listings had required claimants to show a medical condition so severe that it resulted in a complete restriction in functioning, but the new Listings lowered the bar. The old rules granted awards only to claimants who showed a complete inability to perform activities of daily living or to relate to other people, a total lack of interests, or deterioration in personal habits. Advocates objected that this posed an unreasonably high standard, insofar as a judgment about functioning was a simple "yes or no" decision: yes, the claimant was completely incapacitated and thus was disabled, or no, he was not. Examiners made no inquiry into whether claimants could perform these activities on their own without supervision or whether they performed them appropriately and effectively.[16] Bolstering these claims, congressional investigators looking into the SSA's use of functional measures during the disability reviews found that examiners had ended the benefits of a schizophrenic man who told them he spent his days meeting friends and playing the piano. When investigators visited the man at his home, they found that his "friends"

16. Letter of James Folsom, American Psychiatric Association, in U.S. Senate, Committee on Finance, *Social Security Disability Insurance Program*, 97th Congress, 2nd Session, 1982, 25.

Table 7.1 Old and New Listings for Affective Disorders

1979	1985
Functional Psychotic Disorders (mood disorders, schizophrenias, and paranoid states)	Affective Disorders (bipolar disorder, hypomania, and unipolar depression)
Claimant must satisfy both Part A (clinical) and Part B (functional) criteria:	Claimant must satisfy both Part A (clinical) and Part B (functional) criteria:
A. Manifested persistence of one or more of the following clinical signs:	A. Medically documented persistence, either continuous or intermittent, of one of the following:
1. Depression (or elation); or	1. Depressive syndrome characterized by at least four of the following:
2. Agitation; or	a. Anhedonia or pervasive loss of interest in almost all activities; or
3. Psychomotor disturbances; or	b. Appetite disturbance with change in weight; or
4. Hallucinations or delusions; or	c. Sleep disturbance; or
5. Autistic or other regressive behavior; or	d. Psychomotor agitation or retardation; or
6. Inappropriateness of affect; or	e. Decreased energy; or
7. Illogical association of ideas;	f. Feelings of guilt or worthlessness; or
B. Resulting persistence of marked restriction of daily activities and constriction of interests and seriously impaired ability to relate to other people.	g. Difficulty concentrating or thinking; or
	h. Thoughts of suicide; or
	i. Hallucinations, delusions, or paranoid thinking; or
	2. Manic syndrome characterized by at least three of the following:
	a. Hyperactivity; or
	b. Pressure of speech; or
	c. Flight of ideas; or
	d. Inflated self-esteem; or
	e. Decreased need for sleep; or
	f. Easy distractibility; or
	g. Involvement in activities that have a high probability of painful consequences which are not recognized; or
	h. Hallucinations, delusions or paranoid thinking; or
	3. Bipolar syndrome with a history of episodic periods manifested by the full symptomatic picture of both manic and depressive syndromes (and currently characterized by either or both syndromes);
	B. Resulting in at least two of the following:
	1. Marked restriction of activities of daily living; or
	2. Marked difficulties in maintaining social functioning; or
	3. Deficiencies of concentration, persistence, or pace resulting in frequent failure to complete tasks in a timely manner (in work settings or elsewhere); or
	4. Repeated episodes of deterioration or decompensation in work or worklike settings, which cause the individual to withdraw from that situation or to experience exacerbation of signs and symptoms (which may include deterioration of adaptive behaviors).

turned out to be his psychiatric social workers and his "piano playing consisted of aimless doodling."[17]

To remedy these abuses, the new Listings completely reworked the functional measures. Under the revised guidelines, an individual could qualify if he suffered two or three marked limitations in activities of daily living; social functioning; or concentration, persistence, or pace so that he often failed to complete tasks in a timely manner, or if he suffered from repeated episodes of deterioration in work or worklike settings. To advocates, these new measures were clearly superior to the old approach in determining work capacity. The emphasis on sociability and deficiencies in concentration, persistence, or pace more closely resembled the level of functioning required to survive in a competitive workplace, while the attention to deterioration took into consideration the effect of work-related stress on the claimant's mental status. Moreover, the claimant did not have to show complete incapacity, as had been the case in the past, only a "marked" restriction in functioning. And because these functional measures rated the extent to which they could be performed "independently, appropriately and effectively" in a workplace setting, they led examiners to consider the social context of the claimant's behavior. So for example, an aggressive individual who was otherwise "tolerated" by shopkeepers could still be found to have a marked restriction in social functioning if his behavior would not be tolerated were he an employee rather than a customer.[18] By taking into consideration the reaction of potential employers to the prospective employee, this approach helped bridge the gap between whether a claimant theoretically could work and whether in reality he would be hired for a particular job. And it shifted attention away from strictly medical criteria toward some of the social or environmental determinants of unemployment.

Finally, the Listings expanded eligibility by requiring examiners to be much more thorough in their gathering of evidence and much more circumspect when denying an application. The new rules cautioned examiners to appraise the claimant's medical condition over time and to adopt a comprehensive view of his ability to function in a worklike setting. They explicitly stated that even claimants with mild clinical signs could still be unprepared for employment. Medication, for instance, could con-

17. U.S. Senate, Special Committee on Aging, *Social Security Reviews of the Mentally Disabled*, 98th Congress, 1st Session, 1983, 19–20 (hereafter Senate Special Committee on Aging, *Mentally Disabled*).

18. The Listings of Mental Disorders, 20 C.F.R. 404, Subpart P, Appendix I, sections 12.00 C and C2 (1985) (hereafter Listings). Also explanations of the effect of the revisions are from Howard Goldman, phone interview with author.

trol the outward signs of a mental disorder, but it did not cure the illness. In fact, its side effects could exacerbate the functional limitations imposed by the underlying medical disorder. Thus, chronically mentally ill individuals, the guidelines warned, "may be much more impaired for work than their signs or symptoms would indicate."[19] And because an individual's "functioning may vary considerably over time," the revised rules urged examiners to obtain information from the claimant's treating physicians, friends, family, and other sources familiar with the claimant to ensure that he "has been observed over a considerable period of time" and his true capacity to work had been accurately determined.[20] What emerged from the mental impairments workgroup, therefore, was a much more comprehensive set of Listings that led to greater attention to claimants' functional limitations, social settings, and individual circumstances.

Reforming Childhood Disability

While reforms to the adult mental disorders rules were not controversial, revisions to the childhood disability rules set off a political firestorm. The same collaborative effort between sympathetic administrators and advocates occurred when the SSA revamped the children's Listings in 1990 following the *Zebley* decision. In fact, *Zebley*, according to one SSA official, became a pretext to "do the right thing for children" so that in the end, the SSA went above and beyond the Supreme Court's requirements.[21] From the beginning, officials in the Office of Disability determined that, rather than fretting about how liberal or restrictive the eventual rules were, their goal would be to write rules that were in keeping with the recommendations of the medical and pediatric community. As one official explained, the Office of Disability was not overly concerned with how many children would end up on SSI following the *Zebley*-mandated administrative reforms. Capturing the outlook of many within the SSA, he noted the growth that took place in SSI after the release of the new rules was not surprising given rates of childhood poverty. "It was more surprising," he argued, "that there were times when we only had a quarter of a million kids on the rolls."[22]

19. Listings, sections 12.00 E, F, and G.
20. Listings, sections 12.00 D, 12.02 A, 12.03 A, 12.04 A, 12.06 A, 12.07 A.
21 John Ritter, SSA interview.
22. Barry Eigen, executive program policy officer in the Office of Disability, interview with author, Baltimore, Maryland, September 6, 2000.

Following *Zebley*, the SSA made three important changes to the evaluation of childhood disability. The first of these was the addition of the test of functioning that the Supreme Court had ordered. Known as an Individual Functional Assessment (IFA), this was by far the most problematic of the post-*Zebley* changes. In lieu of employment, the court had urged the SSA to use playing, feeding, learning, and caring for oneself as the functional measures of disability. And after consulting a workgroup of legal advocates, pediatricians, and specialists in child development, the agency settled on an "age-appropriate" standard. This meant that the IFA measured the extent to which the child's medical condition limited his ability to attain developmental milestones, perform like children of the same age, and acquire the skills necessary to become a productive and self-sufficient adult. In administrative practice, therefore, a child was disabled if he had limitations in two or three of seven functional areas that were rated in the IFA: response to stimuli; cognition; communication; motor functioning; social functioning; personal and behavioral functioning; and concentration, persistence, and pace.

Nevertheless, the SSA's traditionally strong attachment to the medical foundations of disability led officials to take the *Zebley* ruling two steps further. These two steps amounted to reforms designed to loosen the medical rules so that officials could maximize the number of children entering through the Listings, the clinical step of the disability certification process, rather than through the untested and amorphous IFA.[23] Thus, the second change the SSA initiated after *Zebley* was the release of a new set of Listings for many childhood disorders. The Supreme Court had been critical of the SSA for failing to update its medical criteria to keep track of advances in pediatrics and to issue specific Listings for rare but recently recognized childhood disorders. In response, shortly following the court's decision, the Office of Disability released new Listings for multiple body dysfunctions, such as Down syndrome, phenylketornuria, mental retardation with other bodily complications, and fetal alcohol syndrome. The office also used the occasion to publish a new set of Listings for childhood mental disorders, which were patterned after the changes that had been made to the adult mental disorders Listings in 1985.[24] The new childhood mental disorders Listings, like the revisions made to the adult Listings, broadened the number of conditions considered impairments. Attention deficit/hyperactivity disorder and psycho-

23. Ibid.
24. Dale Cox, chief of exertional and nonexertional impairments in the Office of Disability, interview with author, Baltimore, Maryland, September 6, 2000.

active substance abuse disorders, for example, appeared in the SSA's Listings for the first time. Moreover, the revised children's Listings emphasized functioning. Under the old Listings, a child with behavioral or emotional problems that interfered with his schoolwork but that nevertheless allowed him to feed and dress himself would fail to qualify. Also excluded were children with a range of cognitive and behavioral disorders, such as speech difficulties, learning disabilities, and hyperactivity, which while frequently limiting were not fully debilitating. Under the new rules, children could qualify if they had a "marked" restriction in a few measures rather than a complete absence of functional abilities across all measures.[25]

Finally, the Office of Disability decided to allow children to win awards on the basis of what it called "functional equivalency." In the past, the SSA had only admitted children whose impairments were specifically described in the Listings. Functional equivalency essentially allowed a child to qualify for benefits if examiners could not find the clinical signs of her disorder in the Listings but considered her symptoms as functionally limiting as a listed impairment.[26] For instance, a child who had recently undergone a major organ transplant would be deemed to be suffering limitations that were "functionally equivalent" to a listed impairment even though organ transplants themselves are not described in the medical rules.[27] Brian Zebley was a perfect example of the type of child who would qualify under functional equivalency. Although prior to 1991, his specific set of impairments—paralysis, vision problems, and mental retardation—were not contained in any specific Listing, had functional equivalency been in place, he would have been able to qualify for SSI if an examiner looked at the overall impact of the combined impairments and decided that together they limited his activities as much as impairments that were included. Thus, under functional equivalency, children

25. These examples are taken from Leonard Rubenstein, amicus brief for the American Academy of Child and Adolescent Psychiatry et al., in *Zebley v. Bowen*, United States Court of Appeals for the Third Circuit, No. 87–1692, 9–10, in the Archives of the American Psychiatric Association, Washington, D.C.

26. Prior to functional equivalency, if a child claimant failed to meet the Listings, he then had to show that his impairment or impairments "medically equaled" a listed impairment. In other words, he had to demonstrate the clinical signs or symptoms were of equal severity to the listed impairment that most resembled the claimant's impairment or combination of impairments. If the clinical factors were not as severe as a Listing, the child claimant was denied benefits even though the overall functional impact of the nonlisted impairment might be as severe as the functional impact of a listed impairment. See 20 C.F.R. 416.926(a) (1989).

27. Barry Eigen, interview with author.

needed only to meet the Listings' overall functional standard of severity rather than satisfy specific clinical indicators.

Trouble on the Horizon

The effect of these administrative reforms on the size and composition of the Social Security disability rolls was enormous. Following the 1984 disability amendments and the revision of rules governing the evaluation of adult mental disorders in 1985, mental disabilities became an even more visible and distinct part of the DI and SSI programs. Only 10 percent of DI benefits awarded in 1981 went to people with mental disorders, but in 1986, the year after the new adult rules were put in place, almost a third of new benefits went to applicants with a mental disorder. In later years, the mentally disabled constituted between 20 and 25 percent of all DI awards. The effects of the rule changes were especially pronounced for SSI. While in 1986, individuals with mental disabilities made up less than one-quarter of the disabled people on SSI, within ten years that proportion had grown to almost one in three. Today half the SSI awards are made for reasons of mental retardation or psychiatric impairment.[28]

The transformation of the SSI children's program was even more striking. By pushing disability certification toward greater emphasis on a child's overall functioning rather than the clinical indicators of an impairment, the post-*Zebley* reforms not only expanded eligibility for SSI but also opened the program to more children with mental disorders. From fewer than 300,000 children in 1989, the program hit its peak in the summer of 1996, with just over 1 million children enrolled. Lawmakers and bureaucrats attributed much of the expansion to the addition of the IFA, which brought 219,000 children into SSI between 1991 and 1994, and accounted for one-third of the growth during that time period. Even more contentious, however, were the types of children the IFA admitted. Of the children who entered SSI through the new functional test, 84 percent had a mental disorder listed as their primary limitation. As a combined result of the IFA and the revised childhood mental disorders List-

28. U.S. General Accounting Office, *Social Security: Disability Rolls Keep Growing, While Explanations Remain Elusive*, GAO/HEHS-94–34, 1994, table IV.6, 40, and U.S. General Accounting Office, *Supplemental Security Income: Recent Growth in the Rolls Raises Fundamental Program Concerns*, GAO/T-HEHS-95–67, 1995, 15–16.

ings, by 1994 kids with either mental illness or mental retardation received nearly three-quarters of all SSI awards made to children.[29]

The IFA and Mentally Disabled Children

The IFA was inherently expansive, but it became controversial because it benefited primarily children with mental disorders. There are three ways in which the IFA liberalized children's eligibility for SSI. First, because a child needed to show only functional deficits rather than clinical signs, the IFA helped those children who tended to fare poorly under the Listings. Children with mental disorders, multiple impairments, and rare disorders that were not specifically cataloged in the Listings and infants and toddlers who were too young to take part in clinical examinations now had recourse to the IFA. For instance, in the past, examiners had to wait until an infant suspected of having hearing problems was old enough to respond to clinical tests of auditory capacity. But under the IFA, the examiner needed only to see if the infant reacted to stimuli in the same way as children of a similar age did. Second, the IFA set a lower standard for qualification than the Listings. The Listings generally required that the impairment cause "marked" restrictions in functioning while in some circumstances the IFA allowed children with only "moderate" functional limitations to qualify for payments. Finally, the IFA encompassed a broader inquiry into functioning than the adult functional test, which pegged its standard to work capacity. By contrast, the IFA measured functioning across virtually every activity in which children could participate: studying, playing, socializing, communicating, dressing and feeding oneself, and carrying out activities performed in school as well as at home. In other words, the children's assessment was a much more global evaluation of functioning than was the adult test, and because more areas of functioning were examined, there were more chances for children to qualify.

The IFA, however, did not necessarily let in children with all types of impairments; instead, it advantaged mental disorders. This occurred because the SSA did not know how to graft a work-oriented standard of disability designed for adults onto a program for children. "All we knew to do," one policy official explained, "was provide some way that a child . . .

29. GAO, *Recent Growth in the Rolls*, 3, 5, and U.S. General Accounting Office, *Social Security: New Functional Assessments for Children Raise Eligibility Questions*, GAO/HEHS-95–66, 1995, figure 2, 9–10.

who has a less severe impairment than it takes to meet the Listings could be found disabled, just as we say that an adult who has a less severe impairment than in the Listings could be found disabled" under the adult test of functional capacity. Without much guidance from the Supreme Court and forced to write and implement a brand-new test in less than a year, planners in the Office of Disability patterned the IFA after its revised Listings for childhood mental disorders, which already contained a template for evaluating the functional capacity of children.[30] Used to assess the severity of a child's mental disorder, these functional measures gauged a child's ability to communicate and understand, socialize, take part in activities of daily living, refrain from destructive behavior, and maintain the concentration, persistence, and pace needed to complete tasks in a timely manner. Officials decided that the measures did not have to remain limited to mental capacity but could instead be easily adapted to cover all manner of functional restrictions in children. They reasoned that for each functional area contained in the Listings of childhood mental disorders, there were analogous limitations that could be imposed by physical impairments. For example, a child confined to a wheelchair would have limited abilities to relate to others in the same way that a child with a conduct or learning disorder would. Similarly, a heart condition might reduce the ability of a child to keep pace with his peers in activities such as play and physical education in the same way that a learning disability would impede the ability of a child to keep pace in school assignments.[31] The IFA, therefore, retained all the functional areas used in the Listings for childhood mental disorders and added a measurement for motor function that would be used only for children with physical impairments.

Nevertheless, because it was based on functional measures initially designed for impairments of the mind, the IFA lowered the overall disability standard for children with mental disorders. Since it contained the same functional domains as the Listings, this meant that several areas were examined more than once, first under the Listings and then again under the more lax standard of the IFA. Thus, a child who failed to meet the rigors of the mental disorders Listings could still qualify for benefits by meeting the lower thresholds in basically the same functional areas once he got to the IFA step.[32] As a result, a study conducted in 1995

30. Barry Eigen, interview with author.
31. Ibid.
32. Jerry L. Mashaw, James M. Perrin, and Virginia P. Reno, eds., *Restructuring the SSI Disability Program for Children and Adolescents* (Washington, DC: National Academy of Social Insurance, 1996), 27–29.

found that 42 percent of children with mental disorders qualified through the IFA while only 7 percent of children with physical disorders did.[33]

Given its close ties to mental disorders, the IFA was soon under fire, especially since it had been added by judicial fiat and without congressional sanction. Designed to rectify the disadvantages that the clinical model of disability posed for children of all impairments, it instead became a gateway for children exhibiting what critics regarded as just plain bad behavior, children like Lisa T's son. In fact, many of the kids entering through the IFA were plagued with behavioral, speech, and learning problems, disorders that were relatively common among children but rarely severe enough to be totally incapacitating.[34] "It would make one think," one administrator complained, "that almost any adolescent or preadolescent child going through the typical socialization experiences and 'growing pains' may qualify for SSI."[35]

The Problems with the Functional Approach to Disability

The revision of the adult mental disorders Listings occasioned little outcry. But with the IFA, the drive to incorporate individual functioning and social disadvantage ground to a halt, as the subjectivity of functional assessments frustrated the SSA's efforts to maintain consistent and precise evaluations of disability. The IFA was besieged with criticism and derailed by several difficulties that emerged following its implementation. In general, there were four problems with the new test.

First, despite extensive training, disability examiners struggled to place impairments in the correct functional domains. This is because, although the domains were conceptually distinct, they were closely related to one another, and the same impairment could affect multiple areas of functioning. For example, in the case of a child that lied, behaved aggressively, and fought in school, the examiner had to decide whether the child suffered a deficit of social skills, personal and behavioral skills, or both. The child could have one or two areas of functional limitation depending on how the examiner classified the child's behavior. In an internal study

33. GAO, *New Functional Assessments*, figure 2, 9–10.
34. U.S. General Accounting Office, *Supplemental Security Income: Growth and Changes in Recipient Population Call for Reexamining Program*, GAO/HEHS-95-137, 1995, 17.
35. Quoted in L. Scott Mueller and Peter M. Wheeler, "The Growth in Disability Program as Seen by SSA Field Office Managers," in *Growth in Disability Benefits*, ed. Kalman Rupp and David C. Stapleton (Kalamazoo, MI: W. E. Upjohn, 1998), 214.

conducted in 1994, the Office of Disability discovered that its examiners tended to classify impairments in more categories than it believed was appropriate, thus overstating the functional impact of the impairment.[36]

Second, examiners had trouble rating the extent of a child's functional restrictions. Under the IFA, examiners graded the severity of the limitation according to a five-point scale that ranged from "no evidence of impairment," to "mild," "moderate," "marked," and finally "extreme." The Office of Disability stipulated that a child would be awarded benefits, in general, if he had one marked and one moderate limitation or three moderate limitations. While examiners had a relatively easy time identifying severe and minimal impairments, they could not differentiate between moderate and marked ones. The Office of Disability also found that examiners rated the same children differently; what one examiner rated a moderate limitation, another examiner graded as marked. Nevertheless, the office could provide only limited direction on how to determine severity. In its instructions to examiners, it defined a moderate limitation as "more than a mild or minimal limitation but less than a marked limitation." It did not define mild or minimal but instead explained that a moderate limitation was one that resulted in "considerable" interference with the child's ability to function in an age-appropriate manner.[37] But this only begged the question: What did "considerable" mean? "Marked," "moderate," "considerable"—these were conceptual terms that still did not provide the necessary operational guidance to adjudicators.

In addition, the SSA itself was ambiguous about how to interpret the cumulative results of the IFA. The Office of Disability had stated that three moderate impairments—if they were "three good, solid moderates"—would be enough to justify an award. But here officials equivocated by cautioning examiners that even this was a "general guideline, not a firm rule." Instead, they encouraged examiners to "step back" and evaluate whether the child met the overall standard of disability. Officials noted that in some cases, depending on the individual child's circumstances, "other possible combinations of ratings, such as two strong moderates," might warrant a finding of disability.[38] Yet this raised more questions than it answered. What did two strong moderates look like, and how were they different from three good, solid moderates? In which circumstances might two strong moderates be acceptable? Childhood dis-

36. GAO, *New Functional Assessments*, 12–13.
37. Ibid., 13.
38. Ibid., 14, 29–30.

ability, therefore, looked like something officials could not adequately describe but that examiners should recognize when they saw it.

Finally, the disability determination process for children raised an age-old problem for the SSA: how to distinguish medical from social handicaps. In its 1994 study, the Office of Disability found that examiners tended to base awards on limitations that, in the eyes of SSA officials, stemmed from the child's living circumstances rather than his medical condition.[39] But this was asking too much of examiners. Separating functional impairments that result from environmental conditions from those resulting from a medical condition was a theoretical exercise that did not make much sense in the real world where these factors were intricately and inextricably intertwined.

The real issue, however, was not that the Office of Disability did not provide enough instruction or that state disability examiners were not applying the rules correctly. The fundamental problem with the IFA rested in the inherent subjectivity of the decision rather than in the operational guidelines that governed it. Though judging disability in adults was also subjective, the SSA did not confront this predicament to the same extent when the agency's evaluation of functioning was confined to assessing the effect of an impairment on a specific social role, such as employment. The evaluation of children, on the other hand, was very different and more challenging. To begin with, the functional evaluation of children crossed many behaviors and activities and was pegged to the imprecise and indeterminate standard of "age-appropriate behavior." Indeed, the SSA's disability examiners were confused about what "age-appropriate" meant. The Office of Disability found that examiners tended to overrate the severity of childhood impairments because they frequently compared the child not to age-peers but to the idealized child of that age.[40] Not surprisingly, this meant that many children had the hallmarks of a disability. All children, at some point, act in a manner that is not appropriate for their age. Witness the common admonition of parents to their children to "act your age." To be sure, inappropriate behavior was only a disability if it stemmed from a medical condition, but drawing the line between individual shortcomings and medically imposed functional deficits was exceedingly difficult, if not impossible. The underlying dilemma, put simply, was not that the SSA could not define age-appropriate behavior; rather it is that we all have different ideas about what is "age-appropriate." And when children fail to act appropriately, we disagree about whether this is the re-

39. Ibid., 29.
40. Ibid., 29.

sult of a medical problem, the home and social environment, or the idiosyncrasies of individual children.

Also complicating the determinations of childhood disability was the fact that when looking into the functional capacities of a child, examiners were not simply looking at a child's minimal ability to perform an activity. They were required to assess whether the child could perform that activity with a fair degree of success, and if not, decide whether that failure was the result of a medical impairment. For example, suppose for the moment that the functional assessment of children were confined to the evaluation of their activities at school, the closest analogy to the adult workplace. A significant difference between children and adults lies in the fact that employers do not have to hire impaired workers. Schools, on the other hand, cannot turn away children who want to be educated. Because of this difference, for an adult, the ability to stay on the job is enough to indicate adequate functioning; there is no requirement that the adult actually excel at his job. But it is not enough that the child stays in school. Even severely disabled children can physically stay situated in the school building. In the case of children, therefore, functioning must be assessed according to the impairment's impact on the child's ability to succeed in school. To be considered functional, a child must also succeed to some degree in his schoolwork. Nevertheless, almost every child, whether medically impaired or not, falls short of expectations; almost every child could be a little bit more successful in school. Functional evaluations of children, in short, raised a number of conceptual problems that were not present in the adult programs.

The Growth of Disability Benefits, the Deterioration of Disability Determination

A confluence of several related events sparked a far-reaching reexamination of Social Security disability policy between 1994 and 1996. In the early 1990s, DI and SSI enrollment grew rapidly, so rapidly that lawmakers became worried. In 1994, the number of all disabled persons receiving DI, SSI, or both reached 7.2 million, an increase of 70 percent in less than a decade. Over the same time period, spending for DI grew by 45 percent after controlling for inflation and for SSI by 97 percent. SSI gave lawmakers particular reason to pause because its expansion was so dramatic. Whereas the number of disabled workers rose by 41 percent between 1985 and 1994, the participation of the disabled poor in SSI had more than doubled, and over half that growth had occurred since 1990.[41] In addition, there were signs that the expansion of SSI was having a "spillover effect" on the larger, more expensive Disability Insurance program. Since one of the first questions explored in the disability application is whether the claimant is eligible for DI as well, congressional researchers suggested that the outreach the SSA had conducted for SSI between 1986 and 1990 fueled the rise in DI applications too. In 1992, almost three-quarters of disability claims were for either SSI or concurrent SSI/DI benefits, and for the first time, the number of people awarded SSI due to disability exceeded the number of disabled workers granted Social Security payments. This development led researchers to conclude that "a significant portion of the growth in DI is attributable to the factors driving up enrollment in SSI."[42]

While SSI's expansion could continue unabated, its linkages to DI compelled policymakers to step in to arrest growth in both programs. Because Disability Insurance was financed through a self-sustaining trust fund, its expansion had grave fiscal consequences. In April 1992, actuarial estimates showed that if current trends persisted, the disability trust fund would be exhausted within three months. Although Congress was able to shore up the program by transferring money from the retirement trust fund, many lawmakers, including long-time allies of the advocates, were anxious, given that Old Age Insurance would be caught in its own financing crisis with the aging of the Baby Boom generation. "At the same time we've been assuring senior citizens that we will leave Social Security untouched," Senator William Cohen complained, "a very real threat has been silently creeping up on the solvency of the Social Security trust funds—namely, the unfettered growth of the Social Security Disability Insurance Program."[43]

Finally, more troubling than growth itself was the administrative deterioration that accompanied it. By the early 1990s, it appeared that DI and SSI would break under the combined weight of judicially and congressionally mandated reforms. Courts overturned old disability rules, imposed new ones, and ordered the SSA to readjudicate thousands of old

41. U.S. General Accounting Office, *Social Security: Federal Disability Programs Face Major Issues*, GAO/T-HEHS-95-97, 1995, 3, 4–5.

42. U.S. Congressional Research Service (CRS), prepared by David Koitz, Geoffrey Kollman, and Jennifer Neisner, *Status of the Disability Programs of the Social Security Administration*, 12–13, 14.

43. U.S. Senate, Special Committee on Aging, *Problems in the Social Security Disability Programs: The Disabling of America*, 104th Congress, 1st Session, 1995, 1.

claims. Congress demanded that the SSA modify its programs to accommodate the homeless and mentally disabled and engage in aggressive outreach activities to various troubled groups, including migrant workers, AIDS patients, and legal immigrants. Meanwhile, the SSA watched growth in its program for drug addicts and alcoholics and struggled to patch together some semblance of a treatment referral program.[44] At the same time, between 1986 and 1990, Congress repeatedly slashed funding for administrative staffing to meet tight budget targets, thus leaving the SSA ill-prepared for the more extensive examinations required by the 1984 disability amendments and the surge in caseloads that followed *Zebley* after 1990.[45] To some within the SSA, the situation made congressional concern over outreach a laughable proposition given that the agency suffered from too many rather than too few applicants.[46]

The crushing workload that the SSA faced in the early 1990s took a toll on the quality of the agency's evaluations of disability. In 1991, the SSA faced an excess of more than 500,000 applications that needed processing, and the backlog was expected to reach 1 million cases within two years.[47] The situation was so dire that even advocates were alarmed. Disability reformer Gay Gellhorn declared in frustration, "Disability determination has to change." She noted the litany of problems that had cropped up: "The process costs too much and takes too long. . . . From the claimants' point of view, there is a crisis of confusion and delay. They do not understand how to navigate the system successfully, why it takes so long, and why different levels of the same agency reach opposite conclusions."[48] Moreover, knowing that members of Congress promptly reprimand them when cases take too long to process and constituents complain, SSA officials, forced to do more with less, slowed the agency's reviews of continuing eligibility to a trickle.[49] As a result, the number of persons leaving the DI or SSI rolls because they recovered or were found

44. John Ritter, SSA interview.

45. U.S. General Accounting Office, *Social Security: Reforms in the Disability Determination and Appeals Process*, GAO/T-HRD-91–24, 1991, 3–4, and U.S. General Accounting Office, *Effects of Budget Constraints on SSA Disability Programs*, GAO/T-HRD-88–1, 1987, 1–2, 4–5, 9–11. Staff at state disability determination agencies has remained fairly constant, but applications have increased from about 1.2 million to close to 2 million between fiscal years 1988 and 1993. See 59 *Federal Register* 47887, 47891, 47893–94 (1994).

46. John Ritter, SSA interview.

47. CRS, *Status of the Disability Programs*, 17–18, 60.

48. Gay Gellhorn, "Disability and Welfare Reform: Keep the Supplemental Security Income Program but Reengineer the Disability Determination Process," *Fordham Urban Law Journal* 22 (1995): 968–69.

49. Patricia Owens, phone interview with author.

no longer disabled fell to all-time lows.[50] Thus, when media allegations of widespread fraud and abuse surfaced in 1994, the SSA could not rebut them given how few resources it had been able to devote to maintaining the integrity of its programs. It was a situation strangely reminiscent of the late 1970s.

With the Social Security disability programs condemned from both the Left and the Right, the stage was set for a thorough reexamination of disability benefits policy. That opportunity came in 1992 when President Bill Clinton pledged to "end welfare as we know it." During the debate over welfare reform, lawmakers finally confronted the tensions between the medical model and the inclusive ideals of the advocacy community. Though conservatives tried to roll back the programmatic expansions of the previous decade, like the liberal advocates that preceded them, they too found comprehensive policy change a challenging enterprise.

50. CRS, *Status of the Disability Programs*, 7–8.

8

From Welfare Reform to Welfare Retrenchment

When Republicans won control of the House and Senate in the fall of 1994, Robert Rector, a conservative policy analyst at the Heritage Foundation, promised, "We're not going to have a debate about AFDC. We're going to have a debate on the 'War on Poverty.'"[1] Although the debate over welfare reform first focused on family assistance, soon it encompassed virtually every social welfare program, including SSI and Disability Insurance. This chapter examines these conservative efforts to roll back the program expansion that advocates had achieved over the previous decade. On the one hand, retrenchment of DI and SSI seemed an easy venture. By the early 1990s, liberal antipoverty reformers had succeeded in largely supplanting the SSA's restrictive, clinical approach to disability with a broad functional understanding of impairments. Yet the administrative deterioration that accompanied this transformation cast doubt on the integrity of the disability rolls. Criticism of the two programs was widespread. Carolyn Weaver, for instance, asked—tongue in cheek—whether the unfettered growth of Social Security disability benefits was "making America sick," while Christopher Wright dubbed SSI "the black hole of the welfare state," "a troubling case study of how federal entitlements continually expand beyond their original mission."[2] Moreover, the passage of the ADA

1. Quoted in Jeffrey Katz, "Broad Plan Alters Nature of Welfare Debate," *Congressional Quarterly Weekly Report* 52 (November 19, 1994): 3334.
2. Christopher M. Wright, "SSI: The Black Hole of the Welfare State," *Policy Analysis* 224 (April 27, 1995), http://www.cato.org/pubs/pas/pa-224.html, and Carolyn L. Weaver, "Welfare Payments to the Disabled: Making America Sick?" *American Enterprise* 6, 1 (1995): 61.

called into question the whole premise of providing income support in the first place, and commentators pointed out that generous disability benefits programs and broad disability rights guarantees were incompatible.[3] By the time Bill Clinton entered office in early 1993, long-term dependency—not poverty, hardship, or community living—had become the policy problem to attack.

What stands out most about the drive for retrenchment, however, is its feebleness. Conservatives in Congress tried to fundamentally alter the premises of the liberal welfare state. Republicans proposed converting entitlements into block grants, capping annual spending for many programs, and drastically limiting eligibility. But in the end, they were only able to make dents in the most controversial aspects of DI and SSI, and AFDC, the one program that they did manage to scale back, had few defenders. Begun with high hopes, conservative efforts to restructure programs for the poor ended mostly in frustration.

The Problems with the Social Security Disability Programs

By 1993, problems with the Social Security disability programs were legion, and the issue was not simply one of costs. Growth had occurred among the most unpopular and suspect groups of the disabled. According to congressional studies, legal immigrants, disabled children, and the mentally disabled, especially alcoholics and drug addicts, accounted for nearly 90 percent of the expansion in DI and SSI between 1991 and 1995.[4] Given that this growth was so rapid and unexpected and that it had taken place largely among people with intangible impairments, critics questioned whether those entering the programs were "truly disabled" and whether benefits were being used as Congress intended. The historical irony was that, although at the time it was created lawmakers had praised SSI as a program that would not be subject to fraud and abuse, less than twenty-five years later they found in it many of the same problems that plagued the disreputable AFDC program.

Criticism revolved around three themes. First was fraud. By 1994, the media was filled with stories of recipients who had supposedly cheated

3. James M. Taylor, "Facilitating Fraud: How SSDI Gives Benefits to the Able Bodied," *Policy Analysis* 377 (August 15, 2000): 1.

4. U.S. General Accounting Office, *Supplemental Security Income: Growth and Changes in Recipient Population Call for Reexamining Program*, GAO/HEHS-95–137, 1995, 14.

their way onto the Social Security disability rolls.[5] In a well-known example, *Washington Post* reporter Bob Woodward, famous for uncovering the Watergate scandal, reported that some parents encouraged their children to fail tests or misbehave in class so that they could establish a case for mental disability. There were stories of unscrupulous parents denying their children needed medication so that they remained disabled. Meanwhile, other news sources claimed that rings of shady translators and physicians were faking medical reports and coaching immigrant applicants to feign mental illness.

Second, with so little oversight, abuse appeared to be rampant. Lawmakers expected SSI to remain a program of last resort for "deserving" individuals. But the media featured stories of parents who spent their child's SSI check on luxuries such as cars, televisions, or even family vacations rather than on needed medications or medical treatment.[6] Some news outlets charged that well-to-do naturalized citizens placed their im-

5. See, among others, Bob Woodward and Benjamin Weiser, "Costs Soar for Children's Disability Program: How 26 Words Cost the Taxpayers Billions in New Entitlement Payments," *Washington Post*, February 4, 1994, A1; Jennifer Dixon, "After 20 Years of Helping Poor, Fast-Growing SSI Dogged by Questions," Associated Press, February 23, 1994, Lexis-Nexis document, no page numbers available; Associated Press, "Agency is Faulted for Fraud in Disability Payments to Immigrants," *New York Times*, September 5, 1995, D9; Ashley Dunn, "For Elderly Immigrants, a Retirement Plan in U.S.," *New York Times*, April 16, 1995, Section 1, 1; E. Clay Shaw and Lamar Smith, "Immigrants, Welfare, and the GOP," *Washington Post*, May 28, 1997, Op-Ed, A19; William S. Cohen, "Playing Social Security for a Sucker," *Washington Post*, February 23, 1994, Op-Ed, A17; Spencer Rich, "Congress Planning Cutoff for Addicts on Disability Rolls," *Washington Post*, June 20, 1994, A1; and Associated Press, "House GOP Targets Cash to Drug, Alcohol Addicts," *Washington Times*, January 27, 1995, A12. The General Accounting Office lent legitimacy to the accounts of fraud and abuse by including these anecdotal stories within its more systematic studies of SSI and Disability Insurance presented to Congress. For example, see U.S. General Accounting Office, *Social Security: Major Changes Needed for Disability Benefits for Addicts*, GAO/HEHS-94-128, 1994; and U.S. General Accounting Office, *Supplemental Security Income: Disability Program Vulnerable to Applicant Fraud when Middlemen are Used*, GAO/HEHS-95-116, 1995.
6. To some SSA officials, the charges of fraud and abuse were an unfair misrepresentation of the facts. These were retroactive lump sum payments that families received, typically after winning on appeal. The families had to spend the money quickly because if they saved it, they would no longer qualify under SSI's means test. SSA officials had assured parents that they could spend the lump sums on anything they wanted, and it is not too far-fetched to imagine low-income families suddenly blessed with lots of money to spend in a short period of time might treat their children to a luxury like a family vacation. Janet Bendann, policy officer for childhood disability in the Office of Disability, Social Security Administration, interview with author, Baltimore, Maryland, March 7, 2001.

migrant elderly parents on SSI even through they had the resources to provide for their needs. Even allies of disability advocates found fault with the way DI and SSI were managed. Senator William Cohen, for instance, was critical of the SSA for not assuring that disabled addicts on SSI were enrolled in treatment, as required by the Social Security Act, and that representative payees were properly managing the funds of addicted recipients. Claiming that addicts were "playing Social Security for a sucker," he recounted an outrageous story about a San Francisco drug addict who used his disability checks to buy high-grade drugs that he then diluted and resold for a profit and another about forty alcoholic SSI recipients who listed a Denver liquor store owner as their representative payee. Disability checks, Cohen alleged, were sent directly to the owner who used them to run a tab for the recipients.[7]

A final concern of critics was the perverse incentives that disability benefits seemed to have developed. By 1993, it was hard to ignore the fact that the original purposes of SSI and DI had been eclipsed by the program liberalizations of the 1980s and early 1990s. DI and SSI provided lifelong benefits with little emphasis on return-to-work initiatives. But this was because the programs had been designed to provide compensation for older workers who had lost their earning capacity due to a severe medical impairment. This structure made less sense when a large proportion of beneficiaries were young and had worked little, if any, in their lives. In addition, according to Carolyn Weaver, an expert on Social Security at the American Enterprise Institute, the broad income guarantees of DI and SSI, which were "premised on the complete inability to work," did not appear to comport with disability rights. In light of the passage of the ADA in 1990, Weaver argued, the "'once disabled always disabled' paradigm of social policy," though "deeply embedded in current government policy," was not longer "congruous with modern views of the potential and the abilities of people with disabilities."[8] Long-time supporters of DI also noted the disconnect in the nation's disability policy. Senator Cohen explained to his colleagues on the Senate aging committee that "the Federal Government is sending a very mixed message on disability. We are making the workplace more accessible through the Americans with Disabilities Act, but the Social Security disability pro-

7. Cohen, "Playing Social Security for a Sucker," A17.
8. U.S. House of Representatives, Committee on Ways and Means, Subcommittee on Human Resources, *Contract with America—Welfare Reform*, 104th Congress, 1st Session, 1996, 416–17 (hereafter House Subcommittee on Human Resources, *Contract with America*).

grams weave a web of dependency and undermine efforts toward independence."[9]

A disability benefit program for the contemporary era required a program that provided rehabilitation, encouraged employment, and facilitated young people's transition from welfare to the adult world of work. Social Security disability policy afforded none of these. The General Accounting Office found that few DI or SSI beneficiaries recovered and left the disability rolls once admitted, and while on the rolls, the SSA did a poor job of ensuring that beneficiaries were referred to vocational rehabilitation services or, if they were alcoholics or drug addicts, to treatment programs. Nor did the agency have a plan to teach disabled children how to be independent once they reached age eighteen. For this reason, the provision of benefits to disabled children was especially objectionable. According to investigators at the GAO, "Children who cannot function at an age-appropriate level may be able to develop so that they can work by the time they reach adulthood." But older children had no incentive to prepare themselves for a career so long as the SSA focused on indefinitely paying out cash benefits rather than on "work[ing] with recipients more actively to help them increase their self-sufficiency."[10]

Lawmakers were disturbed by the specter of long-term dependency in such a substantial proportion of Social Security's disabled beneficiaries, especially those who received SSI, since they tended to be younger than DI beneficiaries. In fact, the more lawmakers looked at SSI, the more it looked like AFDC. Some critics even drew direct parallels between the two programs. For example, Carolyn Weaver noted, that although "SSI does not present problems at the forefront of the welfare reform debate—teen pregnancy, out-of-wedlock births, and the cycle of dependency," lawmakers could not ignore the problems it posed. "SSI discourages work and, in providing cash support with basically 'no strings attached,' tends to perpetuate the very conditions that preclude work and promote dependency."[11] In fact, it could be more insidious than AFDC. One study estimated that a family of three living in Maryland could increase its income by more than $3,500 if one of the children transferred

9. U.S. Senate, Special Committee on Aging, *Problems in the Social Security Disability Programs: The Disabling of America?* 10th Congress, 1st Session, 1995, 3 (hereafter Senate Special Committee on Aging, *Problems in the SSD Programs*).

10. GAO, *Growth and Changes*, 21, 22.

11. House Subcommittee on Human Resources, *Contract with America*, 416–17.

from AFDC to SSI.[12] Because SSI benefits tended to be higher than AFDC benefits, were coupled with Medicaid eligibility, and carried no work requirements, families faced strong incentives to shift from the latter to the former program (which states, hoping to reduce their welfare obligations, happily assisted).[13]

Apprehension over dependency was nothing new. In fact, the seeds of SSI's disordered future were present from the very beginning. Children, addicts, and adults with mental disorders had been part of the original legislation. And even back then, policy analysts had worried about the program's open-endedness and its propensity to encourage dependency and undermine recovery.[14] What made the 1990s different was that in the 1970s, suspect groups were a small part of Social Security's disabled clientele. Twenty-five years later, they were hard to miss.

Advocates protested that the reports of fraud and abuse were overblown. True enough, despite numerous investigations, neither the GAO nor the HHS inspector general was able to verify accusations of deceit, at least in the children's program. The GAO noted, "Unless parents admit it, coaching is almost impossible to substantiate." It also acknowledged that "the extent of coaching cannot be measured with much confidence," and in cases where coaching or malingering might be present, only a handful had resulted in an award.[15] Yet the dearth of evidence missed the political significance of even anecdotal reports of dishonesty. According to Kent Weaver, "Concerns about the deservingness of entitlement recipients are closely tied to policymakers' concern for avoiding waste, fraud, and abuse and gaining good value for expenditures."[16] What

12. Jeffrey Kubik, "Incentives for the Identification and Treatment of Children with Disabilities: The Supplemental Security Income Program," *Journal of Public Economics* 73 (1999): 187–215, cited in Mary C. Daly and Richard V. Burkhauser, "Left Behind: SSI in the Era of Welfare Reform," *Focus* 22, 3 (2003), 41.

13. U.S. General Accounting Office, *Social Security: Federal Disability Programs Face Major Issues*, GAO/T-HEHS-95-97, 1995, 12.

14. Martha N. Ozawa and Duncan Lindsey, "Is SSI Too Supportive of the Mentally Ill?" *Public Welfare* 35, 4 (1977): 48–52, and Richard H. Lamb and Alexander S. Rosawski, "Supplemental Security Income and the Sick Role," *American Journal of Psychiatry* 135, 10 (1978): 1221–24.

15. U.S. General Accounting Office, *Social Security: New Functional Assessments for Children Raise Eligibility Questions*, GAO/HEHS-95–66, 1995, p. 17. See also U.S. General Accounting Office, *Supplemental Security Income: Noncitizen Caseload Continues to Grow*, GAO/HEHS-96–149, 1996, 8.

16. R. Kent Weaver, "Controlling Entitlements," in *The New Direction in American Politics*, ed. John E. Chubb and Paul E. Peterson (Washington, DC: Brookings Institution Press, 1985), 337.

mattered for the reform debate was not whether allegations of fraud, abuse, and perverse incentives were true. The fact that they existed at all undermined the perceived "deservingness" of certain disabled beneficiaries, directing attention away from their needs and toward the inherent slipperiness of disability's categorical boundary. Urging Congress to address the matter, the GAO contended that even the perception of impropriety was unacceptable. "Regardless of the actual extent of such abuse," it stated, "reports [of abuse] can significantly erode public confidence in the program's integrity."[17]

Moreover, the media stories had some grounding in reality insofar as they hinted at a larger problem with Social Security disability benefits, especially as they related to SSI. The allegations were not simply the result of the willful misconduct of recipients but also a consequence of SSI's open-ended structure, which no longer suited current expectations about disability. What Democratic representative Gerald Klezcka, one of SSI's most vocal critics, said of children's benefits could easily be applied to the entire program. Calling it a "rudderless program," he argued, "It is impossible to talk about abusive payments when there is no clear statement how payments should be used."[18] Similarly, twenty-five years after SSI's inception, an expert commission charged with making recommendations for improving the program found it necessary to devise its own post hoc statement of program goals because the "ambiguity in the fundamental purpose . . . ma[de] it difficult to assess the program's success."[19] Al-

17. GAO, *Growth and Changes*, 10.

18. House Subcommittee on Human Resources, *Contract with America*, 367.

19. National Commission on Childhood Disability (NCCD), *Supplemental Security Income for Children with Disabilities* (Washington, DC: National Commission on Childhood Disability, 1995), 40. The commission eventually recommended the following four objectives for the children's SSI program: (1) to provide the basic necessities to maintain a disabled child at the home or another appropriate institution; (2) to cover the additional medical and nonmedical costs of caring for a disabled child, costs that are not covered by traditional health care coverage, Medicaid, or other public programs; (3) to enhance the child's opportunities for development; and (4) to offset the loss of family income when a parent drops out of the labor force or remains underemployed in order to care for a disabled child. A panel of the National Academy of Social Insurance looking into the children's disability program cited the additional rationales of preserving family structure by keeping the child at home with her parents and alleviating the marital stress that can accompany the financial strain of raising a disabled child. The NASI panel also noted that keeping a child at home and in the community eased the process of mainstreaming when the child reached adulthood and lessened the stigma that disabled children faced by raising community awareness of disability. Jerry L. Mashaw, James M. Perrin, and Virginia P. Reno, eds., *Restructuring the SSI Disability Program for Children and Adolescents* (Washington, DC: National Academy of Social Insurance, 1996), 17–18.

though the commission came up with a list of objectives, these represented the purposes the program was currently serving or those that commission members believed it should serve rather than the purposes lawmakers themselves had in mind when they enacted the program. Thus, for the first time in many years, lawmakers were asking the right questions about Social Security disability policy. There emerged bipartisan consensus that the system was broken, but little agreement on how to fix it.

Conservative Ambitions Meet Political Reality

Given the far-reaching problems in DI and especially SSI, many policy experts urged Congress, rather than simply making incremental patches to the programs, to undertake a fundamental reassessment of Social Security disability policy in order to adapt it not only to a changing clientele but also to the new expectations about disability that had arisen since the enactment of the Americans with Disabilities Act. But like so many other previous episodes, policymaking became piecemeal as Social Security disability reform found itself entangled in the drive to revamp family assistance. Questions about disability were soon subsumed by concern for meeting budget-cutting targets, and efforts to overhaul the DI and SSI programs gave way to largely incremental tightening. Instead of reforming disability benefits, lawmakers merely squeezed them somewhat.

As had been the case in 1972, during debate over welfare reform in 1994–96, SSI took a backseat to AFDC. It remained the province of just a few members of Congress and of secondary concern in the larger dispute over welfare dependency. This time, however, budget imperatives added a new twist. When candidate Clinton promised to "end welfare as we know it," he was not speaking of SSI or DI. But because of budget rules enacted in 1990, Clinton could not spend more on the child-care, job training, and job placement programs that he envisioned as part of his welfare reform initiative without either raising taxes or making corresponding cuts in other entitlement programs to offset the increased expenditures. Having ruled out tax hikes for fear that such a move would damage the president's moderate, "New Democrat" credentials, the White House also dismissed the idea of squeezing funds from the popular Old Age Insurance program. Also, savings that were to be realized from restrictions in Medicare and Medicaid were already earmarked for Clinton's health care reform initiative. This left the administration scavenging for money from programs with clientele even more unpopular than welfare mothers; this was not easy.[20] Given the controversy surrounding SSI, the program was a natural choice. Citing the allegations of fraud and abuse, one White House official defended the administration's singling out of addicts, legal immigrants, and children. "Just because a program is targeted on the poor," he argued, "doesn't mean we shouldn't touch it. It might not be doing a good job." In early 1994, Clinton's task force on welfare reform broached the subject of saving $800 million annually by dropping 250,000 children from SSI and redirecting savings toward funding reform of family support. But the task force shelved the idea after several White House officials objected.[21]

Once Republicans gained control of Congress after the 1994 midterm elections, they set out to enact welfare reform on their own terms. Welfare reform quickly became welfare retrenchment. With Clinton having already suggested cuts in SSI, the program was an easy target. Congressional Republicans, however, sought to go much further than Clinton, converting the White House's efforts to tighten SSI into a full-scale assault on the program. As the newly installed Republican leaders, headed by House speaker Newt Gingrich, laid out their policy agenda for SSI and DI, four objectives emerged:

- Reduce fraud by reducing the incentives for beneficiaries, especially children, to fake impairments, which could be accomplished by either tightening of the definition of disability so that only the most severely disabled qualified or reducing payments so that SSI was no longer an attractive a source of income;
- End abuse by providing closer monitoring of representative payees and parents; converting children's benefits from a cash payment to a voucher for medical services; and ending benefit payments for substance abusers;
- Control SSI expenditures by capping annual spending or enrollment, or by converting the program from an individual entitlement into a block grant;
- And reserve disability benefits for the most severely disabled persons by emphasizing the medical instead of social components of disability,

20. R. Kent Weaver, *Ending Welfare as We Know It* (Washington, DC: Brookings Institution Press, 2000), 226–27.

21. Quoted in Jason DeParle, "Democrats Face Hard Choices in Welfare Overhaul," *New York Times*, February 22, 1994, A16. Also see Jason DeParle, "White House Memo Sees Higher Costs for Welfare Plan," *New York Times*, April 5, 1994, A1, and Jason DeParle, "Cabinet Expresses Fears about Plan to Alter Welfare," *New York Times*, March 23, 1994, A1.

especially mental disability, and making SSI available only to children needing institutionalization.[22]

Even so, like Clinton, Republicans were driven largely by budget constraints. The House leadership hoped to use SSI cuts not only to finance modest increases in spending for the Temporary Assistance for Needy Families (TANF) block grant, which would replace AFDC, but also to help the party meet its goal of simultaneously enacting a balanced budget and a middle-class tax cut. Dropping the 800,000 noncitizens on SSI alone would generate over $3.6 billion. This measure coupled with cuts in other benefits to legal immigrants represented 40 percent of the savings that would be realized by enacting welfare reform.[23] Retrenchment, though, fell far short of the party's initial ambitions. Rather than overhaul DI and SSI, lawmakers merely picked off the most controversial and vulnerable parts of the programs while the structural reforms conservatives envisioned fell by the wayside.

Drug Addicts and Alcoholics

Reform of Social Security's benefit program for drug addicts and alcoholics began as an attempt to enforce personal responsibility; it ended as an all-out attack on the program. While certainly a highly controversial part of SSI, the number of people on SSI with a primary diagnosis of addiction was never more than about 250,000, a figurative "drop in the bucket" in a program that served more than 6 million disabled adults and children. Overall addicts comprised no more than 3 percent of the DI and SSI rolls. Yet it was not the size of the addicts' program that got into trouble but rather budget pressures and concern about mismanagement and abuse. Initially, lawmakers tried tightening the treatment and monitoring requirements, but soon gave up and eliminated benefits for addicts entirely.[24]

22. U.S. House of Representatives, Committee on Ways and Means, Subcommittee on Human Resources, "Analysis of Legislation, Justification, and Comparison with Present Law," report transmitting H.R. 4 to the Committee on Ways and Means, February 24, 1995, 30–37 (hereafter House Subcommittee on Human Resources, "Analysis of Legislation"); Wright, "SSI: The Black Hole of the Welfare State;" and Weaver, "Welfare Payments to the Disabled," 61–64.

23. GAO, *Noncitizen Caseload Continues to Grow*, 1.

24. Paul Davies, Howard Iams, and Kalman Rupp, "The Effect of Welfare on SSA's Disability Programs: Design of Policy Evaluation and Early Evidence," *Social Security Bulletin* 63, 1 (2000): 6.

Opponents were bothered, not necessarily by the growing number of addicts, but by the SSA's failure to supervise them once they were on the rolls. Senator Cohen explained in a hearing before the Finance Committee's Subcommittee on Social Security and Family Policy, "What is most striking is . . . the fact that there is very little in the way of oversight in terms of how these dollars are being spent . . . because the focus has not been on rehabilitation."[25] In August 1994, Congress resurrected the treatment rules for all SSI and DI beneficiaries whose addiction was a contributing factor "material to the finding" of disability. Addicts were now required to take part in a substance abuse treatment program and to have a representative payee, preferably an organization, managing their disability checks. (This was the first time that the treatment and representative payee requirements of SSI were applied to DI.) To ensure that addicts took treatment seriously and that disability benefits did not subsidize long-term addictions, payments were limited to thirty-six months over a lifetime. In addition, Congress ordered the SSA to establish referral and monitoring agencies in each state to oversee compliance. According to the Congressional Budget Office (CBO), the provisions would lead to a reduction in the rolls, either as addicts recovered or were dropped as they hit the time limit. This would lead to budget savings of $840 million over five years. Hoping to use the savings generated by the restrictions for its reform of AFDC, the Clinton White House enthusiastically supported the measures.[26]

These initiatives, however, did not slow the drive to crack down on addicts. Conservative analyst Carolyn Weaver objected to the "bureaucratic nightmare" that would ensue as a result of the treatment requirements. She pointed out that the SSA would "have to identify, notify, track, and monitor all SSI recipients with a substance-abuse disorder, evaluate the suitability of treatment facilities and make referrals, periodically test SSI recipients for substance abuse, and ultimately suspend payments." In the end, all this work could end up for naught since denying benefits to uncooperative addicts "will no doubt be endlessly appealed in court."[27] Others complained that the new provisions were too expensive. Even

25. U.S. Senate, Committee on Finance, Subcommittee on Social Security and Family Policy, *Rising Costs of Social Security's Disability Programs*, 104th Congress, 1st Session, 1995, 2, 3, 13–14.

26. Sharon R. Hunt, "Drug Addiction and Alcoholism as Qualifying Impairments for Social Security Disability Benefits: The History, Controversies, and Congressional Response," Ph.D. diss., Brandeis University, 2000, 154–155, and House Subcommittee on Human Resources, "Analysis of Legislation," 30–31.

27. Weaver, "Welfare Payments to the Disabled," 63.

after paying an additional $4 billion over five years for the new referral and monitoring agencies and treatment programs, the federal government would still spend for addicts who hit the time limit because they would still continue to receive Medicaid. Critics, moreover, contended that the time limit suffered from a fatal loophole: addicted recipients who had reached the limit could still requalify under another impairment, a scenario that was highly likely given the SSA's broad interpretation of mental disability.[28]

With the GOP in charge after 1994, efforts to scale back the addicts' program gathered steam. In February 1995, on the same week that the SSA began notifying addicts about the new treatment rules, the newly elected Speaker of the House, Newt Gingrich, questioned whether the government should be providing cash benefits at all. A few days later, the Subcommittee on Human Resources of the House Ways and Means Committee voted to eliminate SSI benefits for addicts entirely as part of the GOP's welfare reform bill, the Personal Responsibility Act of 1995. President Clinton vetoed the bill for other reasons, but the restrictions were enacted a few months later as part of the Contract with America Advancement Act of 1996.[29]

There are several reasons why the addicts program became an early and easy target of budget cutters. First, the medical community was divided over the question of whether open-ended cash benefits were an appropriate way to help aid individuals with addiction problems. While the American Psychiatric Association classified addiction as an illness, some physicians argued that the cash payments encouraged the behavior that had disabled the addicts in the first place. Outspoken Yale psychiatrist, Sally Satel, told the Human Resources Subcommittee, "[SSI] is a destructive program and I say this based on the patients I have treated. . . . I have had patients who were progressing in treatment but once their payments began, they dropped out. And also I have had patients who were actively looking for jobs and abandoned that job search once their first check came through."[30] While treatment was supposed to accompany benefits, some experts noted that it was unclear which types of programs actually worked and that there was evidence that indicated treatment had

28. John O' Donnell and Jim Haner, "Crackdown on Addicts Looks Costly," *Baltimore Sun*, October 13, 1994, Lexis-Nexis document, no page numbers available; and John O'Donnell and Jim Haner, "Outrage Follows Crackdown Costs," *Baltimore Sun*, October 14, 1994, Lexis-Nexis document, no page numbers available.
29. Hunt, "Drug Addiction and Alcoholism as Qualifying Impairments," 154–155.
30. House Subcommittee on Human Resources, *Contract with America*, 489–503. See also testimony of Herbert D. Kleber, in ibid., 482–83.

little, if any, effect on recovery.[31] This division in the medical community over the proper approach to addiction diminished the influence of professionals who supported payments. Moreover, with an election fast approaching, no politician wanted to be seen as the defender of addicts, especially with many programs for the "deserving" poor on the cutting block. Neither liberals in Congress nor the White House stepped up to defend the program or even attempt to temper its restrictive language. In fact, reining in the addicts' program was one of the few things on which Democrats and Republicans could agree. For its part, the SSA did little to defend the program, which ever since its inception had been nothing but an administrative and political albatross for the agency.[32]

Disabled Children

Though wracked with controversy as well, the SSI children's program was a different story. The children's program was certainly much larger and more expensive: With almost 1 million children receiving payments at its peak in the summer of 1994, the children's program was four times the size of the addicts' program. Yet, opponents soon learned that it was also much more resilient.

Between 1995 and 1996, Congress considered a number of sweeping plans designed to revamp the SSI children's program. Proposals ranged from giving disabled children vouchers for medical services instead of cash payments to scaling the amount of the benefit according to the severity of the child's impairment. Others suggested doing away with the program's status as an open-ended entitlement by placing a cap on annual spending. The most restrictive measures were drafted by representatives Gerald Kleczka and Jim McCrery, the GOP pointman on the children's program, and folded into the House leadership's first version of welfare reform legislation, the Personal Responsibility Act of 1995. The act divided recipients of children's benefits into three categories. First, children who had qualified under the Medical Listings and were currently on the rolls would continue to receive benefits. But in the future, the bar would be raised; only children with physical or mental impairments so severe that they required institutionalization or constant personal assistance would be eligible for cash payments. Second, future applicants who met the Listings but who did not require institutionalization would receive medical services provided under a new block grant to the states. The block grant gave states funding equal to only 75 percent of the SSI

31. Weaver, "Welfare Payments to the Disabled," 63.
32. Hunt, "Drug Addiction and Alcoholism as Qualifying Impairments," 150–54.

benefits that children in the state would have received under the current law. It did not require states to offer any specific services to children or even guarantee that every child would have access to the services that were offered. Last, children who qualified through the functional test established by *Zebley* rather than the Listings would be cut from SSI. The McCrery-Klezcka proposal was an administratively complex plan that would have slashed payments to disabled children by $12 billion over five years, a spending reduction of 33 percent. As a proportion of program spending, this was far more drastic than the cuts proposed for Food Stamps or AFDC. More than 250,000 children then on the SSI rolls would be dropped, and less than one-third of future applicants would be eligible for cash benefits.[33]

But with Senate moderates wary of cutting children's programs, the McCrery-Klezcka plan went nowhere. A Republican veteran of the Finance Committee, Senator John Chafee of Rhode Island, possessed a long-standing interest in children's health issues and would not allow conservatives to gut foster care, Medicaid, and SSI.[34] Meanwhile, uncertain about the effects of the proposals, the Senate Finance Committee refused to go along with the House. A GAO official confessed to the committee that her office knew little about the level of services required by disabled children. Because she did not fully understand the ways in which the families spent their SSI payments, she concluded that the House plan to "cash out that program and provide services" was a "worrisome" development.[35] Nor were states eager to assume responsibility for SSI children. The National Governors Association expressed fears that the demand for services would quickly outstrip the money allocated for the block grant.[36] Policy experts, moreover, remained skeptical even if unlimited block grant funding were available. Jerry Mashaw, representing the National Academy of Social Insurance (NASI), cautioned the Finance Committee that determining which services were "medical" was

33. House Subcommittee on Human Resources, "Analysis of Legislation," 31–37.

34. On the role that Chafee played in defending children's programs, see Marilyn Weber Serfani, "Mr. In-Between," *National Journal* 27 (December 16, 1995): 3080–84, and Helen Dewar, "Lonely Fight for Republicans in the Middle," *Washington Post*, October 28, 1995, A1. A description of the role that Chafee played in blocking cuts to SSI was provided by Ronald Haskins, former staff member of the U.S. House of Representatives, Subcommittee on Human Resources, 1986–2000, phone interview with author, July 10, 2001.

35. U.S. Senate, Committee on Finance, *Growth of the Supplemental Security Income Program*, 104th Congress, 1st Session, 1995, 16 (hereafter Senate Committee on Finance, *Growth of the SSI Program*).

36. Spencer Rich, "GOP Plan for Disabled Children Draws Fire," *Washington Post*, February 25, 1995, A12.

nearly impossible. Also, developing the service plans and overseeing how parents spend medical funds would be "extremely time consuming and bureaucratically expensive," and it would inevitably "involve significant micromanagement of family affairs." He explained, "The question is whether you want to give discretion to families about their children, or whether you want to give it to bureaucrats, however well motivated."[37] The senators sided with the families and jettisoned the plan for a medical services block grant.

The members of the Finance Committee agreed that most of the children on SSI had severe disabilities but that there was a smaller number with impairments of questionable severity. Most of these were the children who had qualified through the IFA. The problem, however, was that no one knew what the proper measure of disability should be for children if lawmakers overturned either the IFA or the "comparable severity" standard. An expert panel convened by NASI suggested broadening the functional measures used in the IFA to include more children with physical impairments so that the test did not become identified exclusively with mental and behavioral problems. Meanwhile, the National Commission on Childhood Disability (NCCD), a panel of pediatric, rehabilitation, and education specialists appointed by Congress, was internally divided. To placate warring factions, the NCCD ended up releasing two sets of recommendations, one with only incremental tightening of the IFA and the other with a much stricter standard. Members of the Finance Committee had wildly different ideas as well. Senators John Chafee and Kent Conrad suggested raising the bar in the IFA by getting rid of awards based on moderate impairments. Bob Dole, however, suggested a two-tiered system of payment in which children with less severe disabilities received only 75 percent of the full benefit.[38]

At last, in 1995, House and Senate reached agreement on a drastically scaled down plan, which was then included in the final version of the Personal Responsibility and Work Opportunity Reconciliation Act (PRWORA). Congress scrapped plans to block-grant part of the children's program or set up a tiered system. Instead, SSI remained an individual entitlement that paid cash benefits to all children who were found eligible. Congress, however, tightened the disability standard. Lawmakers deleted the phrase stating that a child was disabled if he had an impairment of "comparable severity" to an impairment that disabled an adult. Borrowing from the language already used in the regulations, the

---

37. Senate Committee on Finance, *Growth of the SSI Program*, 26.
38. Mashaw et al., *Restructuring the SSI Disability Program*, 27–29, and NCCD, *Supplemental Security Income for Children with Disabilities*, 54–60.

new definition stated a child would be found disabled if he had a "medically determinable physical or mental impairment, which resulted in marked and severe limitations."[39] Lawmakers also abolished the individualized test of functioning, which had become a lightening rod for criticism. Perhaps, in the end, many senators shared the convictions of the GAO, which argued that the problems in the children's program stemmed from the IFA and that these problems could not simply be fixed by the tightening standards used in the test.[40] Or perhaps moderate lawmakers on the Finance Committee were assured that the elimination of the IFA would not prevent assessments of functioning. In fact, the conference report on PRWORA went to great pains to emphasize the importance of functional measures to the determination of disability. Though the conferees stated that they wanted to limit SSI to "only needy children with severe disabilities," they also reiterated that Congress did "not intend to limit the use of functional information" if it was the best way of assessing the severity of an impairment. The conference report also reminded the SSA to "ensure that the combined effects of the physical and mental impairments" of a child were taken into account in determining disability, and it emphasized that determining functional equivalency (that is, whether a child's impairment, though not included in the Listings, was as severe or more severe than a listed impairment) was a crucial component of decision making in the cases of infants and children with rare disorders. While Congress explicitly overturned *Zebley*, therefore, the conferees nevertheless underscored their support for the functional approach to disability and the liberalizations—other than the IFA—that had been instituted in the wake of *Zebley*.[41] Children would still receive an evaluation of functioning, albeit a more narrowly drawn assessment, even without the individualized test.

39. In addition, following the recommendations of the NCCD and NASI, the PRWORA deleted the counting of "maladaptive behavior" when determining a child's personal and behavioral functioning in the Part B functional criteria of the childhood Listings for mental disorders. Maladaptive behavior, however, is still counted when assessing social functioning. Members of the NCCD voiced concern that maladaptive behavior was "double counted" under the "personal/behavioral domain" and the "social domain" of the Listings. The PRWORA also required the SSA to conduct continuing disability reviews on children at least once every three years if the child's medical condition is expected to improve. The legislation authorized additional $150 million in FY 1997 and $100 million in FY 1998 to conduct continuing disability reviews and removed caps on discretionary spending for the SSA's administrative budget.

40. GAO, *New Functional Assessments*, 18–19, and Senate Special Committee on Aging, *Problems in the SSD Programs*, 12–13.

41. U.S. House of Representatives, *Personal Responsibility and Work Opportunity Reconciliation Act of 1996, Conference Report to Accompany H.R. 3734*, H. Rept. 104–725, 104th Congress, 2nd Session, 1996, 327–28 (hereafter House, *PRWORA Conference Report*).

Enfeebled Retrenchment

The changes to SSI, along with a measure barring legal immigrants from receiving any SSI benefits, nutritional aid, family assistance, and Medicaid, were rolled into the Personal Responsibility and Work Opportunity Reconciliation Act. The law converted AFDC into the TANF block grant, set limits on the number of years recipients could receive family benefits, and added work requirements and additional restrictions. Clinton signed PRWORA into law in the summer of 1996, shortly before the presidential election. Afterward, several HHS executives resigned in protest. One official, Peter Edelman, dubbed the passage of the welfare reform law "the worst thing Bill Clinton has done" and singled out the SSI reform for much of his invective. Conceding that the children's program needed some tightening, he nonetheless asserted that the cuts in benefits to legal immigrants did not "have anything to do with welfare reform" and were "just mean." The new law, Edelman argued, "gave new meaning to the word 'draconian.' "⁴² Bill Archer, chair of the House Ways and Means Committee, was more sanguine, dismissing such complaints as "the dying throes of the federal welfare state."⁴³

But much of what both liberals and conservatives claimed was hyperbole, at least with respect to SSI. No sooner was the ink dry on the 1996 welfare reform bill than lawmakers faced political pressure to ameliorate the harshest cuts made to benefits for legal immigrants and disabled children. In fact, Republicans were soon on the defensive, scrambling to reassure the voters that were not being mean spirited. When advocates charged that the cuts to SSI and Medicaid unfairly singled out the disabled, Representative Jim McCrery responded, "The tide has not turned against disabled people. The tide has turned against abuse of federal programs, against waste of federal dollars, but not against disabled people."⁴⁴ To many advocates, this was a distinction without a difference. But just as the innovations of the past decade reflected the advocates' skill in sneaking liberalizations past opponents instead of a political consensus in favor of expansion, by the same token, the policy changes endorsed by conservative reformers enjoyed only precarious popular support. Not only did

42. Peter Edelman, "The Worst Thing Bill Clinton Has Done," *Atlantic Monthly* 279, 3 (March 1997), 43, 45, 48.

43. Quoted in Jeffrey Katz, "House Passes Welfare Bill: Senate Likely to Alter It," *Congressional Quarterly Weekly Report* 53 (1995), 872.

44. Quoted in Barbara Vobejda, "Disabled People See Budget-Cutting Fervor as Threat, New Attitude," *Washington Post*, August 3, 1995, A12.

Congress fail to hold the line on the initial cuts it had made, but it soon found itself unable to close the door that judicial and administrative expansion of disability had created. It could whittle away at the edges, but it could not reverse the gains advocates had made.

Rolling Back

The rolling back of PRWORA highlights how different family assistance is from other welfare programs. President Clinton made the rescinding of the noncitizen provisions a promise of his presidential campaign (a fact that liberals found infuriatingly ironic given that the restrictions would not have been enacted in the first place had he vetoed the legislation as they had wished). Moreover, dissension in the ranks of the Republican Party made sustaining momentum for retrenchment difficult. Not wanting to pick up the tab for immigrants forced to rely on state and local supports, Republican governors from states that would be affected disproportionately by the cuts argued for a restoration of aid to noncitizens. Said one state official, "Most of the welfare reform debate focused on work and employment and training opportunities. Denying services to legal immigrants was just not part of the mainstream debate." Suggesting that they might have been rash, another added, "The pressure to move a welfare bill through Congress as quickly as possible caused us not to look at the impact and consequences of these provisions as deeply as we might otherwise have."[45] As the push to rescind or at least reduce the cuts in benefits to legal immigrants gathered momentum, some Republican members of Congress asserted they had not recognized the unfairness of the law. Only after voting for it did they learn that some legal immigrants would never be able to become citizens (and thus get around the restrictions) because they were either mentally incompetent and could not take the oath or were too old to learn English and pass the citizenship test. Summing up his change of heart, Republican senator Mike DeWine of Ohio explained, "It seemed wrong to change the rules for" these individuals.[46]

Facing intense political pressure, Republican congressional leaders relented. Bit by bit, the harshest cutbacks in aid to legal immigrants were rescinded. As part of the Balanced Budget Act (BBA) of 1997, Congress agreed to restore eligibility for SSI for the 420,000 legal immigrants that

45. Quoted in Robert Pear, "GOP Governors Seek to Restore Immigrant Aid," *New York Times*, January 25, 1997, Sec. 1, 1.
46. Quoted in ibid., 1.

had been enrolled in the program and had entered the country before passage of the PRWORA on August 22, 1996. Later, Congress took another step, extending eligibility to legal immigrants who entered the country after the enactment of welfare reform, stayed five years, and then became disabled after entering. These modifications were estimated to cost $11.4 billion over five years, thus wiping out almost all of the budget savings that had been realized under the PRWORA. The following year, Congress restored Food Stamps to the 225,000 children, aged persons, and disabled individuals who legally entered the United States before enactment of PRWORA as well as the future eligibility of legal immigrants in the United States before welfare reform became law. It also reinstated some Medicaid benefits to pregnant mothers.

Furthermore, shortly after the PRWORA passed, it became clear that because eligibility for SSI and Medicaid was linked in several states, many children who were cut from SSI were also losing their health care coverage. During his budget negotiations with Republicans after the 1996 elections, Clinton pushed Congress to address this concern. In response, the 1997 Balanced Budget Act "grandfathered" former SSI children into Medicaid until they turned eighteen. Thus, children who otherwise would have lost their health care benefits along with SSI were allowed to continue receiving Medicaid coverage, hindering Republican efforts to cut this rapidly growing program. In addition, the BBA also established the new State Children's Health Insurance Program (SCHIP). SCHIP pledged $40 billion in federal funds through 2007 to encourage states to expand Medicaid eligibility for low-income children or create separate (non-Medicaid) child health insurance programs for low-income children ineligible for Medicaid. This move ameliorated some of the harshness of welfare reform and further chipped away at the potential budget savings contained in PRWORA.[47]

Finally, lawmakers had second thoughts about the harshness of the cuts imposed on disabled children. The PRWORA stated that children must have a "marked and severe limitation," but it did not define the phrase. It stated only that the SSA was to give "severe" its "common sense meaning" without going further to clarify what that meant. SSA officials, therefore, had a fair degree of latitude in drawing up the new regula-

47. SCHIP was established as Title XXI of the Social Security Act. It is a voluntary program, and states must supply matching funds though at a lower rate than under Medicaid. As of August 1, 1999, all fifty states and the District of Columbia had developed plans for expanding children's health insurance under SCHIP, and all but three had received federal approval. For an overview of the program, see Frank Ullman, Ian Hill, and Ruth Almeida, "CHIP: A Look at Emerging State Programs," *New Federalism: Issues and Options for States*, Urban Institute, Series A, No. A-35, September 1999.

tions.[48] Initially, the CBO projected that as many as 170,000 of the nearly 1 million children on the SSI disability rolls would lose their benefits. After the release of interim regulations implementing the new standard, the CBO lowered its projections to 131,000 children while the SSA's own estimates hovered around 135,000.[49]

Once the SSA began its review of the children's rolls, however, it immediately confronted demands to ease its application of the new disability standard. In August 1997, the SSA revised its estimates of how many children would loose SSI benefits. It was now looking at about 148,000 children who would be affected. Senators Kent Conrad and John Chafee of the Senate Finance Committee were alarmed. Throughout congressional debate over welfare reform, the two lawmakers had unsuccessfully opposed proposals to eliminate the IFA, and having failed in that endeavor, they saw implementation as a second chance to moderate the severity of the PRWORA cuts. In a letter to the SSA, Conrad and Chafee claimed that officials had "misinterpreted the intent of Congress" by applying the "marked and severe" standard too strictly.[50] The following month, during Senate hearings on the nomination of Kenneth Apfel to the post of SSA commissioner, Conrad extracted a promise from Apfel to investigate whether examiners were being overly harsh.[51] Once confirmed, Apfel made good on his promise. The SSA revisited its handling of the PRWORA reviews of children and put new safeguards in place.[52] As a result, the SSA lowered its estimate to only 100,000 children cut.[53]

Closing the Back Door

In 1988, conservatives took a parting shot at SSI in an effort to roll back the gains that mental advocates had made in the 1980s. Critics rec-

---

48. House, *PRWORA Conference Report*, 328.

49. The interim regulations were published on February 11, 1997. See 62 *Federal Register* 6408 (1997).

50. Robert Pear, "After Review, 95,180 Children Will Lose Cash Disability Benefits," *New York Times*, August 15, 1997, A1.

51. U.S. Senate, Committee on Finance, *Nominations of Rita Hayes Kenneth S. Apfel, Nancy-Ann DeParle, Olivia A. Golden, David A. Lipton, Timothy F. Geither, Gary Gensler, and Nancy Killefer*, 105th Congress, 1st Session, 1997, 29–31, 72–73, 80–81, 83–84.

52. The details of these measures can be found in U.S. Social Security Administration, *Review of SSA's Implementation of New SSI Childhood Disability Legislation*, 1997, http://www.ssa.gov/policy/child.htm.

53. U.S. Social Security Administration, News Release, "SSA will review 45,000 cases of children who had SSI disability benefits ceased, offer second chance for appeal to all," December 17, 1997, http://www.ssa.gov/press/childhoodpress.html.

ognized that the disability rules, vastly loosened by the courts, served as a back door into SSI that undercut the limits they tried to impose on the front end. In fact, during debate over the abolition of the addicts' program, congressional staffers warned legislators that even if they eliminated addiction as a qualifying disability as many as 80 percent of addicts could be found eligible for disability benefits under another impairment category, most likely another mental disorder. Bearing out the wisdom of those words, as of December 1997, nine out of every ten addicts that had managed to requalify for SSI or DI had done so on the basis of either a psychiatric disorder or mental retardation.[54] In response, some conservatives suggested repealing the liberalizations Congress and the SSA had made to mental impairments as part of the 1984 disability amendments.[55]

Republicans took a step in this direction but faltered once again. Even after the enactment of PRWORA, concern about fraud and abuse in SSI persisted, and in the summer of 1998, Clay Shaw, chair of the House Subcommittee on Human Resources, floated a plan to tighten the program further. The plan would have required the SSA to look at only the clinical signs and symptoms of an impairment unless a determination regarding work capacity required more evidence. Only then would the SSA take into consideration evidence concerning how the impairment actually affected functioning. A second provision required the SSA to accord equal weight to medical evidence from the claimant's treating physician and evidence from a consulting physician hired by the SSA (often when the claimant's medical record was incomplete or the examiner doubted the conclusions of the treating physician). This measure would have reversed rulings by the federal courts ordering the SSA to give greater weight to the treating physician (unless the SSA could state a specific reason not to), provisions of the 1984 disability amendments emphasizing the importance of evidence obtained from the treating physician, and changes made to DI and SSI rules in 1985 that accorded equal weight to functioning and clinical signs.[56]

54. Lewin Group and Westat, "Policy Evaluation of the Effect of Legislation Prohibiting the Payment of Disability Benefits to Individuals Whose Disability is Based on Drug Addiction and Alcoholism," Interim Report, 1998, ES1–ES2. The overall number who requalified, however, was much lower than estimated. Only 34 percent or 71,000 addicted beneficiaries that had been targeted for removal had been found reeligible, half as many as expected. Most who did requalify did so on the basis of a psychiatric disorder. Overall, 138,000 DI and SSI beneficiaries with addiction problems lost their eligibility as of December 1997.
    55. Wright, "SSI: The Black Hole of the Welfare State."
    56. U.S. House of Representatives, Committee on Ways and Means, Subcommittee on Human Resources, *Supplemental Security Income Fraud and Abuse*, 105th Congress, 2nd Session, 1998, 50, 52, 56–58, 59.

Advocates rightly saw the proposed bill as an assault on the advances they had made in disability determination, and they objected vociferously to it. The MHLP, now called the Bazelon Center, warned its members in its "action alert" that, though the increased emphasis on clinical factors seemed minor and even "reasonable," the subtle shift was "fraught with potential problems." It argued that "particularly in the cases of individuals with mental illness," "medical evidence is not generally decisive or even the most important" indicator of work capacity. In response to the provisions relating to evidence from treating and consulting physicians, the Bazelon Center protested that the shift in influence would mean that "a doctor who sees a person for perhaps an hour and has no knowledge of the individual's illness over time will have as much [say] . . . as a physician who has treated the person for years." Though the changes would affect the evaluations of all type of disabilities, the effect on the adjudication of mental disability would be especially adverse because of the complex and cyclical nature of mental disorders.[57] Responding to objections from advocates and medical professionals, Shaw dropped his proposal.[58]

From the Reagan Revolution to the Gingrich Revolution

Despite the fact that more than ten years separated the Reagan Revolution from the Gingrich Revolution, both President Reagan and Speaker Gingrich confronted strikingly similar impediments. Both leaders tried to preserve disability benefits for only those who were "truly disabled," and by this they meant the most severely disabled of the disabled. But this impulse ran headlong into the logic of deinstitutionalization. Reserving disability benefits for only those most severely disabled entailed resurrecting the medical underpinnings of disability determination. It stranded those individuals who were unable to work but still needed social assistance to live in the community. It failed to acknowledge the fact that Social Security disability policy had evolved beyond its original purpose. It was no longer simple compensation for disabled workers. DI and SSI now maintained deinstitutionalized patients in the community and subsidized the wages of parents who cut back on employment to care for their disabled children who might otherwise become institutionalized. In

57. Bazelon Center for Mental Health Law, "Action Alert: House Subcommittee Plans to Narrow Access to Disability Benefits," June 1, 1998, http://www.bazelon.org/601alrt.html, and U.S. House of Representatives, Committee on Ways and Means, Subcommittee on Social Security, *Supplemental Security Income Fraud and Abuse*, 105th Congress, 2nd Session, 1998, 56–57.

58. Ronald Haskins, phone interview with author.

doing so, however, they also provided cash to addicts and offered payments to parents whose children did not need around-the-clock care. But separating the former from the latter without creating hardship among sympathetic and deserving individuals was all but impossible.

Furthermore, both Reagan and Gingrich found retrenchment could reach only the most objectionable groups or programs, leaving the structure of the welfare state in place. To be sure, conservatives had succeeded in fundamentally altering AFDC, pushing program restrictions further than Clinton had ever intended. But this was only one program and an especially unpopular one at that. Medicaid, Food Stamps, foster care, school lunches, and special education all survived intact. Moreover, the impetus for retrenchment was difficult to sustain, and entreaties to expand programs that served sympathetic groups or morally worthy causes were difficult to resist.

Finally, despite achieving some restrictions in eligibility, neither Reagan nor Gingrich could accomplish a fundamental reassessment of disability benefits. Indeed, during the 1994–96 round of welfare reform, conservatives believed that the structural changes they sought, such as caps on spending, were as important as eligibility restrictions. This was because the Reagan years had taught conservatives that structural maneuvers were crucial to slamming the door on state efforts to cost-shift. In 1981, Reagan packed fifty-four social programs valued at $7 billion into nine large block grants and turned them over to the states to administer. Yet between 1982 and 1985, inflation-adjusted federal spending for those grants quickly increased by 14 percent because of the ingenuity of state governments in shifting fiscal burdens. For example, some states offset cutbacks in social services and health care block grants by transferring those services to the Medicaid program. Asked to comment on the potential effect of the 1995 welfare reform law on his state's treasury, one Michigan official stated frankly, "I've been here for 17 years, and we've always done a good job in maxing out federal dollars. . . . We'll find new ways of being creative."[59]

The failure of conservatives to impose a structural ceiling on SSI expenditures had repercussions for their effort to reduce overall spending for means-tested programs. An Urban Institute study conducted in 1995 found that as many as one-fifth of adult recipients of AFDC suffered from physical or mental problems that limited their functioning, and

59. Quoted in Christopher Georges, "As GOP Governors Discuss Block-Grant Funding, Ghost of a Failed Reagan-Era Plan May Visit," *Wall Street Journal*, January 26, 1995, A16.

more than one in ten children on AFDC had similar impairments that adversely affected their ability to function in an age-appropriate manner.[60] The initial purpose of the study had been to convince Congress to increase the proportion of TANF recipients that states could exempt from work requirements. But after the passage of PRWORA, advocates seized on the study's implications to promote a strategy of categorical program shifting. Antipoverty attorney Michael O'Connor explained in a study circulated to advocates, "Substantial opportunities exist to move many thousands of parents and children from TANF to SSI." Documenting the efforts some states were beginning to take, O'Connor contended that state "investment in screening and advocacy to secure SSI benefits for disabled TANF recipients—both adults and children—will more than pay for itself through savings in TANF cash assistance."[61] Though most states have yet to engage in large scale shifting of TANF recipients, the door remains open.

By 1998, the retrenchment juggernaut had run its course. Congress had repealed many of its cutbacks on welfare benefits for legal immigrants, cautioned the SSA to go easy during its review of the SSI children's program, and extended health care coverage to many previously uninsured children. Conservatives could tinker with social programs, tightening standards here and there if it seemed appropriate. But as disability and mental health advocates had learned years earlier, remaking these programs through comprehensive, structural reforms was a Herculean task. This litany of failed ambitions left aggravated conservatives complaining that trying to scale back the American welfare state was like "trying to sweep a sidewalk during a blizzard."[62]

60. Pamela Loprest and Gregory Acs, "Profile of Disability among Families on AFDC," Washington, D.C., the Urban Institute, 1995.

61. Michael A. O'Connor, "Supplemental Security Income—An Underused Resource for Disabled TANF Recipients in Illinois," Center for Urban Research and Learning, Loyola University, March 8, 1999, 1, 8.

62. James L. Payne, "Welfare 'Cuts'?" *The American Enterprise* 8 (1997): 38–41, 38, 40.

Conclusion:
The Lessons of Reform

In his seminal work on the development of capitalist democracies, famed sociologist T. H. Marshall argued that advanced societies could be recognized by their attainment of full citizenship. By this, he meant the establishment of civil rights, such as the freedom to own property or make contractual obligations; political rights, such as the right to vote; and social rights. At the pinnacle of this trajectory were social rights, those rights that allowed individuals to participate effectively and meaningfully in the social and cultural life of a society. They included the right to education, the right to be free from discrimination, and the right to a modicum of economic well-being.[1] The rights of the disabled and the right to welfare are forms of social rights, demands from disadvantaged groups for full equality, acceptance, and belonging. Franklin Roosevelt gave voice to the call for social rights when in his second inaugural address he declared, "The test of our progress is not whether we add more to the abundance of those who have much; it is whether we provide enough for those who have too little."

Nevertheless, because of its traditionally strong antistatist political culture, the United States has found positive social rights more problematic than civil and political rights, which were established relatively early in the nation's history. But the demand for the rights of the individual is difficult to resist. Thus, during the 1960s and 1970s, America witnessed a revolution in which practically every public issue was redefined "in terms of legally protected rights of individuals. Rights of the handicapped;

---

1. T. H. Marshall, *Class, Citizenship, and Social Development* (Chicago: University of Chicago Press, 2003).

rights of workers; rights of students; rights of racial, linguistic, and religious minorities; rights of women; rights of consumers; the right to a hearing; the right to know—these have become the stock and trade of American political discourse."[2]

This book recounts the development of a rights movement at the crossroads of disability and social welfare policy, one that had a profound impact on Social Security disability policy. As I argue throughout the book, the American political system is replete with many windows of opportunity for meaningful reform, and rights advocates are clever at exploiting those pathways. The road is not always easy, however, and it frequently lacks excitement and glamour. Instead, advocates often find themselves wading through mundane administrative matters or dry court cases involving statutory and administrative law, rather than traversing the more thrilling avenues filled with landmark pieces of legislation or high-profile disputes over constitutional law. But as the transformation of Social Security disability policy makes clear, what the advocates do matters nonetheless.

Throughout this book, I have chronicled the enormous gains that disability advocates made in convincing able-bodied Americans to respect the dignity and equality of fellow citizens with disabilities. Social Security has grown over the past three decades to cover many vulnerable groups of the disabled that were once excluded. Congress passed the Americans with Disabilities Act to ban discrimination and mandate equal access, and mental health care today is a far cry from the back wards of the dilapidated asylums that launched the patients' rights movement. Yet all is not well either. A recent government report found that adults with severe disabilities are almost twice as likely as the general population to live in poverty, to be unemployed, and to live in a family with an annual income of less than $20,000.[3] It appears that that although the social safety net may have grown wider over the decades, it still leaves many voids, and disability policy in general remains unable to facilitate work or provide adequate support for many disabled people.

There are limits, therefore, to how far reform efforts can go, and this chapter explores some of them. The nature of the American political system and of policymaking itself makes comprehensive reform exceedingly rare. The policy world is thick with holdover policy frameworks and pro-

2. R. Shep Melnick, "The Courts, Congress, and Programmatic Rights," in *Remaking American Politics*, ed. Richard A. Harris and Sidney M. Milkis (Boulder, CO: Westview Press, 1989), 188.

3. U.S. General Accounting Office, *Adults with Severe Disabilities: Federal and State Approaches for Personal Care and Other Services*, GAO/HEHS-99-101, May 1999, 9–10.

grams from previous years. Advocates cannot always anticipate how their strategies and arguments will play out over the long term, and a good deal of policymaking is contingent, driven one way or the other by events that are difficult, if not impossible, to predict and control. Institutional changes, too, can abruptly close some valuable windows that advocates have come to rely on. These were all challenges that disability advocates confronted, and these constraints left their mark. Thus, the revolution in disability policy remains incomplete. International comparisons suggest that this void is in part the result of the residual nature of the American welfare state. But, I argue, this condition is also the outcome of decisions made by the advocacy community as it adopted its tactics and arguments to fit the political windows of opportunity. Strategic choices, such as the tendency to treat rights and welfare as antithetical rather than complementary, ultimately compromised larger ambitions for a broad and generous social safety net. Though advocates were able to secure sweeping disability rights protections, they also lost much along the way.

The Possibilities for Reform

This book charts the efforts of disability advocacy groups to reorient Social Security along principles compatible with the integrative principles of disability rights, and it shows how reform groups converted Disability Insurance and SSI from compensatory programs, designed primarily for workers and the aged, into vital threads in a community-based social safety net for disadvantaged people with disabilities. As I have explained in the preceding chapters, the transformation of Social Security disability policy reflects the vast possibilities for innovation and advocacy even in the face of tenuous and hostile circumstances. Public policies may be institutionally rooted, but they are not frozen. Rather, because it is fragmented, the American political system is highly accessible to organized interests and new ideas. Thus, though neither numerically nor financially powerful, disability and antipoverty groups were able to take advantage of the many strategic openings available to them. Policy entrepreneurs both within and outside of government refreshed political discourse with new ideas and new perspectives drawn from the rights movements. When the advocates found traditional pathways to reform blocked, they searched out alternative channels, activating institutions that once lay dormant or calling on old ones to serve new ends. By galvanizing state governments, advocacy committees in Congress, and sympathetic administrators to their cause and by politicizing once quiescent institutions, like the federal courts, the advocates incrementally broadened the categorical boundaries of disability.

What emerges from this dynamic is a two-level political contest. At the macrolevel, high-profile legislation still drove policy. In 1980, Congress passed the Disability Benefits Reform Act to stem an unprecedented rise in the Disability Insurance rolls. Four years later, it enacted a second Disability Benefits Reform Act in order to resolve the political controversy engendered by the Reagan administration's ambitious purge of disabled beneficiaries. And in the mid 1990s, legislators scrambled to deal with rapidly mounting SSI expenditures, a predicted shortfall in the DI trust fund, and widespread concern about welfare fraud and abuse. These were highly visible, conflict-ridden partisan battles involving the president, Congress, and many mobilized interest groups. But these events were few and far between. Since 1972, elected officials have rarely ventured into Social Security policymaking, and when they have, they did so only when their hands were forced by a fiscal or political crisis of major proportions. At the microlevel, however, innovation was continuous, as the courts mandated numerous administrative reforms in DI and SSI, as the states instituted plans to shift their welfare burdens onto the federal government, and as the SSA grappled to stay abreast of these developments. These changes attracted little public attention but they are no less consequential than the major legislative initiatives pursued by Congress and the White House.

This picture of social welfare politics, in many ways, runs counter to conventional expectations. According to Theodore Lowi and James Q. Wilson, because social welfare programs are redistributive, political conflict over these programs will be both broad and intense as large numbers of interest groups wade into the political fray to defend their stake in the programs.[4] In the case of antipoverty programs, the conflict is heightened by the fact that programs for the poor often touch on volatile issues of race, sexual norms, and family and gender relations. But disability presents a different picture. To be sure, in those few instances in which Congress debated reform alternatives, the scope of the conflict was wideranging. But the "pyrotechnic politics" of the culture wars—to borrow the colorful imagery of James Morone—seldom surfaced.[5] Instead, because support for social assistance to the disabled was difficult for elected

4. Theodore J. Lowi, "American Business, Public Policy, Case Studies, and Political Theory," in *Public Policies and Their Politics*, ed. Randall Ripley (New York: Norton, 1966), 27–40; and James Q. Wilson, *Political Organizations* (New York: Basic Books, 1973), 327–46.

5. James A. Morone, "American Ways of Welfare," *Perspectives* 1, 1 (2003), 138.

officials to oppose, the focus on disability tended to blunt the ideological nature of the political debate. This did not preclude ideological clashes over the meaning of disability and the proper scope of social welfare programs. But to the extent that conflict usually took the form of disagreements over administrative rules, these conflicts were hardly the type of the broad partisan battles that engage the American public.

Thus, if we look only at legislative skirmishes, we miss a great deal of politics. Congressional enactments in DI and SSI are few and far between, and on the surface, the two programs look largely as they did in the early 1970s. But beneath the surface, extraordinary policy change has occurred. This change took place, however, through mundane administrative measures rather than through high-profile legislation, making it easy to overlook because political conflict was buried deep in the details of the programs out of the public eye. The subterranean and technical nature of this reform limited the number of political actors involved, and allowed advocacy groups to exert a great deal of influence on policy outcomes despite their limited popular base. Policymaking essentially became a dialogue limited to the small circle of political actors who were conversant in the many technical intricacies of disability. As long as we are concerned with the spectacle of cultural or partisan conflict rather than the routine details of administration, we will continue to give this sort of reform politics little critical scrutiny. And we will miss the significant policy changes that can occur through even small variations in program rules and operating practices.

The Limits of Reform

Opportunities for reform are not infinitely open, however, and within the advocacy strategy, we also find the limits of reform, rooted in both the institutions and ideas of American politics. The constraints that the advocates confronted took three forms: the institutional and policy fragmentation of the American political system, policymakers' affinity for the medical model of disability and their corresponding ambivalence toward the social model, and the advocates' tendency to downplay the true costs of integrating the disabled into mainstream society.

Reorienting a Policy Morass

First, the institutional decentralization of the American political system, though conducive to innovation, also frustrates sweeping reforms.

Instead, it tends to encourage the development of a complicated and maddening morass of programs and laws. Thus, because it required giving coherence to many fractured programs, erecting the "new asylum of the community" was an inherently daunting challenge. Ironically, the same institutional arrangements that generated windows of opportunity so that advocates could advance their cause also frustrated their efforts to build an inclusive social safety net in the community. Therefore, they could not capitalize on the momentum they had after the Reagan administration's failed disability reviews to realize ambitious policy goals.

Advocates could not, for instance, align DI and SSI with the hundreds of other state, local, and federal disability programs to combat the structural disadvantages of the poor and the disabled. In part, this was because of the fragmentation of disability policy itself. There were programs for people who were poor: SSI, TANF, state- and local-level general relief, food stamps, housing assistance, and Medicaid. There were programs for people who were homeless, such as homeless shelters funded through a mix of federal, state, and local aid as well as private charity. There were separate programs for veterans with disabilities: veterans' pensions and care in Veterans' Administration hospitals. There were community mental health clinics specifically for people with mental disorders, and centers of independent living that served all the disabled. There were middle-class entitlement programs for workers: Medicare, Disability Insurance, and workers' compensation. There were special education programs for children, and programs designed for adults to promote employment, such as programs that helped pay for assistive devices and personal attendants, initiatives in DI and SSI that adjusted benefits according to income earned on the job, vocational rehabilitation, and government incentives for the private employers to hire the disabled. And there were equal access laws mandating job accommodations, accessible transportation, and accessible public facilities. Some of these programs were created to serve the disabled, some to serve only a particular group of the disabled. For other programs, the disabled were only one of the groups in a clientele that could include welfare mothers, low-income families, legal immigrants, the able-bodied homeless, and the senior citizens. Some programs provided cash; others, health care, housing, food, or access to jobs and schools. The social safety net for the disabled, in other words, was a patchwork of programs and laws, each administered by different levels of government, by different agencies, with different missions and areas of concern, and different definitions of disability. Bringing coordination and coherence to this chaotic field was a daunting undertaking.

The nature of the political system in which the advocates operated further complicated the task. With programs spread across different levels of government and different agencies, advocates could not remake policy in one fell swoop. Often reform had to be accomplished program-by-program, state-by-state, sometimes locality-by-locality.[6] In fact, DI and SSI, seen from this perspective, were particularly easy programs to reform because they were relatively centralized. Despite the fact that disability determinations are conducted by states, DI and SSI are both federal programs administered by one agency, the Social Security Administration. By contrast, Medicaid, another important safety net program for the disabled, is a program in which the federal government and the states share costs and administrative responsibilities. As a result, not only does Medicaid vary widely across states in terms of the groups covered and the quality of services provided, but reforms secured in one state do not necessarily translate into advances in other states.

The dilemma that disability advocates face is one of historical sequencing. They had the unfortunate luck to launch their revolution into a health care delivery system and social welfare structure that was both mature and scattered among various political actors and levels of government. Over time, as programs were enacted, they were layered one on top of the other. Efforts to revamp policy, therefore, required combating intense opposition from the organized interests, political institutions, and social expectations that had crystallized around the prevailing policy structure. A perfect example of these frustrations is the campaign by mental health reformers to bring parity to private health benefits, which provide more restrictive coverage of mental health services than they do for services pertaining to physical health. The equal access principles of the ADA offered reformers the first opportunity to challenge this disparity, but during debate over the ADA, business and insurance groups successfully fought attempts to require equal treatment of mental and physical illnesses in private health care plans. A few years later, conservatives defeated President Clinton's proposals for universal coverage, which would have provided extensive though still limited mental health benefits. Then, in 1996, although Congress enacted the Mental Health Parity

6. For an example of some the difficulties advocates face with respect to one particular group of people with disabilities, the homeless, see Jonathan L. Hafetz, "Homeless Legal Advocacy: New Challenges and Directions for the Future," *Fordham Urban Law Journal* 30 (2003): 1215–65. Also telling is the analysis of Medicaid and the mental health system in April Land, "Dead to Rights: A Father's Struggle to Secure Mental Health Services for his Son," *Georgetown Journal on Poverty Law and Policy* 10 (2003): 279–343.

Act, taking the first steps toward parity, the law was a watered-down proposal that left many restrictions on mental health care coverage in place.[7] The conundrum for mental health advocates is the fact that a substantial proportion of the U.S. health care system is privatized while mental health care, "for which little financial demand exists," receives substantial funding from Medicaid and other various government sources. As a result, services and coverage are fractured between the public and private sector as well as from state to state, complicating efforts to achieve a uniform national policy to redress the inequities created by disability.[8]

Finding Certainty through Science?

Second, despite reform efforts to articulate a new understanding of disability, as Peter Hall reminds us, innovations are easier to accomplish if, rather than being seen as radical changes, they correspond to existing policy conceptions. Thus, to win over skeptical policymakers, advocates couched their reforms in the language of the prevailing policy frameworks. In the case of Social Security disability policy, this meant that advocates never fully challenged the premises of the medical model. A compromise that left disability benefits policy caught between its strict, compensatory origins and the new integrative goals advocates promoted.

The pervasive hold of the medical model on policymaking limited advocates in three key respects. The first constraint is related to the advocates' decision to ground their arguments for disability benefits expansion on the standards and norms of medical professionals—ironically, the very professionals whose authority earlier rights activists had sought to free the disabled from. Because members of Congress viewed disability as a medical phenomenon, experts in medical science, not necessarily the disabled or the poor themselves, were empowered to speak on the issue of disability determination. By arguing that disability standards should conform to the prevailing medical diagnostic standards, advocates appealed to the congressional penchant for dodging the contentious dis-

7. Christopher Aaron Jones, "Legislative 'Subterfuge'? Failing to Insure Persons with Mental Illness under the Mental Health Parity Act and the Americans with Disabilities Act," *Vanderbilt Law Review* 50 (1997): 753–93, and Maggie D. Gold, "Must Insurers Treat All Illnesses Equally?—Mental v. Physical Illness: Congressional and Administrative Failure to End Limitations to and Exclusions from Coverage for Mental Illness in Employer-Provided Health Benefits under the Mental Health Parity Act and the Americans with Disabilities Act," *Connecticut Insurance Law Journal* 4 (1997/1998): 767–806.

8. Simon Goodwin, *Comparative Mental Health Policy: From Institutional to Community Care* (Thousand Oaks, CA: Sage), 1997, 12.

tributive decisions by delegating the truly difficult decisions to experts. But expert decision making is not the same as apolitical decision making. Experts are not neutral political observers. They may not necessarily be partisans or ideologues, but they have their own norms and policy preferences that color how they understand policy and in turn present information to lawmakers and the public. Moreover, as Marc Landy and Martin Levin point out, those experts who feel strongly enough about an issue to wade into the political fray "may or may not be a microcosm of the broader scientific or social scientific community whose research and analysis is relevant to the policy issues at stake."[9] Given their alliances with reform-minded physicians and rehabilitation specialists, it is understandable that advocates would draw on the specialized knowledge of these respected experts.

The language of experts, however, proved ill-suited to the passion aroused by calls for social justice. The statutory and administrative definition of disability was a categorical boundary used to resolve redistributive questions. Where to locate that boundary is ultimately a political choice.[10] But by grounding much of the debate on the intricacies of medicine, advocates missed an opportunity to build political support for definitional boundaries expanded in the name of fairness. Philosophical arguments about the appropriate boundaries of welfare became reduced to technical discussions of medical diagnostic standards, hardly the kind of the discourse that resonates with American citizens. As a result, the expansion of DI and SSI took place without widespread public support. The outcry over the Reagan disability reviews revealed that the public was not willing to curtail dramatically the scope of these programs. But neither did it necessarily support broadening the boundaries of disability, as the controversy that engulfed SSI in the early 1990s demonstrates.

In this sense, Social Security was like a lot of other policy issues—health care, tax, and deregulation, to name a few. Because citizens "have no direct experience with the problem," they have "few ways of evaluating the merits of alternative proposals."[11] Thus, policymaking empowers

9. Marc K. Landy and Martin A. Levin, "The New Politics of Public Policy," in *The New Politics of Public Policy*, ed. Marc K. Landy and Martin A. Levin (Baltimore: Johns Hopkins University Press, 1995), 292.

10. Indeed, Peter Hall notes, "The process whereby one policy paradigm comes to replace another is likely to be more sociological than scientific. That is to say, although the changing views of experts may play a role, their views are likely to be controversial, and the choice between paradigms can rarely be made on scientific grounds alone." Peter A. Hall, "Policy Paradigms, Social Learning, and the State: The Case of Economic Policymaking in Britain," *Comparative Politics* 25, 3 (1993): 280.

11. James Q. Wilson, "New Politics, New Elites, Old Publics," in *The New Politics of Public Policy*, ed. Landy and Levin, 262.

elites, experts, and insiders, "the masters of detail who have their fingers on the pulse of change," and it "debilitates ordinary citizens, who find it difficult to keep track of a rule that is subtle and changing in appearance." They remain "greatly baffled" by a political world that is "dense with organized interests and policy advocates" who do not speak their language.[12] Because it relied heavily on policy expertise to give political form to the principles of disability rights, the reform strategy fostered a politics in which the grand, moving principles that had animated the movement in the first place were condensed into arcane rules that few outsiders could understand.

Second, the medical model constrained the advocates because of the difficulty associated with adapting an old policy paradigm to a new cause. According to Peter Hall, "because so much of it is taken for granted and unamenable to scrutiny as a whole," policy paradigms are exceedingly difficult to displace. Policy reforms that maintain some connection to preexisting modes of thinking are more likely to gain acceptance than radical breaks.[13] Thus, charting the course of least resistance, advocates did not replace the medical model with the social model but instead made peace with it by proposing a functional approach to disability determination. While functionalism folded into disability certification some consideration of social context and individual disadvantage, it was essentially an adaptation of the medical perspective. It drew heavily from the norms of psychiatric, pediatric, and rehabilitation medicine, and it did not radically alter the SSA's evaluation practices, which still operated on the assumption that disability was a medical condition resulting in incapacity. Because of this perspective, though debates about Social Security disability policy took place in a policy world heavily influenced by the new ideas of the social model and disability rights, lawmakers did not seriously consider how DI and SSI could be restructured to conform to the emerging paradigm of rights.

However, the disconnect between the medical model that grounds Social Security and the social model that informs ADA and other disability rights legislation incites political controversy. Since the enactment of the ADA, many critics have faulted the SSA for "turning a blind eye to all standards and common sense when passing out benefits." For example, in an article for the conservative think tank, the Heritage Foundation, James M. Taylor, a disability consultant for businesses, noted that the SSA often awarded benefits to individuals "who pursue disability dis-

---

12. Wilson Carey McWilliams, "Two-Tier Politics and the Problem of Public Policy," in *The New Politics of Public Policy*, ed. Landy and Levin, 268–269.

13. Ibid., 279.

crimination claims under the Americans with Disabilities Act." Taylor noted that in order to file such a claim, the plaintiff had to be "fully capable of performing" the job in question, yet Social Security disability standards state that a claimant must be unable to perform any substantially gainful work. "How," Taylor asked indignantly, "can a person be simultaneously able and unable to work?" He then went on to recount case after case of ADA plaintiffs winning DI or SSI benefits, even though many these individuals could perform part-time work or would have been capable of continuing on their jobs with some slight modifications of the work environment.[14] Fraud certainly takes place in some circumstances, and well-intentioned people may disagree with how strictly or liberally the SSA interprets disability. Yet blaming the SSA for failing to take into account possible ADA accommodations that would allow a claimant to work fails to acknowledge that policymakers made no provision to protect all disabled employees. Some inevitably fall though the cracks of the ADA because they require job modifications that pose an undue burden on their places of work. These employees could work, but they are "disabled" insofar as accommodations are not forthcoming. Nor have policymakers made an attempt to scale disability benefits to the degree of impairment or to fold into disability evaluation any consideration of the effect of assistive devices or job accommodations.

A final constraint emerged from the advocates' failure to fully supplant the medicalized understanding of disability that motivated social welfare policy. Simply put, there are inherent limits to how far the medical concept of functionalism could be stretched to resolve deep-seated social problems. All compensation programs based on the medical model have strict and invasive eligibility criteria precisely because they are to remain limited to people with the most severe medical impairments, a relatively small group. But to serve as the sort of social safety net that advocates wanted, the boundaries of disability must be much more inclusive because medical condition alone is not the sole reason that people are unable to meet social expectations of work, schooling, and self-sufficiency. Medicalizing disadvantage, however, is an indirect and sometimes not terribly effective way of dealing with these issues. For instance, criticizing the expansive understanding of mental illness that accompanied DSM-III and its successive revisions, Herb Kutchins and Stuart Kirk describe the illustrative example of a young girl diagnosed with oppositional defiance disorder. They relate that the intern examining her noted

14. James M. Taylor, "Facilitating Fraud: How SSDI Gives Benefits to the Able Bodied," *Policy Analysis* 377 (August 15, 2000): 1, 6–23.

that the root of the child's behavioral troubles rested not in her medical condition but instead in her disruptive home. She lived in a small apartment with her two siblings, mother, grandmother, and uncle. Her derelict father had threatened to kill himself in front of her, and authorities suspected her older brother of molesting her. Without a doubt, the young girl confronted severe social limitations, and she could not or did not perform at an age-appropriate level. But when asked why she diagnosed the young girl with a mental disorder instead of attributing her troubles to a chaotic family life, Kutchins and Kirk's intern responded:

> The answer is, simply, money. Funding and the need for service delivery. . . . The clinic receives 80% of its funding from public money, particularly Medicaid. . . . To be eligible for services at the clinic, a child must have a DSM-IV diagnosis. . . . Sibling or parent-child relational problems, which provide more accurate descriptions of the dysfunctions in the lives of my young clients than do the diagnosis with which they have been—and are required to be—labeled, [do not qualify for reimbursement]. . . . Clinicians at the clinic are forced to manipulate diagnoses in order to secure reimbursement from third-party payers.[15]

Whether health care was offered on a fee-for-service or managed care basis, if assistance was to be rendered at all, it would be offered for reasons of medical dysfunction, not social disadvantage. No diagnosis meant no service. But by channeling aid through the medical concept of disability, the range of possible solutions is narrowed. Attention to familial discord and the wider pathologies of poverty fall by the wayside, and the need for social reform is collapsed into a call for behavioral therapies or pharmaceutical regimens for the individual. As disability law professor Samuel Bagenstos cautioned, "In pursuing medicalized social welfare strategies to achieve the goals of the disability rights movement, activists risk further entrenching the salience of the medical model of disability."[16]

Hiding Costs

Finally, the historical timing of the disability rights movement served to channel the strategic choices of the advocates in ways that limited their ability to realize the movement's larger ambitions. Ambivalence within the disabled community regarding the role that the welfare state should

15. Herb Kutchins and Stuart A. Kirk, *Making Us Crazy: DSM: The Psychiatric Bible and the Creation of Mental Disorders* (New York: Free Press, 1997), 259–60.

16. Samuel R. Bagenstos, "The Future of Disability Law," *Yale Law Journal* 114 (2004), 76.

play in making disability rights meaningful further hampered efforts to shift the goals of social welfare policy from compensation to inclusion. When they finally dedicated themselves to cultivating the safety net, advocates were forced to contend with a political climate marked by fiscal austerity and growing disenchantment with governmental activism. Because they had to advance their agenda at the same time that the New Right's critique of the liberal regulatory-welfare state gained acceptance, advocates had to align their movement with conservative principles. They portrayed the reforms as cost-neutral, even cost-saving, and so hid the depth of commitment required to realize meaningful social inclusion.

Hiding the true costs of reform was in part a strategic adaptation to the fact that, even though the advocates' vision of community integration struck a chord among policymakers, no political institution was committed enough to provide the resources needed to make this vision a reality. Democratic presidents from Kennedy to Carter may have talked the rhetoric of deinstitutionalization and community mental health. They may have established special commissions and passed bills authorizing spending for the construction of community mental health centers. But as fiscal times became increasingly dire, presidents shunned more far-reaching reforms that would have greatly improved the situation for de-institutionalized patients. Carter, for example, endorsed spending for small grants targeted at the mentally ill, but he avoided more sweeping revisions of mainstream social welfare programs. The federal courts, too, were enthusiastic guardians of mental patients, but only so long as they were confined within the asylum. Advocates learned that it was state custodial power that concerned the courts, not necessarily the autonomy and inclusion of former patients. Judges simply refused to mandate from the bench the construction of sorely needed community programs. Congress also supported community mental health but only because it was convinced that this would cost less than maintaining asylums, and it supported relaxing the disability standards for DI and SSI only after advocates persuaded lawmakers that this would be cheaper than institutionalization. In a similar vein, lawmakers backed equal access laws after they were convinced that these would reduce spending for entitlement programs.

In this regard, Senator William Cohen's discussion of deinstitutionalization policy is telling. During the midst of the Reagan administration's disability reviews, he told his fellow lawmakers that deinstitutionalization was intended to take people with disabilities that are not so severe that they needed institutionalization and "put them back into the community to reduce costs and make them a better part of the community." The problem with the Reagan administration's disability reviews was that "if you take away their subsistence . . . what you do is force them back into the institution because they have no place else to go. . . . Costs are dramatically higher, which totally reverses the policy that we have pursued in the past decade."[17] The logic of community mental health was compelling—yet for reasons of fiscal prudence as much as social justice.

Under the surface of the technical jargon of disability measurement and cost estimates, therefore, was a pitched ideological battle over the scope of welfare state activism. Humane community living could occur only with a generous social safety net available. But by obscuring the costs of reform, advocates allowed politicians to get away with talking the talk of rights but not providing a commitment of public resources to make the attainment of those rights meaningful. The connections between the welfare state and the ability to bring about the social equality of an excluded group remained obscured.

Inadvertent Consequences: The Undercutting of the ADA and the Closing of Windows

As many episodes of this book illustrate, there is a great deal of contingency and historical accident in policymaking. SSI became law, in part, because Russell Long mistakenly thought he could use it to kill the drive for the Family Assistance Plan. The expansion of mainstream social welfare programs, though not undertaken with the disabled in mind, altered the incentives of state governments in ways that fueled deinstitutionalization. The Reagan administration inadvertently gave rise to the reform coalition that fostered the expansion of DI and SSI. Judicial efforts to make the SSA's evaluation of disability more accurate unintentionally contributed to the widespread perception of rampant fraud. None of these events was planned, none of their outcomes anticipated. But they mattered. Policy outcomes simply would not have played out the same way in their absence.

These historical quirks highlight the uncertain nature of policymaking and cast doubt on any notions that political actors can make decisions with full knowledge of the consequences of those decisions. More often than not, the choices we make bring with them unintended consequences and unforeseen events that reverberate over time, structuring choices

---

17. U.S. Senate, Special Committee on Aging, *Social Security Reviews of the Mentally Disabled*, 98th Congress, 1st Session, 1983, 11–12.

much farther down the temporal road. This sort of historical contingency, Margaret Weir observes, "means that decisions about policy—defining a problem, delimiting its scope, and devising a strategy of intervention—are often the product of circumstances that cannot be readily anticipated or controlled."[18] The tendency of disability rights activists in the late 1980s and early 1990s to define civil rights laws and social welfare programs as incompatible approaches to the problem of disability was one such contingency. While the strategic choice was understandable given that activists needed to broaden the appeal of disability rights to conservative Republicans, in retrospect, it is now evident that this choice carried grave consequences for the disabled. Since the passage of the Americans with Disabilities Act in 1990, the policy gains of disability rights movement have stalled as governing institutions prove resistant to the social change that activists seek. Activists today confront the inherent limits of the ADA and its judicial mechanisms for enforcement.

Ironically, proponents of the ADA argued for a civil rights law in which the disabled would be able to seek redress for discrimination primarily in federal court rather than through direct administrative enforcement in part because they did not trust bureaucracies.[19] But the ADA came to suffer from all the drawbacks of a policy premised on litigation, including long delays before reaching resolution of cases, high costs associated with resolving a dispute, unpredictable penalties, and distrust and defensiveness on the part of employers.[20] In addition, the courts have not been able to provide a coherent definition of the ADA's categorical boundaries. Judges have found that people with carpal tunnel syndrome, asthma, paranoid schizophrenia, epilepsy, and multiple sclerosis are not disabled under the statute, while separate judges, somewhat paradoxically, held that pregnancy and infertility were legitimate disabilities.[21]

Even more maddening to disability advocates, however, is that the Supreme Court has practically eviscerated the protections offered under the ADA. Through a series of cases, the Supreme Court has held that

18. Margaret Weir, *Politics and Jobs: The Boundaries of Employment Policy in the United States* (Princeton: Princeton University Press, 1992), 164.

19. Thomas F. Burke, "On the Rights Track: The Americans with Disabilities Act," in *Comparative Disadvantages? Social Regulations and the Global Economy*, ed. Pietro S. Nivola (Washington, DC: Brookings Institution Press, 1997), 271–72. Burke identifies other reasons including the decentralized structure of the American political system, the limits of administrative versus judicial sanctions, and the vagaries of budget constraints and political control of the executive branch.

20. Ibid., 272–79.

21. Ibid., 273, and Ruth O'Brien, *Crippled Justice: The History of Modern Disability Policy in the Workplace* (Chicago: University of Chicago Press, 2001), 177–81.

plaintiffs must prove they have an impairment that substantially limits a major life activity before they can be considered "disabled" under the law. In *Sutton v. United Airlines, Murphy v. United Parcel Service*, and *Albertson's v. Kirkingburg*, a trilogy of cases handed down in 1999, the justices ruled that persons who could correct the limitations of their condition through mitigating factors, like medication or assistive technology, were not disabled even if they were not using such devices.[22] Three years later in *Toyota v. Williams*, the court further explained that in order for a person to be disabled, a limitation on job-related activities was not enough; the impairment had to be one that "prevents or severely restricts the individual from activities that are of central importance to most people's daily lives."[23] In essence, the justices and the lower courts following their lead have created an impossible bind for people with disabilities. Plaintiffs must show that they suffer a substantial limitation of a major life activity in order to be considered disabled under the ADA, but by making this case, they may also undermine their argument that they are otherwise qualified for employment. The restrictiveness of the courts' approach means that some people may be functionally limited enough to be fired from their jobs yet not limited enough to meet the courts' high standard of disability. Additionally, critics argue that by requiring plaintiffs to prove that they are substantially limited before they can qualify for protection, the courts have disempowered the disabled, precisely the opposite of the ADA's intent.[24]

The Supreme Court's attempt to chip away at the ADA is not an isolated incident. Instead, it is indicative of larger institutional changes in American government that may signal the demise of the conditions that facilitated the success of the reform movement. The rights revolution was predicated on a certain political foundation that included activist federal courts, divided government, the demise of state governments (and the concomitant nationalization of political authority), and heightened public expectations of government. Unfortunately for liberals, these political mainstays have eroded significantly in the last decade. The Republican dominance of Congress since 1994 has thrown sizable hurdles into the path of advocates. Although "Congress may not succeed in enacting legislation" that would roll back the gains of the rights revolution, "committee leaders certainly are not going to engage in the sort of entrepre-

22. *Sutton v. United Airlines*, 527 U.S. 471 (1999); *Murphy v. United Parcel Service*, 527 U.S. 516 (1999); *Albertson's v. Kirkingburg*, 527 U.S. 555 (1999).

23. *Toyota Motor Manufacturing v. Williams*, 534 U.S. 184 (2002).

24. Samuel R. Bagenstos, "Subordination, Stigma, and 'Disability,'" *Virginia Law Review* 86 (2000): 472–73.

neurial activity that has expanded programmatic rights."[25] Thus, even though after 1996, Republicans have failed to significantly scale back the reach of DI and SSI benefits, neither have disability advocates been able to build legislatively on their successes with Social Security or the ADA. In similar fashion, the Supreme Court and the lower federal courts have grown increasing conservative with the appointments by Reagan, Bush, and now George W. Bush. Beginning in the early 1990s, the Supreme Court, under the leadership of Chief Justice William Rehnquist, sought to rein in the reach of federal power and reassert the autonomy of the states, by restricting its interpretation of the Commerce Clause, enlarging the scope of state immunity from private lawsuits, and refusing to infer "legally binding commands in federal statutes."[26] Thus, much to the chagrin of disability advocates, the Supreme Court in 2001, struck a blow against disability rights by ruling that the provisions of the ADA requiring employers to provide job accommodations to workers with disabilities did not apply to states.[27]

Of course, the judicial rollback of the ADA may have run its course. To the relief of advocates, in 2004, the justices held off on advancing states' rights any further. In *Tennessee v. Lane*, they narrowly upheld provisions of the ADA requiring states to make public facilities accessible to the disabled.[28] Moreover, in the 2000 case of *Olmstead v. L.C.* the Supreme Court ruled in a fractured and complicated 6–3 decision that the ADA required states to place individuals who had qualified for out-patient care in an appropriate community program.[29] Endorsing the principle that "unjustified isolation" of the disabled in mental institutions "is properly regarded as discrimination based on disability," the court held that, though subject to certain qualifications, failure to provide community alternatives could constitute a violation of the ADA.[30] *Olmstead* was a significant victory for mental health advocates. In response, President George W. Bush, when he assumed office in 2001, pledged to encourage states to quickly implement the decision. Several states began drawing up

25. Ibid., 339–42.

26. R. Shep Melnick, "Federalism and the New Rights," *Yale Journal on Regulation* 14 (1996), 339–42.

27. *Board of Trustees of University of Alabama v. Garrett*, 531 U.S. 356 (2001).

28. *Tennessee v. Lane*, 541 U.S. 509 (2004).

29. *Olmstead v. L. C.*, 527 U.S. 581 (1999). The qualifications include: if a health professional determined that a community setting was the most appropriate, the individual desired such a placement, and the state could reasonably accommodate the request taking into account its resources and the needs of other state hospital residents.

30. Ibid., at 597.

plans for transferring institutionalized disabled patients into community-based programs and reducing long waiting lists for those programs, actions the Supreme Court described as a way of showing reasonable progress toward community placement. Advocates also seized on the *Olmstead* precedent to sue states, compelling them to revise their Medicaid programs, which strongly favored institutionalized care, to provide more supports for disabled persons living in the community, and they have met with some success.[31] But whether a particular state has, in fact, committed an ADA violation will have to be determined on a case-by-case basis by state officials and ultimately by the federal courts, thus leaving the eventual impact of *Olmstead* uncertain, at least for the time being.

What is clear, however, is that the ADA has failed to live up to its expectations. The ADA has not led to people with disabilities flooding the workplace, as its proponents promised it would. In fact, studies showed that employment among the disabled dropped during the 1990s even as the economy flourished and the employment rate of other demographic groups, including welfare mothers, rose. During this same time, entitlement spending for disability increased rather than decreased as expected.[32] Therefore, as a tool to further the employment and community integration of the disabled, the ADA remains insufficient. Thomas Burke puts it bluntly: rights do not create jobs.[33] The limits of the ADA suggest a need for a multifaceted approach to disability rights, one that incorporates public guarantees for assistance. In this respect, lessons from abroad may prove useful.

American Exceptionalism: Disability Policy across the Pond

No nation has been particularly effective at integrating the disabled into schools and workplaces. And some European nations have begun to

31. Bagenstos, "Future of Disability Law," 56–58, and Mark C. Weber, "Home and Community-Based Services, *Olmstead*, and Positive Rights: A Preliminary Discussion," *Wake Forest Law Review* 39 (2004): 283–87. Bagenstos, however, has an intelligent discussion of why these efforts to reform Medicaid are inherently limited by the structure of the program itself on 58–62.

32. Richard V. Burkhauser, Andrew J. Houtenville, and David C. Wittenburg, "A User's Guide to Current Statistics on the Employment of People with Disabilities," in *The Decline in Employment of People with Disabilities: A Policy Puzzle*, ed. David C. Stapleton and Richard V. Burkhauser (Kalamazoo, MI: W. E. Upjohn Institute, 2003), 72–73.

33. Burke, "On the Rights Track," 280.

replicate the antidiscrimination and equal access laws pioneered in the United States. But it is also the case that Americans have pursued a brand of disability policy that is exceptionally libertarian by international standards. It combines strong legal mandates for the civil rights of disabled individuals with weak acknowledgment of the collective need to provide for the economic well-being of disabled citizens. It provides a relatively narrow view of the range of options to integrate the disabled into society. Of course, continental disability policy is not without its problems. Some scholars find that the medical model is just as prevalent in nations such as Germany as it is in the United States, and as a result, services are often more likely to be delivered in a segregating setting.[34] Nonetheless, in their struggle to integrate income support with work and to further the social rights of the disabled, Europeans also bring a diverse set of policy tools to the table, including quotas and tax incentives to encourage businesses to hire the disabled and generous income support and health care programs that smooth the transition to employment.[35] By comparison, many European nations—even those moving in the direction of American-style disability rights activism—take a more comprehensive view of disability and so offer American policymakers a glimpse of the possibilities.

Take the example of Sweden and Germany. The two countries not only recognize the social components of disability but also state that integration is a goal of their programs. In Germany, workers are disabled if they are "limited in their capacity for integration into society" because of an impairment. A disability in Sweden "is not looked upon as a characteristic of a person, caused by injury or illness," but as a mismatch between the person's functional capabilities and the work environment.[36] Moreover, both countries also explicitly recognize that a disabled person "has a social right . . . to secure a place in the community, in particular in working life, in accordance with his or her abilities" and to the social support necessary to achieve these goals. Thus, in addition to employment and accessibility rights, disability policy in Germany and Sweden emphasizes early intervention, personal assistance, and social welfare as

34. See Fiona Geist, Bernd Petermann, and Volker Widhammer, "Disability Law in Germany," *Comparative Labor Law and Policy Journal* 24 (2003): 575–76, and Samuel R. Bagenstos, "Comparative Disability Employment Law from an American Perspective," *Comparative Labor Law and Policy Journal* 24 (2003): 660 n. 62.

35. Burke, "On the Rights Track," 286–88, and Joann Sim, "Improving Return-to-Work Strategies in the United States Disability Programs, with Analysis of Program Practices in Germany and Sweden," *Social Security Bulletin* 62, 3 (1999): 41–50.

36. Sim, "Improving Return-to-Work Strategies," 42.

well.[37] On the other hand, the United States uses a particularly strict medical definition of disability for its benefit programs that encompasses only the most disabled of the people with disabilities, thus complicating later return-to-work initiatives. Indeed, broader disability programs that catch people early—before they become completely incapacitated, physically and emotionally—may do a better job of promoting employment that strict, residual American-style programs. Germany and Sweden recognize degrees of disability and pay partial as well as full benefits; by contrast, the Social Security disability programs pay only a full benefit and only to those who are completely disabled.[38] Because the Swedish and German systems allow for early intervention, disabled persons can be identified near the beginning of the process and promptly referred to vocational rehabilitation programs. Moreover, Swedish and German claimants can rely on income from sickness benefits while undergoing rehabilitation. In the United States, however, claimants tend to wait several months before finally applying for DI or SSI benefits. By that time, they have exhausted all options and may be feeling disheartened. Thus, the "optimum period for early intervention may have already passed by the time an applicant walks into the Social Security office." Claimants then undergo a lengthy examination process and sometimes an appeal to prove they are completely unable to engage in any remunerative work whatsoever—not a process conducive to fostering a mindset for returning to the workplace.[39]

American policymakers have tried to align Social Security disability policy with the new expectations of work and productivity articulated by the ADA. In late 1980s, Congress added programs that would allow the disabled who returned to work to keep their Medicaid coverage and to set aside a portion of their SSI benefits to pay for personal attendances and other work expenses. DI beneficiaries, meanwhile, were permitted to keep Medicare coverage for up to thirty-nine months after completion of a trial work period. In 1999, Congress passed the Ticket to Work and Work Incentives Improvement Act, the latest in a long line of proposals designed to get the disabled back to work. It allowed people with disabilities to receive a voucher for use in any participating public or private vocational rehabilitation or employment services program, and it suspended continuing disability evaluations for beneficiaries trying to return to work. Similarly, as one of his first acts on assuming office, President George W.

37. Ibid., 43.
38. Ibid., 42.
39. Ibid., 43, 47.

Bush tried to enhance independence and employment among the disabled. In February 2001, Bush announced his New Freedom Initiative, which included a plethora of proposals: low-interest loans so low-income people with disabilities could purchase assistive devices, investment in the development of assistive technology, tax incentives to business to help disabled workers commute to their jobs, decreased regulations of home offices for disabled people working from home, vouchers to increase home ownership among the disabled, and the appointment of an expert panel to make recommendations for improving the delivery of mental health care. And to help people with disabilities make sense of the chaos of programs out there, the White House unveiled DisabilityInfo.gov, a website providing information on disability-related government programs spanning the areas of education, employment, housing, welfare, transportation, health and health care, and civil rights.

These measures, however, may have only a limited impact on employment of the disabled. Large scale return-to-work demonstration projects show that the increased income that beneficiaries earn on their jobs hardly offset the value of SSI and DI payments—certainly not enough to cover the costs of the support services the typical working beneficiary requires. In fact, often it is cheaper to pay disability benefits than pay the total costs of accommodations and support services.[40] Moreover, American policymakers are generally reluctant to spend money on the transitional services that are necessary for the disabled to achieve employment. Both Germany and Sweden spent a higher percentage of their GDP on vocational rehabilitation, work programs for the disabled (like sheltered workshops), and disability benefits than the United States.[41] Germany, in addition, has a range of policy tools to help beneficiaries who return to work, "including wage subsidies, job modifications, technical aids, transportation allowances, and a variety of other assistive devices. There are also provisions for part-time reintegration into the workforce while receiving partial benefits."[42] By comparison, for every hundred dollars the Social Security Administration spends on disability benefits, it spends less than ten cents on vocational rehabilitation.[43] Federal expenditures for transportation allowances, assistive devices, and subsidies to employers who make job accommodations are also meager, and partial benefits are lacking.

40. Mary C. Daly and Richard V. Burkhauser, "Left Behind: SSI in the Era of Welfare Reform," *Focus* 22, 3 (2003): 41.
41. Sim, "Improving Return-to-Work Strategies," 44.
42. Ibid., 43–47.
43. U.S. General Accounting Office, *Social Security: Federal Disability Programs Face Major Issues*, GAO/T-HEHS-95-97, 1995, 13.

Perhaps the greatest barrier to return-to-work initiatives is the residual, layered, and fragmented nature of the American welfare state itself. Studies show that SSI recipients rely on a number of other means-tested programs that they risk losing if they return to work. For example, because some states provide more coverage of mental health services under Medicaid than is available under private insurance plans or Medicare, Medicaid is an especially valuable benefit. When disability advocates suggested that the fear of losing public health insurance coverage deterred the disabled from returning to work, Congress enacted the Health Insurance Portability and Accountability Act of 1996, which limited to twelve months the exclusions that private health care plans can place on preexisting conditions. But fundamental reform of health care—particularly in the area of mental health—is unlikely anytime soon. And while efforts like the New Freedom Initiative are laudable, they do not contemplate any significant change in the current state of affairs.

Of course, this is not to say that German and Swedish disability policy is superior to America's in all respects or that the two countries are not without their own problems. In fact, some analysts suggest that the quotas used in many European nations for promoting employment are ineffective because they are rarely enforced vigorously and they rely on the presumption that the disabled are less capable workers than able-bodied persons.[44] Moreover, like the United States, Germany, Sweden, and most European nations face fiscal pressures that have forced governments to reduce entitlement spending and expenditures for rehabilitation services. Nevertheless, they still may do a better job of reintegrating disabled workers because the divide between welfare and work is not so gaping as it is in the United States.[45] The European approach to disability, put simply, is more comprehensive because their welfare states are more comprehensive.

The Need for a Balanced Approach to the Disadvantages of Disability

The final lesson of reform is the need to keep in mind those who are truly disadvantaged but whose voices are often lost in deliberations about policy. During congressional debate over the Americans with Disabilities

44. See also Lisa Waddington and Matthew Diller, "Tensions and Coherence in Disability Policy: The Uneasy Relationship between Social Welfare and Civil Rights Models of Disability in America, European, and International Employment Law," 2000, http://www.dredf.org/international/waddington.html.
45. Sim, "Improving Return-to-Work Strategies," 43, 45.

Act in 1990, Elizabeth Gaspard, a representative with the National Rehabilitation Association, told lawmakers of how proud she was that, even though she used a wheelchair, she had been able to graduate from college and become "a taxpayer, not a tax user," a worker, not a welfare recipient.[46] This sort of language, pitting equal access rights against social welfare programs, surfaced often during congressional testimony over the historic disability rights law. But disability rights and social aid were not always seen as antithetical to each other. For example, in 1949, a representative for the National Federation of the Blind told Congress that blindness was both "a social condition that involved discriminatory exclusion . . . from the main channels of social and economic activity" as well as "a physical condition that incurred significant expense and limitations . . . and therefore required societal aid."[47] It is time to revisit this older understanding of disability. To argue that rights alone are enough to bring about the integration of the disabled is to assume that the only barrier an individual with a disability faces is the discriminatory attitudes of the able-bodied people she encounters. This leaves policy inadequate along several dimensions.

First, this negative conception of disability rights fails to recognize the multiple barriers that many people with disabilities confront. According to Samuel R. Bagenstos, the problem of social exclusion extends deeper than "the discriminatory acts of particular employers" and rests on "deeply-rooted structural barriers." Some of these structural barriers are the same impediments that confront all disadvantaged individuals regardless of their ability or disability. Simply put, opportunities for education, networking, and mobility are not equally available to all workers. Sometimes disability impedes a worker's ability to access these opportunities, but other times, the cause is not disability alone. Thus, the antidiscrimination provisions of the ADA "can prohibit employers from discriminating against qualified people with disabilities who apply for jobs, but they cannot put people with disabilities in a position to apply and be qualified for jobs in the first place."[48] Simply being in a position to apply for a job is a tall order when disability intersects with race, class, age, and gender to deepen discrimination and further social isolation. Indeed, the disadvantage can become a vicious cycle. The harsh living conditions associated with poverty may exacerbate the functional restrictions of a dis-

46. Joseph P. Shapiro, *No Pity: People with Disabilities Forging a New Civil Rights Movement* (New York: Times Books, 1993), 136.

47. Paul K. Longmore, "The Second Phase: From Disability Rights to Disability Culture," an online document from 1995, Independent Living Institute, http://www.independentliving.org/docs3/longm95.html.

48. Bagenstos, "The Future of Disability Law," 23.

ability, while the structural impediments created by poverty further com-
plicate efforts of disabled individuals to find and hold employment.[49] By
focusing on negative rights alone, the rhetoric of employment rights may
not resonate for minority and low-income people with disabilities who
face these compounded hurdles to economic self-sufficiency.

In addition, the provisions of the ADA are of limited use to individuals
who require extensive or expensive accommodations. Though the ADA
requires employers to adapt jobs to compensate for the functional restrictions of disabled workers, they are excused if such modifications
would pose an "undue hardship." Thus, a worker whose accommodations
require an ongoing expense, such as the services of a personal attendant,
may be disadvantaged relative to someone who needs a one-time expense, such as the construction of a wheelchair ramp. Today, more sober
students of disability policy argue that policymakers need to recognize
that the costs of disability will continue to accrue after the individual re-
turns to work.[50] And in some cases, these costs may be substantial. Indeed, Ellen Smith Pryor points out, "The patchwork quilt of American
disability policy does not lie evenly over both mental and physical work
disabilities."[51] Simply put, some impairments are more burdensome to
accommodate than others. Bifurcating equal access rights from social
welfare could also disadvantage whole classes of impairments, like mental
disorders or pervasive developmental disabilities, which require more extensive or far-reaching accommodations. Moreover, work often entails
ongoing expenses for services that are not strictly work-related—expenses
such as personal assistance in dressing and preparing for work, assistive
technology to allow an individual to commute to work, affordable health
care, or rehabilitation services to enhance functional abilities. The ADA
requires neither employers nor private health insurance plans to cover
these expenses.[52] And so long as policymakers believe that disability

49. John K. Kramer, "The Right Not to be Mentally Retarded," in The President's
Commission on Mental Retardation, *The Mentally Retarded Citizen and the Law*, ed.
Michael Kindred, Julius Cohen, David Penrod, and Thomas L. Shaffer, report spon-
sored by the President's Committee on Mental Retardation (New York: Free Press,
1976), 32–59; and Henry Brehm, "The Disabled on Public Assistance," *Social Security
Bulletin* 33 (1970), 29.

50. Susan Lonsdale, quoted in Helen Barnes, *Working for a Living? Employment,
Benefits, and the Living Standards of Disabled People* (Bristol, England: The Policy Press,
2000), 11.

51. Ellen Pryor Smith, "Mental Disabilities and the Disability Fabric," in *Mental
Disorder, Work Disability, and the Law*, ed. Richard J. Bonnie and John Monahan (Chicago: University of Chicago Press, 1997), 153.

52. Bagenstos, "The Future of Disability Law," 25–32, 34–41.

rights will save money, they fail to see the logic for public investment in these sorts of supportive measures.

Finally, the negative conception of disability rights rings hollow for those individuals who are so disabled or otherwise disadvantaged that they may never be able to work. For them, the social safety net is a vital prerequisite to community integration. Orienting the focus of disability policy so squarely on the right to equal access and work to the exclusion of the right to welfare risks making gainful employment and economic self-sufficiency the overriding measure of personal worth. This could have the unintended and unfortunate effect of devaluing and "maintaining and intensifying the exclusion" of those who will never join the productive economy.[53] By presenting policymakers with a false choice between welfare and work, by arguing that the ADA would make income support unnecessary, the rhetoric of disability rights has sometimes, however unintentionally, undercut the foundation needed to build extensive, publicly backed income support and social services programs that, in addition to civil rights, are required for true integration.

For all these reasons, some disability rights advocates today have reconsidered denigration of the welfare state. Some have renewed their focus on social welfare programs, promoting the expansion of aid to the disabled within the context of programs that are universal rather than targeted at the disabled and pressing for increased consumer control of the services that are offered.[54] Like the mental health and children's reformers covered in this book, they recognize that welfare rights are just as significant to social inclusion as antidiscrimination rights. In this sense, without attention to the social safety net, the discourse on disability rights is impoverished. Rights are not simply trump cards held by lone individuals. They are expressions of collective aspirations toward a just society; as such, they must be brought to fruition collectively. Rights without social support are mere paper guarantees.

53. Paul Abberley, quoted in Barnes, *Working for a Living?* 12.
54. Bagenstos, "The Future of Disability Law," 70–81. Bagenstos notes that the return to social welfare advocacy within the broader disability rights movement could fracture the cause, as affluent people with disabilities, who can afford services, abandon the less well-to-do disabled and as different impairment groups wrangle over a limited social welfare pie (see 81–82). Of course, as I point out in this book, the potential for conflict was present from the beginning. The disability rights movement has never been a single, unified entity. Moreover, as it gained strength in the late 1980s, its leaders tended to be white, well-educated, and affluent, and they tended to be people with mobility impairments. Thus, the advocates featured in this book gave voice to people with disabilities whom the disability rights movement did not fully speak for.

INDEX

Numbers in italic are page numbers for tables or figures.

community mental health care, 20, 57, 60;
homeless and, 165–66; logic of, 230–31
community mental health centers, 54,
91–92
Community Mental Health Centers Construction Act, 54
comparable severity standard, 83–85,
132–35, 208–9
Congress, 1; concerns about DI and SSI,
25–26; deadlock, 19, 21; enactment of
Disability Insurance, 32, 33–37; fragmentation of power, 37–38; institutional
environment, 151–54; spending bills,
165. *See also House committees; Senate
committees*
Congressional Budget Office (CBO), 204
congressional committees, 33, 37–38, 127
Conlan, Timothy, 41
Conrad, Kent, 25, 208, 213
conservatives, 3, 234; addiction/alco-
holism, attack on, 203–6; AFDC and,
68–69; approach to advocacy, 167–70;
policy agenda, 1990s, 201–9
constituent politics, 37
contact stations, 164
continuing disability investigations. *See*
disability reviews
Contract with America Advancement Act
of 1996, 205
Cook, Timothy, 170
costs of programs, 5, 21, 57, 66; hiding of,
156, 229–31
courts, 122–23; administrative law, view
of, 125–26; amicus briefs, 126, 134–36;
class action lawsuits, 124, 129–30, 131,
137–40, 142; conservatism of, 234; denials on appeal, 97, 109–10, 145; as expansive force, 123–24, 140, 145–46; inconsistency of disability rules and,
142–43; jurisprudence of disability,
127–40; logic of judicial activism,
146–48; lower courts, 138, 139, 141;
mental impairment cases, 129–31; multiple meanings of disability and, 140–46;
politicization of, 123–26; strategies of
advocates and, 119–20
Crouch, Sam, 89
culture wars, 221

Dart, Justin, 62
Davis, Rhoda, 95n, 173, 175–76
decentralization of American political system, 32–33, 222–23

decision making: incremental adjustments
preferred, 76–77; as politically based,
130–31; subjectivity of, 16–17, 189–90
definitions of disability, 5, 94; ADA con-
version, 167; categorical boundaries,
226; categories, 70–71, 101; strict,
34–35, 98–101; as subjective, 16–17. *See
also* functional model of disability; Listings of Medical Impairments; medical
model of disability; social model of disability
degrees of disability, 40
deinstitutionalization, 44–45, 59, 89–92,
231; experiments in, 53–54; logic of,
215–16. *See also* mental disorders
denials on appeal, 97, 109–10, 145
Department of Health, Education, and
Welfare (HEW), 53, 56
Department of Health and Human Services (HHS), 94, 107, 139, 154, 174
dependency, concerns about, 31, 197–99
Derthick, Martha, 32–33, 36–37, 76,
96–97
deservingness, discourse of, 15–17, 24, 159,
206; allegations of fraud and, 199–200
DeShaney v. Winnebago County, 61
Developmental Disabilities Assistance and
Bill of Rights Act, 57
deviance, social, 28–29, 51
DeWine, Mike, 211
Diagnostic and Statistical Manual (DSM-
III), 113–17, 155, 177–78, 228
disability, 3; as administrative concept, 17;
compared to premature aging, 35–36;
degrees of, 40; expanded understanding
of, 81–82; moral status of recipients,
15–17; multiple meanings of, 140–46;
types of, 5–8, 12, 16. *See also* addiction/
alcoholism; childhood disabilities; mental disorders
Disability Benefits Reform Act of 1980,
94–95, 97–98, 107, 221
Disability Benefits Reform Act of 1984,
138, 154–58, 221; institutional environment and, 151–52; Medical Listings
and, 156–57, 177
disability-centered perspective, 62
DisabilityInfo.gov, 238
Disability Insurance (DI), 2, 5, 22–23; age
limit, 35–36; certification process,
81–82; enactment of, 32, 33–37; enrollment rates, 5, 6, 95–96, 184, 190–91,
195; expansion of, 36–37, 170–71

reform: limitations on, 222–31; possibilities for, 38–39, 220–22
rehabilitation, 28, 44, 116; vocational, 62,
167, 237–38
Rehabilitation Act of 1973, 31, 56–57
Rehnquist, William, 134, 234
reinstitutionalization, 156
representative payees, 86, 162, 197, 204
retirement age, 36
retirement trust fund, 191
retrenchment, 21–22, 27, 40, 93–94,
194–95; Carter years, 94–98; childhood
disabilities and, 206–9; conservative
policy agenda, 201–9; Gingrich era,
215–16; limitations on, 210–17; problems with disability programs, 195–201;
programs alleged to cause lifelong dependency, 197–99; Reagan era, 106–10,
215–16; rolling back of PRWORA,
211–13
Ribicoff, Abraham, 71, 77
rights idea, 3–4, 44, 48–57; mental disorders and, 50–54
right to treatment, 52, 54, 55
Roberts, Ed, 62
Rochefort, David, 92
Roosevelt, Franklin, 1, 218
Rothman, David, 58, 93
Rothman, Sheila, 93
Rouse, Charles, 55
Rouse v. Cameron, 47, 55
Roybal, Edward, 160, 162
Rubenstein, Leonard S., 95, 112, 117–19,
173–74
rule-writing process, 177–84
Rupp, Kalman, 9

Sabatier, Paul, 42
Satel, Sally, 205
Save Our Social Security coalition, 160
Scalia, Antonin, 134
Schweiker, Richard, 174
Schweiker v. Gray Panthers, 126
Scott, Charles, 9
Second Circuit Court, 147–48
Section 504, 31, 56–57, 167, 168
Senate Finance Committee, 33, 76, 79,
151, 152–54; alcoholism debate, 86;
childhood disabilities debates, 84,
133–34; disagreement within, 71–72;
retrenchment and, 207–9; Subcommit-
tee on Social Security and Family Pol-
icy, 204

Senate Governmental Affairs Committee,
152
Senate Special Committee on Aging, 152,
197
Senate Subcommittee on Oversight, 152
Shaw, Clay, 214, 215
sick role, 28
Simmons, Paul, 141
Simpson, Alan, 25
small government approach, 62, 168
social handicaps, 82–83, 87–89
social inclusion, 3–4, 20, 50, 122; 1990s
policies, 170–71; states and, 60–61
social model of disability, 29–31, 39–41,
44–45, 49, 113, 227
social problems, medicalization of, 228–
29
social rights, 218–19
social safety net, 59, 160; concerns of advocates, 58–63; divergence from disability rights, 166, 167–71; inadequacy of
for mental disorders, 90–92; late 1980s
difficulties, 165–66; threatened by Reagan Revolution, 106–10; unraveling of,
late 1970s, 93–94. *See also* deinstitutionalization; *welfare headings*
Social Security: benefit increases, 73–74;
equity and adequacy in, 72–80. *See also*
Disability Insurance (DI); Supplemental
Security Income (SSI)
Social Security Act of 1935: court rulings
and, 150; two-tiered program, 67–68.
See also Old Age Insurance; Unemployment Insurance
Social Security Administration (SSA),
66–72; administrative deterioration,
1990s, 191–92, 194; commissioners, 72,
74, 213; contempt citations, 125; as de-
fendant, 124–25; fragmentation of policy and, 141–42; offices, 97, 175; responsibilities of, 143–45; sympathetic
bureaucrats, 21, 33, 173–76. *See also* Office of Disability
Social Security Advisory Council, 34
Social Security Amendments of 1972,
75–79, 90, 132
Social Security Amendments of 1984, 38,
151–52, 214
Social Security Subcommittee, 107, 153
social workers, 70
soft impairments, 7, 7–9
Southern states, 68–69
spending bills, 165